AUSTRALIAN CLINICAL LEGAL EDUCATION

DESIGNING AND OPERATING
A BEST PRACTICE CLINICAL PROGRAM
IN AN AUSTRALIAN LAW SCHOOL

AUSTRALIAN CLINICAL LEGAL EDUCATION

DESIGNING AND OPERATING
A BEST PRACTICE CLINICAL PROGRAM
IN AN AUSTRALIAN LAW SCHOOL

ADRIAN EVANS, ANNA CODY,
ANNA COPELAND, JEFF GIDDINGS,
PETER JOY, MARY ANNE NOONE
AND SIMON RICE

Australian
National
University

PRESS

ANU PRESS

Published by ANU Press
The Australian National University
Acton ACT 2601, Australia
Email: anupress@anu.edu.au
This title is also available online at press.anu.edu.au

National Library of Australia Cataloguing-in-Publication entry

Creator: Evans, Adrian Hellier, author.

Title: Australian clinical legal education / Adrian Evans, Anna
                  Cody, Anna Copeland, Jeff Giddings,
                  Peter Joy, Mary Anne Noone, Simon Rice.

ISBN: 9781760461034 (paperback) 9781760461041 (ebook)

Subjects: Law--Study and teaching (Clinical education)--Australia.
                  Law--Study and teaching--Australia.

Other Creators/Contributors:
                  Cody, Anna, author.
                  Copeland, Anna, author.
                  Giddings, Jeff, author.
                  Joy, Peter, author.
                  Noone, Mary Anne, author.
                  Rice, Simon, author.

Cover design and layout by ANU Press. Cover photograph: *White-bellied Sea Eagle*, by Jeff Giddings © 2016.

Contents

List of authors

Adrian Evans
Professor of Law,
Monash University

Anna Cody
Associate Professor and
Director Kingsford Legal Centre,
Faculty of Law, University of
New South Wales

Anna Copeland
Director of Clinical Legal
Programs, School of Law,
Murdoch University

Jeff Giddings
Director, Monash-Oakleigh
Legal Service, Professor of Law,
Monash University

Peter A. Joy
Henry Hitchcock Professor
of Law, Washington
University School of Law

Mary Anne Noone
Professor of Law,
LaTrobe University

Simon Rice
Professor of Law,
The Australian National
University

Preface

Australian clinicians have long laboured in law schools and external clinical sites with too little appreciation and too many obstacles, but those days are coming to an end. Clinical legal education has taken a long time to come to the forefront of legal education in Australia, but that moment is here now.

Australian law schools without a reputable clinical presence are fast becoming an anachronism. But as more and more law schools dip their toes into clinical experimentation, we see the potential for superficial courses and lower-quality educational outcomes. In the absence of agreed clinical pedagogies for Australian clinical programs, we may see mediocrity posing as diversity and—worse, to our minds—a diminution of focus on serving clients in poverty and striving for social justice.

This book sets out in detail the many complex issues associated with developing law students' public-interested professionalism in an Australian context. In the process, we offer very practical guidance on how to construct and operate a 'best practice' clinical legal education program, for the benefit of regulators, law deans, associate deans, colleagues and students, now and in the future. To support the book's continuing usefulness, we have used Harvard library permalinks, a reference system that ensures that the web links in the footnotes remain uncorrupted by the passage of time. To the same end, we have chosen to publish with ANU Press, ensuring that the book is accessible free online throughout the world.

We dedicate this book to the contributions of the late Sue Campbell and Guy Powles, as well as Neil Rees, all of whom were pioneers in our discipline and who stood their ground for the twin pillars of Australian clinical legal education: providing the best in both legal education and client service.

Adrian Evans, Anna Cody, Anna Copeland, Jeff Giddings, Peter Joy, Mary Anne Noone and Simon Rice
February 2017

Acknowledgements

We acknowledge with considerable appreciation the contribution of Sandy McCullough to the editing and formatting of this book. Sandy has frequently gone further than many editors would do in helping us get to press. In the early stages of the research that underlies our work here, we were also greatly assisted by Ebony Booth, who managed our research team and ensured we were meeting our deadlines. Both Sandy and Ebony brought professionalism and good humour to their roles and made everything so much easier. There are many others—friends and colleagues—who have contributed ideas, comments and insight as we worked through the complex and challenging issues that this book addresses: Tony Foley, Frances Gibson, Richard Grimes, Vivien Holmes, Richard Johnstone, Michael McNamara, David McQuoid-Mason, Zoe Rathus, Simon Smith, Gai Walker, Kristen Wallwork, Denise Wasley and Leah Wortham, among them. We also acknowledge the many clinicians and law teachers across Australia who have offered their opinions and observations during our research phase. Without them, our prescription for powerful and accountable legal education would be far less confident.

We would not have been able to formulate and agree on our mutual (and sometimes differing) perspectives without the growing sense of shared insight we acquired while working on the underlying research. That project forged a consensus that we have come to value and respect. We therefore thank the Australian Government's Office of Learning and Teaching for the grant that got us going in the first place.

Finally, each of us thanks our families, for their patience and support during our late nights and interrupted weekends and holidays.

1

The reason for this book

Why address Australian clinical legal education now?

Australian legal education is evolving rapidly in response to university competition for more students in perceived high-status courses. The lack of any caps on law enrolments, and the perception that some courses can be delivered less expensively online, have encouraged a belief that much larger numbers of students can be graduated from old and new law schools alike. The typical law school business model is increasingly and inevitably fee-driven, since graduate law students can be charged large amounts of money for their degrees.[1]

At the same time, law schools are delivering larger numbers of graduates into a shrinking or, at best, stable legal jobs market. Regardless of the state of the Australian economy in any one period, overseas legal process providers are succeeding in standardising and commodifying local, routine legal work at such levels that many local law graduates, particularly those without much or any experience of legal practice or who don't have family connections, struggle to get jobs.[2] And there is every indication

---

1   See e.g. M Thornton, 'Deregulation, Debt and the Discipline of Law' (2014) 39(4) *Alternative Law Journal* 213–16; M Thornton, 'Legal education in the corporate university' (2014) 10 *Annual Review of Law and Social Science* 19–35; M Thornton, 'Introduction [to Part IV: Justice in a Comparative Context]', in M Thornton and L Shannon, '"Selling the Dream": Law School Branding and the Illusion of Choice' (2013) 23(2) *Legal Education Review* 249–71.
2   See Law Society of New South Wales, *Future Prospects of Law Graduates Report and Recommendations* (2015), perma.cc/3CPB-HTWF.

that the application of artificial intelligence to many legal processes is only in its infancy, so that the number of local legal jobs may never return to buoyancy under the sheer weight and number of instantly accessible overseas providers, combined with these emerging technologies.

There may be no solution to this economic pincer movement if governments remain unwilling to cap law enrolments. In fact, the opposite may be the case, as free-trade agreements increasingly specify greater access to Australian higher education.[3] But there is also a strong desire for quality legal education through the development of standards, particularly the threshold learning outcomes project,[4] and law school legal educators are increasingly committed to doing things better, not just to withstand the above pressures, but to fulfil their own desires for excellence. Even if legal education and legal employment is being squeezed, many academic law teachers believe that the social and justice values of the Australian legal profession cannot be allowed to wither for want of law graduates who are practice-ready, ethically aware and intending to contribute to justice and social equity.[5] Contemporary major reviews of legal education in the United States and the United Kingdom—discussed in detail in Chapter 10—concur that clinical legal education is a key strategy not just for legal educators determined to strengthen law graduates' professional capacities, but also in support of the wider and more fundamental task of maintaining the rule of law.

This book is dedicated to those teachers and law schools who view academic legal education as a force for good and, in particular, to an aspect of that process—clinical legal education—that has the best chance of strengthening legal education and hence law graduates of the future.

Clinical teachers largely appreciate that they are 'on a mission' to strengthen legal education and have gathered for irregular conferences at different law schools since the 1980s. As referred to in Chapter 3,

---

3   See, generally, Angel J Calderon, J Tangas, 'Trade Liberalisation, Regional Agreements and Implications for Higher Education' (2007) 5(18) *Higher Education Management and Policy* 29–104.
4   These outcomes are a generally accepted set of standards for the learning process in law schools. See Anna Huggins, 'Incremental and Inevitable: Contextualising the Threshold Learning Outcomes for Law' (2015), 38(1) *UNSW Law Journal* 264.
5   See e.g. V Holmes and others, *Submission to LACC Review of Academic Requirements for Admission to the Legal Profession* (26 March 2015); www.lawsociety.com.au/about/StudentHub/LawGraduatesReport/index.htm.

Kingsford Legal Service (a clinical site of the University of New South Wales law school) publishes an annual guide to current Australian clinical programs in an effort to disseminate knowledge of their depth and breadth. Of course, the clinical legal education 'movement' is not alone in a desire to improve legal education. The federal government's Office of Learning and Teaching (OLT),[6] the Council of Australian Law Deans (CALD),[7] the Law Admissions Consultative Committee (LACC)[8] and the Australian Professional Legal Education Council (APLEC),[9] which oversees pre-admission practical legal training, are all attempting to improve educational quality in different ways.

Regulatory bodies are well aware of the potential and the capacity of clinical legal education to improve law courses and they interact routinely with law school deans. The Victorian regulator of that state's law schools' curricula, the then Council of Legal Education,[10] was closely involved in our research phase and is influential in other jurisdictions. Similarly, the Australia New Zealand Law Admissions Consultative Committee (LACC) reports to the Council of Australian and New Zealand Chief Justices and counts CALD among its membership.[11] But these are institutional bodies rather than actual teachers. While this book is addressed to clinical teachers—'clinicians'—and intending clinicians, it will also be of considerable use to law school leaders and legal professionals with an interest in legal education. It is written by clinicians and is informed by empirical research conducted by them. That research led to the September 2012 report known as 'Best Practices: Australian Clinical Legal Education' and then to the larger final published report, *Best Practices: Australian*

6   See www.olt.gov.au. Accessed 4 June 2015.
7   See perma.cc/GT6V-UZY4. Accessed 4 June 2015.
8   See www.lawcouncil.asn.au/LACC. Accessed 4 June 2015.
9   See perma.cc/E8UD-H5UM. Accessed 4 June 2015.
10   This body is now the Victorian Legal Admissions Board (VLAB). See perma.cc/BV66-4EBJ.
11   See Law Admissions Consultative Committee at perma.cc/Y7PC-C9DR. This site states: 'The Law Admissions Consultative Committee (LACC) consists of representatives of the Law Admitting Authority in each Australian jurisdiction, the Committee of Australian Law Deans, the Australasian Professional Legal Education Council and the Law Council of Australia. It is generally responsible to the Australian and New Zealand Council of Chief Justices, which appoints the Chairman of the Committee.'

Clinical Legal Education (2013) (referred to here as *Best Practices*).[12] Throughout this book, we refer to the best practices developed for those reports because, as we describe in Chapter 10, they are the product of a research program and are not just a matter of individual opinion.

Each of the following chapters represents a tangible extension of *Best Practices*. We became acutely aware during the research process that each of the topics we address has individual importance, not just as a descriptor of some aspect of Australian clinical legal education, but as a key element in the best of clinical legal education. These topics did not suddenly emerge in a flash of light. Long and sometimes difficult debates about what the research process had uncovered were followed by agreement and then U-turns, as often as not. Gradually, a shared understanding of what is truly best, and not just good or better, emerged from a digestion of research reports and the literature, and our reflection on both.

This book takes *Best Practices* one step further, or perhaps one step deeper. In that report we condensed the underlying debates into concise statements so that key players, especially law deans, might readily accept that clinical legal education is not just an option within wider legal education, but a necessity for the best of legal education. That task was achieved in the unanimous adoption of our best practices by CALD in November 2012.[13]

Now, our (educational) task is to more clearly inform and persuade Australian colleagues not just of the depth and potential of clinical legal education, but also of the detailed operational issues that, when confronted,

---

12   The development of this report occurred during 2010–12. An application by Adrian Evans in 2009 to the then Australian Learning and Teaching Council (ALTC) (now the Office for Learning and Teaching (OLT)) led to a research grant to investigate clinical teaching practices in Australian law schools with a view to improving and strengthening student learning in clinics and, hence, the wider law curriculum. The authors of this book (other than Peter Joy) were joint researchers (along with Ebony Booth) in this project. Regional surveys of all Australian law schools allowed the identification of all those offering a clinical course or utilising clinical legal methods in their teaching. Analyses of these clinicians' responses to subsequent surveys and interviews permitted the authors to develop best practices in clinical legal education. The document titled 'Best Practices: Australian Clinical Legal Education Sept 2012' contains only those best practices and was uploaded to the CALD website in November 2012 after it had been endorsed by CALD. It is document number 14 and can be found at perma.cc/BY6N-6SRF. For the larger final project report, published in 2013, see Adrian Evans, Anna Cody, Anna Copeland, Jeff Giddings, Mary Anne Noone, Simon Rice and Ebony Booth, *Best Practices: Australian Clinical Legal Education* (cited hereafter as *Best Practices*), which can be downloaded from the OLT website: www.olt.gov.au/resource-best-practices-Australian-clinical-legal-education; perma.cc/2J6E-ZMQX. Ebony Booth was a research assistant on the research project and contributed considerably to its organisation, background research and management. The supporting research material (including summaries of the Regional Reports) is also linked to this site.

13   See footnote 12.

will result in the best clinical legal education. This task is not simple. The greater use of clinical teaching methods in Australian law schools is yet to be matched by a strong understanding of the pedagogical choices required to maximise this most powerful of teaching methods. This lack of strong engagement with the pedagogy of clinical legal education was one catalyst for *Best Practices*, but such a commitment remains elusive. In this book we use the research results that led to *Best Practices* as a pathway into the discussion of these key areas of engagement. Each is canvassed thoroughly by one or two of us as authors of a chapter, with moderation provided by each of the other authors.

Coverage of chapters

The primary authorship of each chapter varies and, to that extent, there will be a difference in voice in each chapter, albeit one that has been moderated by the comments of every other author. Chapter 2 is primarily the work of Jeff Giddings, and dissects the extended context of Australian legal education generally, explaining the regulatory framework and distinguishing clinical legal education from practical legal training, service learning and *pro bono* programs, while discussing the relationship with work-integrated learning. Beyond scene-setting, we discuss in Chapter 2 the need for a functioning 'ethical infrastructure' to strengthen the professionalism of clinical legal practice. Finally, Chapter 2 offers an extended overview of the state of play in Australian legal education and its relationship to clinical legal education, including the currently vexing issues of wellness and depression and their effect on all law students' performance.

Chapter 3 is authored by Mary Anne Noone and Anna Cody. It reflects the multilayered debates about definitions and the proliferation of terms that always come up whenever clinical legal education is discussed. This chapter appears early on in the book so that readers can be clear about what is actually meant by terms such as clinical legal education, a clinic, a client and a 'model'. Different models of clinical legal education are suited to making different contributions to aims and learning outcomes. Phrases such as 'in-house live client clinic', 'in-house live client clinic (some external funding)', 'external live client clinic (agency clinic)', 'externships (includes internships and placements)' and 'clinical components' are all identified, distinguished and justified. Chapter 3 will be of special interest to clinicians and law deans looking at externships because of tight budgets. Externships and agency clinics are increasingly the point of entry to clinical legal education for smaller law schools because of the view that they cost less to implement and run. The conflict about whether a simulated experience is or is not 'clinical' is also addressed, for similar reasons.

In Chapter 4, Simon Rice tackles good course design. It is a first-order mistake to simply begin a clinic and hope for the best, because it is only possible to assess whether a clinic is successful by measuring it against the aim behind its establishment. In clarifying clinical aims and objectives, the design process identifies the potential to shape clinical experiences in order to make them as constructive as possible for students and other communities. The provision of clinical experience involves broader and significantly more complex learning outcomes beyond the acquisition of practical skills. Course aims can include the promotion of legal doctrine, addressing specific social issues, developing legal and/or professional skills, promotion of social values, strengthening of legal theory or social justice, the provision of public service or the development of legal policy and law reform. The chapter also looks at the options for student selection, a topic that will become increasingly important as student pressure for selection into clinical legal education programs increases.

Chapter 5 is composed by Anna Cody and Simon Rice and recognises that notions of justice are the central framework for our endeavours as clinicians. Social justice inspired the emergence of clinics, both in Australia and elsewhere, and should, in our view, continue to guide their development. The chapter explores what justice means for contemporary clinical legal education, whether community legal education, community development, strategic litigation or policy advocacy leading to law reform. But there is a recurring debate—encouraged to some extent by the prevailing conservative political mood of the last decade—should clinics be about social justice at all, or only really about direct service and student learning? In an era when some new clinics may attempt to provide business advice or deliver services for a fee, it might be suggested that our emphasis on a justice focus for clinical programs is passé. We do not agree and are confident that the socially appropriate focus of an Australian clinical program is the promotion of justice for clients and clients' interests, and of students' appreciation of this priority as they grow in confidence and understanding of injustice in contemporary societies. Clinical education is significantly more than a 'mechanistic' educational methodology.

Chapter 6 deals with clinical supervision, perhaps the most neglected of clinical skills as well as the most important for the best clinical legal education. Jeff Giddings makes a strong case for effective supervision as central to clinical pedagogy, and that effective practices need to be developed in order to enable students to learn as much as possible from their (relatively short) clinic experience. And the unexpected benefits for supervisors are not forgotten: because good supervision is mutually enriching for supervisor and supervisee alike, competent supervision training is likely to be a strengthening and re-energising experience for all. Clinicians will be particularly interested in supervision from the point of view of the sometimes problematic externship clinic, where the practice environment can permit less than effective supervision and where clinicians may have less access to good supervision training. Online supervision poses particular challenges, but the underlying principles of effective supervision, affirmed in our research program, are identical regardless of media. Importantly for new clinics, the chapter addresses the sensitive topic of supervision ratios, that is, the maximum number of students that a law school ought to require a clinician to simultaneously supervise; and offers practical, accessible guidance for new supervisors.

A popular but not well understood aspect of clinical legal education is the power of reflection. This issue is explored in great depth by Anna Copeland in Chapter 7. Anna asks rhetorically whether reflection is as important to clinicians and their students as water is to human survival. Clinical legal education cannot do without it. Good reflection by a student means that their mistakes are less likely to be repeated and, in grasping that simple insight, students learn how to learn indefinitely. Optimal clinical legal education involves a circular sequence of experience, reflection, theory, practice, and then further reflection. The best reflective practice exposes students sensitively but sharply to the essentially positivist nature of much law teaching and, in that moment, encourages them to get involved in serious law reform and community development. Students are enabled through reflection to continue to learn from their own experience, long after they have left their clinic. The chapter leads into a wider discussion about clinical assessment in Chapter 8, by raising questions about how reflection can be taught and assessed. For example, should clinical legal education even attempt to assess a student's capacity for reflection, or should the essentially intimate nature of reflection justify its remaining private and unexplored?

The assessment of students' clinical performance is next on our list of 'must discuss' clinical legal education issues. Assessment is often an afterthought in a new clinical legal education program, but not in this book. In Chapter 8, Adrian Evans highlights why assessment is critical to achieving course aims and objectives and can lead to student dissatisfaction if not thought through carefully. For example, if a law school operates a criminal defence or Innocence clinic (the latter aims to achieve post-conviction pardons in the light of new evidence), how will clinic performance be measured if there are few acquittals or releases of clients from custody? Assessment must be thought through so that its components are significantly wider than the success of client representation. It can occur in different forms, with some programs preferring to grade only on a pass/fail basis, while others prefer the full range from fail through to distinction.

Chapter 9 is also authored by Adrian Evans and discusses adequate staffing and infrastructure levels in Australian clinics, depending on the type of clinic and its learning objectives. Under-resourced (that is, underfunded) clinics face major challenges, so that finding ways to involve a range of external partners has potential to promote the contributions clinics can make. Chapter 9 also recognises that even the well-structured clinic will decline if people with inadequate skills are appointed to run it. We pay specific attention to clinical directors, administrators and 'coal-face' clinicians, and provide a table that lists minimum resources needed in different clinic structures.

In Chapter 10, Peter Joy provides international comparisons, along with a very helpful analysis, of the approaches taken to strengthening live client clinical legal education by each of the United Kingdom, the United States of America and Australia. The analysis highlights what is distinctive about Australia's approach (for example, the dual emphasis on both education and service), and helps clinicians reflect on what is generic to all good programs and what ought to be improved in Australian clinical legal education (for example, the academic status of clinicians). The chapter concludes with a cross-referenced table, offering a valuable overview of the general focus of each country's set of best clinical practices.

In our concluding Chapter 11, Mary Anne Noone discusses the links between some recent developments in Australian clinical legal education and emerging trends in legal education, legal practice and the delivery of legal aid services. Mary Anne's focus is the changing legal educational landscape since the 2010–11 collection of data for the *Best Practices* report. Since then, the rise of the JD degree coupled with federal regulatory developments has improved the climate for greater penetration of clinical methods into Australian law schools. And clinicians themselves are strengthening and deepening their commitment, though never in smooth waters. The resilience of clinical teachers in adapting to course restrictions caused by reductions in community legal aid funding, is a case in point. Yet the innovative spirit of these teachers remains constant, particularly in their creation of cross-jurisdictional and multidisciplinary clinics and in their participation in global justice movements of various dimensions. It is for good reason that Australian clinicians are now well-regarded contributors to a number of emerging Southeast Asian clinical programs.

Conclusion

Australian clinical legal education remains a rapidly evolving phenomenon. Our prior efforts to underpin this growth and depth with an empirically based report and analysis of current practices were a necessary precursor to this book. Here we set out our understanding of the thematic history of clinical legal education in this country—and of its transformative potential for legal education—in the light of that research and of our subsequent experiences and reflection.

2

Clinics and Australian law schools approaching 2020

Introduction

In this chapter, we consider the place of clinical legal education in Australian legal education generally.[1] We chart the countervailing currents set to influence the prominence and direction of Australian clinics as they approach 2020 with Australia's entire higher education sector facing very turbulent times. The chapter is designed to set the scene for the key aspects of clinical legal education addressed in subsequent chapters. We argue that clinics can and should make multiple contributions to Australian legal education, including fostering student commitment to concepts of justice and raising awareness of how the law and legal processes impact on people.

Law schools and their clinical programs are subject to a range of powerful influences.[2] The prospects for clinics, being part of the higher education sector, will continue to be shaped by the actions of regulators and by broader university agendas. The judiciary and legal profession have

---

1   This chapter draws extensively on research undertaken by Jeff Giddings as part of his PhD study, 'Influential Factors in the Sustainability of Clinical Legal Education Programs'. See Jeff Giddings, *Promoting Justice Through Clinical Legal Education* (2013) Justice Press (cited hereafter as Giddings (2013)).

2   For an analysis of the range of influential factors, see Giddings (2013), Chapter 5. See also Margaret Barry, Jon Dubin and Peter Joy, 'Clinical Education for This Millennium: The Third Wave' (2000) 7(1) *Clinical Law Review* 1.

important roles to play in supporting the work of clinics. Economic challenges, such as those generated by the Global Financial Crisis in 2008 and, more recently, federal government policy shifts and budget cuts, appear set to slow the recent momentum that has seen many Australian law schools develop new clinical programs.[3]

The contributions of clinical legal education

Experiential learning has the potential to contribute to achieving a range of objectives for students, clients and law schools. This generates both opportunities and challenges for those responsible for clinical programs. The capacity to both broaden and deepen student learning is central to clinical legal education. Students can benefit from a sustained experience enabling them to develop understandings and approaches that foster ethical and reflective practice. Academics, supervisors and students involved in clinical programs can make a broad range of research-related contributions, especially where projects require a breadth of knowledge and expertise.[4] Clinicians are also likely to be able to engage effectively with the public policy dimensions of research issues and identify ways to utilise knowledge from other disciplines. Importantly, clinical programs also provide law schools with a natural point of focus for community service, ethical reflection and professional engagement activities.

The service dimension of clinical legal education can generate substantial community benefits while promoting student awareness of social justice and commitment to *pro bono* values. These benefits are evident from the history of Australian clinical legal education, which reveals an enduring commitment to social justice and service.[5] Many Australian clinics continue

3   Giddings (2013), Chapter 1. See also Kingsford Legal Centre, *Australian Clinical Legal Education Guide 2014–2015*, Kingsford Legal Centre.

4   For examples of student contributions to research, see Liz Curran, 'Innovations in an Australian Clinical Legal Education Program: Students Making a Difference in Generating Positive Change' (2004) 6(1) *International Journal of Clinical Legal Education* 162.

5   Mary Anne Noone, 'Australian Community Legal Centres: The University Connection' in Jeremy Cooper and Louise Trubek (eds), *Educating for Justice: Social Values and Legal Education* (1997) Ashgate, 267; Giddings (2013), 8–10, 46–47.

to view community service as an integral element of their programs.[6] Commitment to justice and client service can usefully be extended beyond clinics to inform other elements of the work of law schools, as we discuss in Chapter 5. A more recent connection between clinical methods and ethical practice is also emerging for law schools, as they seek to respond to broader community calls for lawyers who are ethically aware and resilient. We discuss the concept of 'ethical infrastructure', as it affects clinics, later in this chapter.

Clinical legal education and other forms of experiential legal education offer a more complete package than other pedagogies, but they do so with the cost of often intensive student supervision. At its most effective, Australian clinical legal education is distinguished from other forms of 'learning by doing' by its commitment to social justice and the structured approach taken to student supervision. As will be discussed later in this chapter, the focus of clinical legal education is more developmental than is the case for placement arrangements in the practical legal training (PLT) programs that law graduates must complete prior to professional admission. Clinical programs in Australia also tend to provide greater structure and require greater student responsibility than work-integrated learning experiences and student volunteer programs.

Clinical legal education and service learning share a strong commitment to social justice. As we discuss later in this chapter, service learning involves students and academics working on legal issues often generated by crisis circumstances.[7] The unpredictability involved in responding to crises tends to make it challenging to use such experiences as the centre point of an experiential learning framework. Service learning may have a more important role to play as a site for more advanced clinic-type experiences.

---

6   *Identifying Current Practices in Clinical Legal Education, Regional Report: New South Wales and Australian Capital Territory*, 12–13 (at perma.cc/FU7X-5TNV); *Identifying Current Practices in Clinical Legal Education, Regional Report: Queensland and Northern New South Wales*, 8 (at perma. cc/257Z-6EMR); *Identifying Current Practices in Clinical Legal Education, Regional Report: South Australia*, 7–8, (at perma.cc/3MPF-5U5A); *Identifying Current Practices in Clinical Legal Education, Regional Report: Victoria and Tasmania*, 7 (at perma.cc/J562-X6GU); *Identifying Current Practices in Clinical Legal Education, Regional Report: Western Australia and Northern Territory*, 6 (at perma. cc/4EDN-5SZG). See also Judith Dickson, 'Clinical Legal Education in the 21st Century: Still Educating for Service?' (2000) 1 *International Journal of Clinical Legal Education* 33.
7   Laurie Morin and Susan Waysdorf, 'The Service-Learning Model in the Law School Curriculum' (2011–12) 56 *New York Law School Law Review* 561.

Clinical legal education has potential to make a substantial contribution to legal education generally, through integrating practical insights and theoretical understandings in order to transcend the current doctrinal focus. But there remains a long way to go until this potential is embraced by the legal academy in Australia. Until this integrative potential is harnessed, clinics are unlikely to feature prominently in professional admission requirements and in the standards set for law schools. Those charged with developing clinical legal education face the significant challenge of building the level of awareness of these programs among public policymakers, members of the judiciary and the practising legal profession as well as within both their universities and their law schools.[8]

At the very time that many Australian law schools are responding to university agendas related to experiential learning,[9] the viability of current models of clinical legal education may be called into question by various factors. These include changes to how the legal profession and legal education are structured and regulated, along with dramatic growth in the numbers of law schools and law graduates seeking to enter the legal profession. These changes are examined in the next part of this chapter. We then consider the likely implications for clinical legal education of sector-wide developments, namely the promotion of work-integrated learning and capstone experiences. The chapter ends by addressing the relationship between student wellbeing, learning and service, and the potential for clinical legal education to contribute to the development of resilient legal professionals with an enhanced awareness of ethically appropriate behaviour.

Dramatic growth in the number of law schools

Australia has seen a significant increase in the numbers of law schools and law students over the past 25 years, and this has fostered the development of a range of new clinical programs. Barker refers to an 'avalanche of law schools', with their numbers trebling since the Dawkins reforms to tertiary education in the late 1980s.[10] In 1998, Chesterman described the new

---

8   Giddings (2013), Chapter 11; Mary Anne Noone, 'Time to Rework the Brand "Clinical Legal Education"' (2013) 19 *International Journal of Clinical Legal Education* 341.

9   See Janice Orrell, *Good Practice Report: Work-integrated Learning* (2011) Australian Learning and Teaching Council.

10   David Barker, 'An Avalanche of Law Schools, 1989–2013' (2013) 6 *Journal of the Australasian Law Teachers Association* 153. See also Margaret Thornton and Lucinda Shannon, '"Selling the Dream": Law School Branding and the Illusion of Choice' (2013) 23(2) *Legal Education Review* 249.

'third wave' law schools as having filled some of the many gaps in legal education.[11] Lansdell refers to a dramatic increase in student numbers, from 11,254 studying law in 1984 to 36,331 studying law or legal studies in 2000.[12] More recently, Thornton and Shannon have argued that Australian law schools offer prospective law students an illusion of choice that emphasises employability and glamour. They are rightly critical of law school branding that pays insufficient attention to 'the centrality of justice and critique'.[13] Their analysis could have usefully considered the potential of clinic-based learning and service to make a major contribution to the development of a justice-focused legal education.[14] Those involved in clinical legal education have long emphasised its potential beyond being merely a 'head start' program for those soon to enter the profession.[15] As we noted earlier, Australian clinical legal education continues to be strongly linked to various access to justice agendas.

The Dawkins reforms promoted the establishment of new law schools, but did so in a manner that generated financial pressures to maximise student numbers. Since 1991, the federal government has used a Relative Funding Model to allocate operating grants to universities. Law is placed in the lowest of five discipline funding clusters (along with economics, accounting and various humanities disciplines) with a weighting of 1.[16]

---

11   Michael Chesterman, 'The New Law Schools: What's New in Them?' in John Goldring, Charles Sampford and Ralph Simmonds (eds), *New Foundations in Legal Education* (1998) Cavendish, 204. He identified the achievements of these new entrants in their emphasis on practical skills training and practical experience, integrating law with other disciplines and in distance learning, 205–06.
12   Gaye Lansdell, 'Have We "Pushed The Boat Out Too Far" in Providing Online Practical Legal Training? A Guide to Best Practices for Future Programs' (2009) 19 *Legal Education Review* 149, 151, note 11.
13   Margaret Thornton and Lucinda Shannon, cited at footnote 10, 251.
14   Margaret Thornton and Lucinda Shannon, cited at footnote 10, 261–63. Their criticism of experiential learning relates to how it is marketed 'because it accords with the market's demand for graduates with "job ready" skills—that is, the neoliberal imperative which favours "know how" over "know what"'.
15   Meredith Ross, 'A "Systems" Approach to Clinical Legal Education' (2007) 13 *Clinical Law Review* 779, 781. In her account of the history of the clinical program at the University of Wisconsin, Ross quotes (at 788) the founder of that program, Frank Remington, who criticised skills-focused courses as narrowing the clinical experience to a 'head start program' for people soon to join the profession.
16   Andrew Goldsmith, 'Why Should Law Matter? Towards a Clinical Model of Legal Education' (2002) 25(3) *University of New South Wales Law Journal* 721, 721–30. See also Richard Johnstone and Sumitra Vignaendra, *Learning Outcomes and Curriculum Development in Law: A Report Commissioned by the Australian Universities Teaching Committee* (2003) Higher Education Group, Department of Science, Education and Training, 3–4; Les McCrimmon, 'Mandating a Culture of Service: Pro Bono in the Law School Curriculum' (2003–04) 14(1) *Legal Education Review* 53, 72–73; and Mary Keyes and Richard Johnstone, 'Changing Legal Education: Rhetoric, Reality, and Prospects for the Future' (2004) 26(4) *Sydney Law Review* 556.

By contrast, the top cluster (comprising medicine, dentistry and veterinary science) has a weighting of 2.7. Higher clusters received more funds per student enrolled. Consequently, and perhaps inevitably, less expensive ways of teaching were reinforced as the default approach in Australian law schools.[17]

While some law schools have recently created new experiential learning opportunities, the pedagogy informing some of these programs requires further development. Our research for *Best Practices* revealed considerable variation among clinical programs in terms of the responsibility given to students, supervisory processes and the classroom component accompanying the clinic experience.[18] Further, the resource-intensive nature of clinical programs has contributed to their remaining elective courses rather than becoming a compulsory part of the curriculum. In an effort to reduce costs, some law schools have relied on unpaid and unsupported external supervisors. While external placements have great potential to provide students with excellent learning opportunities, they require careful structuring in terms of the supervision arrangements and the academic component linked to the placement. Some of these newer programs may also be underperforming in any effort to inculcate a justice focus in their students. Unless close attention is paid to the pedagogy that underpins experiential learning, Australian law schools may end up in a 'race to the bottom' that emphasises the practice-oriented experience at the expense of the justice-oriented learning we discuss in Chapter 5.

Regulation of law schools

The Council of Australian Law Deans (CALD) has adopted Standards for Australian Law Schools,[19] which address a range of matters related to the operation of law schools and law courses. The standards facilitated the establishment of the Australian Law Schools Standards Committee

---

17 Giddings (2013), 121.

18 *Identifying Current Practices in Clinical Legal Education, Regional Report: New South Wales and Australian Capital Territory*, 12–13 (at perma.cc/FU7X-5TNV); *Identifying Current Practices in Clinical Legal Education, Regional Report: Queensland and Northern New South Wales*, 8 (at perma. cc/257Z-6EMR); *Identifying Current Practices in Clinical Legal Education, Regional Report: South Australia*, 7–8, (at perma.cc/3MPF-5U5A); *Identifying Current Practices in Clinical Legal Education, Regional Report: Victoria and Tasmania*, 7 (at perma.cc/J562-X6GU); *Identifying Current Practices in Clinical Legal Education, Regional Report: Western Australia and Northern Territory*, 6 (at perma. cc/4EDN-5SZG).

19 Council of Australian Law Deans, The CALD Standards for Australian Law Schools, as adopted 17 November 2009 and amended to March 2013: perma.cc/3EGK-LAW5.

(CALD standards committee). The committee is independent of CALD and has responsibility for certifying whether a law school complies with these voluntary standards,[20] a process that began in 2015.

It remains too early to say whether the CALD standards committee will produce meaningful change, but at least the standards refer to the potential contributions clinics can make to law school engagement with the wider community. However, it should be emphasised that they do so only in aspirational terms, as an example of experiential learning.[21] This lukewarm endorsement of clinics should be contrasted with the references to clinical legal education in the arguments made by CALD in efforts to reverse the history of underfunding of law schools. In its 2007 submission to the Review of the Impact of the Higher Education Support Act 2003: Funding Cluster Mechanism, CALD stated:

> It is now widely accepted that legal education should have a clinical or industry placement component, with students having hands-on experience with real clients; yet clinical programs are so expensive that only a handful of law schools have been able to fund them adequately, usually with substantial external support, to which many law schools do not have easy access.[22]

Australian law schools have also faced other recent regulatory changes. The Tertiary Education Quality and Standards Agency (TEQSA) was established in 2011 with responsibility for ensuring compliance with the Australian Qualifications Framework (AQF). The AQF is the national policy that sets the specifications for regulated qualifications in Australia.[23] One of the key reference points for the operation of the AQF in terms of law studies is the Threshold Learning Outcomes (TLOs) for Law published in 2010 as part of the Learning and Teaching Academic Standards component of the AQF.[24] TLOs have been developed for a range of disciplines and are defined in terms of minimum discipline knowledge,

---

20   CALD Standards Introductory Context Statement March 2014: perma.cc/M3XG-7H96.

21   Council of Australian Law Deans, The CALD Standards for Australian Law Schools, Standard 2.2.4: perma.cc/3EGK-LAW5.

22   See Council of Australian Law Deans, Submission to the Review of the Impact of the Higher Education Support Act 2003: Funding Cluster Mechanism, 26 February 2007, 2.

23   See www.teqsa.gov.au. Accessed 16 September 2016.

24   Australian Learning and Teaching Council, Learning and Teaching Academic Standards Project, Bachelor of Laws Learning and Teaching Academic Standards Statement, December 2010: perma.cc/X93F-GHM5. TLOs have also been developed for Juris Doctor (JD) graduates. CALD has stated that the TLOs for JD studies are designed to ensure they reflect the AQF requirements for a Master's degree (extended) qualification. See perma.cc/KD4J-VQXF

discipline-specific skills and professional capabilities including attitudes and professional values that are expected of a graduate from a specified level of program in a specified discipline area.[25] Clinical legal education can make vital contributions to law students' achieving each of the following six TLOs:

- understanding a coherent body of *knowledge*;
- developing understandings and abilities related to *ethics and professional responsibility*;[26]
- developing relevant *thinking skills*;
- developing research-related skills;
- being able to communicate and collaborate; and
- being able to *self-manage*.[27]

The application of the sector-wide AQF to the law discipline has been strongly criticised. The University of New South Wales Law Dean, Professor David Dixon, described the AQF as providing 'a series of round holes into which our square pegs don't fit'.[28] The AQF specifications for Honours and Master's degrees were identified as likely to damage law programs without benefit, especially in relation to providing significant disincentives for international students to study law in Australia.[29]

The far-reaching higher education reforms announced by the federal government in the 2014 budget have the potential to impact dramatically on the number of law schools in Australia and their focus. The changes may also see the emergence of new private providers in the legal education market with programs designed to fill perceived gaps in the market.

The globalisation of legal education may generate further regulatory requirements for Australia. In a 2011 report, Flood referred to the influence of factors that include the greater mobility of lawyers, technological developments, greater specialisation and outsourcing, and

---

25   The former Australian Learning and Teaching Council (ALTC) implemented the Threshold Learning Outcomes project. See www.olt.gov.au/system/files/altc_standards.finalreport.pdf.

26   See Chapter 5 of this book.

27   See Learning and Teaching Academic Standards Project, 'Bachelor of Laws Learning and Teaching Academic Standards Statement, December 2010', at perma.cc/X93F-GHM5, at 10. See also Chapter 4 of this book on course design.

28   David Dixon, 'The Regulatory Threat to Australian Legal Education', Centre for Law Markets and Regulation, UNSW, at perma.cc/MMP4-EEL2. Accessed 4 February 2017.

29   See David Dixon, cited at footnote 28.

noted 'an inexorable move in the world towards the Americanisation of legal education, in the form of the widespread adoption of the JD degree over the LLB'.[30] Flood's report referred to the significance of the American Bar Association (ABA) Law School Accreditation Standards and its recent moves to 'liberalize legal education by permitting more online instruction, less security for faculty, and various other changes'.[31] The ABA Standards include requirements for provision of clinical legal education opportunities for students as well as safeguards for the status and employment of clinicians.[32] It is likely that Australian law schools wishing to develop and maintain their place in the developing 'Global JD' market may need to provide their students with clinic-based experiences comparable to those offered by United States law schools.

Practical legal training and preparation for reflective practice?

There have also been dramatic changes in the professional training required of law graduates in order to gain admission to legal practice in Australia. Across Australia, the traditional articles of clerkship have largely been replaced with PLT programs (offered by law schools and private providers) and workplace traineeships.[33] While these PLT programs can generate considerable educational benefits,[34] the placement experiences offered to students vary considerably in terms of duration, currently from three weeks[35] to 16 weeks,[36] and nature. Some programs rely on the student to secure their placement, and almost all permit students to claim

---

30   John Flood, 'Legal Education in the Global Context: Challenges from Globabilization, Technology and Changes in Government Regulation', Report for the Legal Services Board, 1 at perma. cc/N37K-H5TX. Accessed 13 September 2016. Flood is referring to the Juris Doctor degree.

31   See John Flood, cited at footnote 30, 17.

32   Giddings (2013), 43–44.

33   Allan Chay and Frances Gibson, 'Clinical Legal Education and Practical Legal Training' in Sally Kift, Michelle Sanson, Jill Cowley and Penelope Watson (eds), *Excellence and Innovation in Legal Education* (2011) LexisNexis Butterworths, see Chapter 18, 511.

34   For a comprehensive analysis of the merits of PLT programs, see John De Groot, *Producing a Competent Lawyer: Alternatives Available* (1995) Centre for Legal Education. See also footnote 33.

35   See *Tasmanian Legal Practice Court Handbook* (2017), 13, at www.utas.edu.au/legal-studies. Accessed 7 February 2017.

36   See Jeff Giddings and Michael McNamara, 'Preparing Future Generations of Lawyers for Legal Practice: What's Supervision Got to Do With It?' (2014) 37(3) *University of New South Wales Law Journal* 1225.

credit for previous practice-based experience.[37] But the placement process is not without its challenges, and in a range of instances the placement appears not to be effectively integrated with other program components.[38]

The Competency Standards for Entry Level Lawyers that frame the content of PLT programs are concerned with competencies developed principally, if not entirely, through classroom-based programmed training.[39] For the vast majority of students, the classroom is a virtual one, with most PLT programs engaged in online delivery. Lansdell has plausibly argued that programs that blend classroom-based work with online study will be more effective than those that are solely online.[40] This analysis could usefully be extended to include making full use of the learning potential of placement experiences. The current standards make no reference to workplace experience requirements, while the standards that came into operation on 1 January 2015 require a workplace experience of only at least 15 days.[41] It is conceivable that these days will be more widely separated than in the past and involve a wider range of placement sites. If accreditation arrangements were to move beyond requiring students to complete a prescribed number of hours of activities, and were to focus instead on key experiences that students must successfully undertake in collaboration with a skilled supervisor, then there might be reduced emphasis on the number of days while enabling recognition of the added value of clinic-based learning.[42]

Playing 'pass the parcel': Confusion in Australia's legal education framework

The place of clinical teaching methodologies in Australian legal education is left uncertain by the continuing lack of clarity around the functions of the different stages of the legal education process. In many instances, the academic stage of legal education provided by law schools and the professional (or vocational) stage provided by PLT programs operate as

---

37   See Jeff Giddings and Michael McNamara, cited at footnote 36, 1232–35.
38   See Jeff Giddings and Michael McNamara, cited at footnote 36, 1232–36.
39   Allan Chay and Frances Gibson, cited at footnote 33, 519. Chay and Gibson refer to classroom and online learning environments in which students can gain 'some or all of the benefits of experiential learning'.
40   Gaye Lansdell, cited at footnote 12.
41   Law Admissions Consultative Committee, *Practical Legal Training Competency Standards for Entry Level Lawyers, Requirements for Each Form of PLT*, 4.1(b)(ii).
42   This is discussed further in Giddings (2013), 257 and 343.

disconnected parts of an uncoordinated system. The most prominent exceptions to this *ad hoc* approach have been the clinic-focused Professional Program pioneered by the University of Newcastle Law School in the 1990s[43] and the integrated PLT programs at the law schools of the University of Technology Sydney (UTS) and Flinders University, but even these programs lack clear alignment with the supervised legal practice period required of all newly admitted practitioners.

Unfortunately, some involved in legal education continue to conflate clinical legal education with the PLT requirements that law graduates must complete prior to admission to practice. As we discuss in Chapters 4 and 5 in this book, the focus of many undergraduate clinical programs is on critique, exploration and the development of real-world judgment, rather than on the need to meet competency requirements. It is a matter of concern that legal education authorities have not taken up the challenge of finding ways for these phases to work constructively together. However, this task may now have become culturally and logistically easier with the advent of uniform regulation of legal practice across Victoria and New South Wales in 2015.

The superior courts in each Australian state and territory play a central role in setting requirements for admission to legal practice. In accrediting law degrees, the focus of the admitting authorities in each state and territory, and of the Law Council of Australia's Law Admissions Consultative Committee, has been on ensuring coverage of particular areas of substantive law with limited attention to the approaches used to foster student learning.[44]

The only regulatory requirements for law students to learn in a practice setting involve requirements in PLT programs, and in most instances they require only an unstructured placement in a legal workplace. Australian regulators should recognise the value of giving law students opportunities to engage in 'learning by doing and reflecting' prior to undertaking their PLT. As discussed earlier, focusing on practical skills development leaves

---

43   For an account of the development of the University of Newcastle Law School Professional Program, see Giddings (2013), Chapter 8.

44   In 2004 Keyes and Johnstone highlighted that the nationally unified requirements for admission to the legal profession are preoccupied with issues of content rather than pedagogy. Minimal attention has been paid to addressing graduate attributes, skills and theoretical perspectives: Mary Keyes and Richard Johnstone, cited at footnote 16, 538. See also Vivienne Brand, 'Decline in the Reform of Law Teaching?' (1999) 10 *Legal Education Review* 109, 125–26; and Richard Johnstone and Sumitra Vignaendra, cited at footnote 16, Chapters 1 and 2.

the full educational potential of clinical legal education unfulfilled. Rather, clinics should be recognised for their capacity to develop students' ability to learn from experience, and to connect their classroom learning to the practice of law. Clinical legal education can make a major contribution to law students' ability to develop their understanding of the ethical dimensions of the law and legal processes.[45] This is particularly the case with undergraduate and JD clinics, where the students can be engaged in understanding and exploring key concepts, rather than in meeting competency standards as is required in PLT programs.

Greater use of experiential learning models, and their integration across the academic and professional stages of legal education would, of course, have resource implications for law schools. Regulators have an important role to play in encouraging universities and governments to address the historic inadequacy of resources committed to legal education.[46] In the face of limited resources, such requirements are unlikely to be voluntarily developed by law schools themselves. The United States' experience of accreditation standards imposed by the ABA provides a valuable example of a regulator fostering law school engagement with clinical methods.[47] If accreditation requirements are to be used to promote the broader use of such methods, then it will be valuable for such arrangements to recognise the additional benefits students derive from participation in effectively structured and supervised clinical experiences as compared to other less coherent forms of exposure to legal practice. Students are likely to learn much more when engaged in collaborative work with an experienced supervisor who will harness the learning potential of clinical experiences.

Limited availability of clinical placements, and the underdeveloped nature of clinical pedagogy in Australia, mean there is heavy reliance on graduates learning 'on the job' without being effectively prepared for the rigours of professional life during their legal education. Often these graduates have had little or no exposure to practice-based learning designed to enhance their capacity for reflective practice, and reliance is placed on up to two years of 'supervised legal practice' that must be completed by newly

---

45   Giddings (2013), 59–61.
46   See Giddings (2013), 121.
47   See Giddings (2013), 43–44.

admitted lawyers before they can hold a full practising certificate.[48] Despite this reliance, only limited guidance is provided in relation to the meaning of supervision and appropriate supervision practices. In particular, there is no guidance on the training and development function of supervision and its place in the overall legal education framework. Nor are there any legislative references to the importance of the concept of reflection and its role in law students' learning. It is noteworthy, however, that the Australian Government Productivity Commission's 2014 *Access to Justice Arrangements Inquiry Report* contains a recommendation for the Australian Government to conduct a holistic review of the current status of the three stages of legal education in consultation with the state and territory governments, jurisdictional legal authorities, universities and the profession.[49]

The disconnection between, and confusion around, the respective roles of each phase of legal education and the place of clinic can be eased by greater 'clinic fluency'. By this we mean the familiarity of people with the characteristics of clinical learning in law.[50] Fluency involves a close familiarity with the range of clinical models available (see Chapter 3), the strengths and limits of each, and the value of integrating and sequencing the use of various clinical models in tandem with other teaching methods.[51] Such fluency enables understanding of the great potential of experiential learning, while also tempering unrealistic expectations around what can be achieved with only limited resources. It also entails an appreciation of the potential for insights from clinical legal education to inform the broader law curriculum.

One of the distinctive contributions made by students having the opportunity to learn through supervised work with clients is the development of frameworks for personal reflection. Chapter 6 examines the learning opportunities generated by supervision arrangements that

---

48 *Legal Profession Act 2006* (ACT) s 50; *Legal Profession Act* (NT) s 73; *Legal Profession Act 2007* (Qld) s 56; *Legal Profession Act 2007* (Tas) s 59; *Legal Profession Act 2008* (WA) s 50. In South Australia, this is a requirement pursuant to r 3 of the *Rules of the Legal Practitioners Education and Admission Council 2004*; in NSW (*Legal Profession Uniform Law Application Act 2014*) and Victoria (*Legal Profession Uniform Law Application Act 2014*, Schedule 1, cl 49), the requirement is two years if practical legal training is undertaken, or 18 months if a law firm traineeship is completed.

49 Australian Government Productivity Commission, *Access to Justice Arrangements Inquiry Report* (2014), Chapter 7, 254. See Recommendation 7.1.

50 See Giddings (2013), Chapters 1 and 2.

51 See Chapter 4 of this book.

systematically assist students to 'learn how to learn from experience'.[52] These circumstances make it more important for both law schools and PLT providers to make informed choices about the design and delivery of experiential learning opportunities. The development of supervision arrangements that enable students and their supervisors to effectively harness the learning potential of practice experiences requires sustained engagement with the pedagogy of experiential learning.

These changes in legal education and legal practice in Australia have created serious and unresolved tensions around how to best prepare current students and recent graduates for the effective and ethical practice of law. As noted earlier, opportunities for law graduates to participate in a closely supervised transition to professional practice appear to have diminished.[53] At the very time that the importance of close supervision is being more clearly recognised, it is no longer uniformly available to law graduates. Some law graduates seek to enter the legal profession with little in the way of direct experience of legal work, and without structured support to assist them in making sense of the exposure to practice they have had. This has the potential to place greater expectations on clinics to play a more substantial role in the preparation of students for the practice of law.

Broader university agendas

Interest in clinics has been generated by a range of sector-wide developments in tertiary education. These include the growing emphasis on 'work-integrated learning' and the importance attached to providing graduates with a capstone experience.[54] Both of these trends are linked to developing graduate attributes and employability skills.[55]

---

52 See Chapter 6 of this book.

53 Joe Cantanzariti, 'The Future of the National Legal Profession', Speech to the Opening of Law Summer School 2013, University of Western Australia, Perth, 22 February 2013. The emergence of larger national law firms and, over the past decade in particular, the internationalisation and digitisation of legal practice have further challenged the structures that have traditionally been used to prepare trainee and junior lawyers.

54 Capstone courses are designed to assist students to develop their professional identity and their transition out of university into work and professional life. See Sally Kift, Des Butcher, Rachael Field, Judith McNamara, Catherine Brown and Cheryl Treloar, *Curriculum Renewal in Legal Education: Final Report 2013*, Office for Learning and Teaching at perma.cc/KH3P-93QR.

55 Carol-joy Patrick, Deborah Peach and Catherine Pocknee, *The WIL [Work Integrated Learning] Report: A National Scoping Study* (2009) Australian Learning and Teaching Council, 3.

Work-integrated learning (WIL)

Within universities, efforts have been made to institutionalise WIL 'as a teaching and learning approach which has the potential to provide a rich, active and contextualised learning experience for students which contributes to their engagement in learning'.[56] Orrell's 2011 Australian Learning and Teaching Council (ALTC) *Good Practice Report: Work Integrated Learning* refers to WIL as 'a chameleon term with a problem of definition', describing programs involving student engagement with workplaces and communities as a formal part of their studies with the expectation of 'gaining new knowledge, understandings and capabilities, and mastering skills considered essential to particular workplace practices'.[57]

The 2008 report of the Bradley Review of Australian Higher Education, and the federal government's response to the report, both acknowledge the need for universities to prepare graduates for the world of work, increasing the interest of the sector in WIL as an educational approach.[58] While law as a discipline has not been central to this agenda,[59] the setting of institutional goals is likely to increase pressure on law schools to make workplace learning opportunities readily available to their students.[60] Clinics appear to be seen by law schools as the easiest way to address such pressure despite their different orientation.

As we have noted earlier, clinical legal education in Australia is distinctive in its focus on social justice concerns. Such concerns are more prominent in Australian clinical legal education than in WIL-related activities in other disciplines.[61] In addressing equity, access and social justice in her *Good Practice Report*, Orrell's concern was with the participation of students rather than with the ethos of the programs.[62] WIL programs also tend to be less structured, with limited focus on linking the experiential aspects

---

56   See Carol-joy Patrick and others, cited at footnote 55.

57   Janice Orrell, cited at footnote 9, 5.

58   Denise Bradley, Peter Noonan, Helen Nugent and Bill Scales, *Review of Australian Higher Education: Final Report* (2008) Department of Education, Employment and Workplace Relations.

59   The WIL literature features little about the particular requirements and operational context of law as a discipline. See Patrick and others, cited at footnote 55; and Janice Orrell, cited at footnote 9.

60   See Melinda Shirley, Iyla Davis, Tina Cockburn and Tracey Carver, 'The Challenge of Providing Work-Integrated Learning for Law Students – the QUT Experience' (2006) 9 *International Journal of Clinical Legal Education* 134.

61   See Giddings (2013), 121–22; see also Janice Orrell, cited at footnote 9, 19.

62   See Janice Orrell, cited at footnote 9, 19.

to an academic component. Clinics need to be able to demonstrate the additional learning opportunities generated by a structured practice-based experience if they are to avoid being confused and conflated with WIL.

Capstone experiences

Australian universities have shown increasing interest in developing so-called 'capstone' experiences for students as part of a broader agenda to develop graduate attributes. Capstone courses are generally completed in a student's final year or final semester. They have been defined as a crowning experience, 'with the specific objective of integrating a body of relatively fragmented knowledge in a unified whole'. They enable undergraduate students to 'both look back over their undergraduate curriculum in an effort to make sense of that experience, and look forward to a life of building on that experience'.[63]

Clinical legal education has great potential to address the set of curriculum design principles identified by a Queensland University of Technology (QUT)-led project on capstone experiences in legal education.[64] The following principles were identified by the QUT project team:

- supporting transition by promoting self-management, developing professional identity and supporting career planning and development;
- providing integration and closure;
- responding to diversity by enhancing students' capacity to engage with diversity in professional contexts;
- promoting professional engagement;
- recognising the experience's culminating nature by requiring students to make appropriate use of feedback and to reflect on their own capabilities; and
- being regularly evaluated.[65]

---

63   Robert Durel, 'The Capstone Course: A Rite of Passage' (1993) 21(3) *Teaching Sociology* 223.
64   See Kift and others, cited at footnote 54.
65   Kift and others, cited at footnote 33, Chapter 5.

Clinical courses in a student's final year have often fulfilled many of these features. By default, many clinical elective courses are capstones. It remains to be seen whether clinical programs can be extended to enable all law students to engage in this type of capstone experience. Resource issues would present the most serious challenge to any such proposal.

Learning and service

Recognition of the capacity for clinical legal education to serve multiple purposes generates the need to balance student learning and community service, as well as the legal professional responsibilities of clinic supervisors.[66] Similar challenges are also raised by other models of engagement such as service learning and *pro bono* work.

Service learning

Service learning has been identified by United States clinicians as having great potential to enhance the potential for law students to serve their communities. A United States review of the literature on service learning emphasises the importance of students being directly involved with the service users while engaging in classroom discussion and activities designed to foster reflection.[67] Although it is not prominent in Australian higher education, service learning has been recognised as aligning with Deci and Ryan's self-determination theory that emphasises the basic human needs of autonomy, competence and relatedness.[68] This theory is considered important in the developing literature on wellbeing in the legal profession, an issue we address later in this chapter.

Morin and Waysdorf have written about service learning as a form of experiential learning that involves responding to humanitarian crises, emphasising its focus on community service, with students receiving

---

66 Gavigan sums up this tension very effectively in her account of the Parkdale Clinic operated by Osgoode Hall Law School: 'Put most baldly, the unspeakable question has been: are law students … learning on the backs of the poor? Put more politely, the question was framed not infrequently as one of "service vs. education".' See Shelley Gavigan, 'Twenty-five Years of Dynamic Tension: The Parkdale Community Legal Services Experience' (1997) 35(3) *Osgoode Hall Law Journal* 443, 457. See also Giddings (2013), Chapter 2.
67 Chantal Levesque-Bristol, Timothy Knapp and Bradley Fisher, 'The Effectiveness of Service-Learning: It's Not Always What You Think' (2010) *Journal of Experiential Education* 208.
68 Richard Ryan and Edward Deci, 'Self-Determination Theory and the Facilitation of Intrinsic Motivation, Social Development, and Well-Being' (2000) 55(1) *American Psychologist* 68.

little, if any, academic credit.[69] They provide an account of a special service learning project involving students responding to needs generated by Hurricane Katrina in the United States. The project was service-driven, while recognising the learning potential such work presents. Behre provides another interesting example involving student volunteers responding to legal needs generated by a tornado.[70] The divide between service learning and clinical legal education appears to relate most particularly to the voluntary nature of student contributions, the limited classroom component, and the principal focus on service rather than student learning.[71]

Pro bono

Clinics are often identified as important sites for fostering student commitment to making *pro bono* contributions.[72] Evans has identified the interest of many clinicians in 'proving that a "clinical experience" in law school will direct law students towards public interest lawyering'.[73] However, establishing such a link with hard data remains a challenge. Sandefur and Selbin have reported on the clinical legal education dimensions of the Beyond the JD Research Project, a national longitudinal study of early-career United States lawyers.[74] They found 'surprisingly little empirical evidence about the relationship between clinical legal education and the practical and professional development of law students'.[75] Their data indicate that early-career lawyers value clinical experience more highly than any other aspect of the formal law school curriculum in preparing them to make the transition to the profession.[76] However, their analysis addresses the contributions made by clinical experiences in a

---

69   Laurie Morin and Susan Waysdorf, cited at footnote 7, 574.
70   Kelly Behre, 'Motivations for Law Student Pro Bono: Lessons Learned From the Tuscaloosa Tornado' (2013) 31 *Buffalo Public Interest Law Journal* 1.
71   Valverde has argued that clinic teachers can harness many of the insights and teachable moments generated by service learning in clinical programs. See Jennifer Rosen Valverde, 'Hindsight is 20/20: Finding Teachable Moments in the Extraordinary and Applying Them to the Ordinary' (2013) 20 *Clinical Law Review* 267.
72   For a review of these sources, see Giddings (2013), 64–67.
73   Adrian Evans, 'Efficacy Beyond Reasonable Doubt?' (2001) 19 *Law in Context* 89.
74   Rebecca Sandefur and Jeffrey Selbin, 'The Clinic Effect' (2009) 16 *Clinical Law Review* 57.
75   Rebecca Sandefur and Jeffrey Selbin, cited at footnote 74, 58. They go on to state that the existing research 'does little to reveal, explain or otherwise inform our understanding of the relationship between clinical legal education and the practical and professional development of law students'.
76   Rebecca Sandefur and Jeffrey Selbin, cited at footnote 74, 58–59; see also Table 1, at 85.

stand-alone sense; it would be interesting to consider whether additional contributions can be made through integration of clinical insights across the broader law curriculum.[77]

Law student *pro bono* schemes have developed in Australia through the work of the National Pro Bono Resource Centre[78] and Pro Bono Law Students Australia.[79] Such schemes have the potential to provide pathways for valuable student contributions, provided they are effectively coordinated and resourced. In Chapter 6, we address issues related to the importance of effective supervision and structure in enabling students to maximise their learning from clinical experiences.[80]

Wellness and depression in legal education and legal practice

Awareness of issues related to the mental health and wellbeing of law students has grown dramatically in the past decade. The work of the Tristan Jepson Memorial Foundation[81] and the Wellness for Law Forum[82] in particular has been important in publicising the difficulties facing both law students and lawyers.[83] The 2009 Courting the Blues project reported that 35 per cent of Australian law students recorded elevated levels of psychological distress as compared to 13 per cent of the general population. Almost 40 per cent of those students with high or very high levels of psychological distress reported distress severe enough to warrant medical or clinical intervention. The research concluded that the problem of 'law student distress' was not confined to the United States.[84]

---

77   While such contributions would be difficult to measure, Sandefur and Selbin refer to the Carnegie Report recommendations regarding a curriculum that integrates the cognitive, skills and civic dimensions of legal education. See Rebecca Sandefur and Jeffrey Selbin, cited at footnote 74, 70.
78   See www.nationalprobono.org.au/. Accessed 12 December 2014.
79   Sebastian De Brennan, 'Rethinking Pro Bono: Students Lending a Legal Hand' (2005) 15 *Legal Education Review* 25.
80   See Chapter 5 of this book.
81   See Council of Australian Law Deans, *Promoting Law Student Well-Being Good Practice Guidelines for Law Schools,* September 2014, at perma.cc/V8YP-RYAW.
82   See www.wellnessforlaw.com/. Accessed 13 September 2016.
83   See also the work of National Teaching Fellow, Dr Rachael Field at www.olt.gov.au/altc-teaching-fellow-rachael-field. Accessed 12 December 2014.
84   Norm Kelk, Georgia Luscombe, Sharon Medlow and Ian Hickie, *Courting the Blues: Attitudes Towards Depression in Australian Law Students and Lawyers* (2009) Brain and Mind Institute.

A 2010 study of law students at The Australian National University (ANU) found that students entered law school with rates of wellbeing no lower than those among the general population but that levels of psychological distress rose significantly in first-year law.[85] Research involving students from Melbourne University Law School has subsequently produced findings consistent with those of the ANU study.[86] The Melbourne University Law School study has also questioned the extent to which these wellness issues are confined to legal education, suggesting the challenges may relate to higher education more generally.[87]

Colin James from the University of Newcastle Legal Centre leads the work of Australian clinicians in addressing issues related to the wellbeing of law students and lawyers.[88] His research has investigated the experiences of law graduates in their transition to practice, and has identified a range of strategies to safeguard law students against depression and enhance their experience of law school.

85   Molly Townes O'Brien, Stephen Tang and Kath Hall, 'Changing our Thinking: Empirical Research on Law Student Wellbeing, Thinking Styles and the Law Curriculum' (2011) 21 *Legal Education Review* 149.

86   See Wendy Larcombe, Letty Tumbaga, Ian Malkin, Pip Nicholson and Orania Tokatlidis, 'Does an Improved Experience of Law School Protect Students against Depression, Anxiety and Stress? An Empirical Study of Wellbeing and the Law School Experience of LLB and JD Students' (2013) 35 *Sydney Law Review* 407; and Wendy Larcombe and Katherine Fethers, 'Schooling the Blues? An Investigation of Factors Associated With Psychological Distress Among Law Students' (2013) 36(2) *University of New South Wales Law Journal* 390. For a cautionary view of the concerns raised by the ANU and Melbourne University Law School research projects, see Christine Parker, 'The "Moral Panic" Over Psychological Wellbeing in the Legal Profession: A Personal or Political Ethical Response' (2014) 37(3) *University of New South Wales Law Journal* 1102.

87   Wendy Larcombe, Sue Finch and Rachel Sore, 'Not Only Law Students: High Levels of Psychological Distress in a Large University Sample', Presentation to the 2014 Wellness Network for Law Wellness Forum, QUT, February 2014. See www.wellnessforlaw.com/wp-content/uploads/2014/03/Wendy-Larcombe_Not-only-law-students.pdf.

88   Colin James, 'Law Student Wellbeing: Benefits of Promoting Psychological Literacy and Self-Awareness Using Mindfulness, Strengths Theory and Emotional Intelligence' (2011) 21(2) *Legal Education Review* 217; Colin James, 'Lawyer Dissatisfaction, Emotional Intelligence and Clinical Legal Education' (2008) 18 *Legal Education Review* 123; Colin James, 'Seeing Things as We Are: Emotional Intelligence and Clinical Legal Education' (2005) 8 *International Journal of Clinical Legal Education* 123.

Larry Krieger is among the United States clinicians who are prominent in the therapeutic jurisprudence literature.[89] Krieger's research, in collaboration with Kennon Sheldon, has emphasised the importance of promoting supported autonomy as part of efforts to overcome the 'corrosive effect' of United States legal education on the 'well-being, motivation and values' of law students.[90] Krieger and Sheldon draw on Ryan and Deci's self-determination theory[91] that explains the need people have for 'regular experiences of autonomy, competence, and relatedness to thrive and maximize their positive motivation'.[92] In the context of their longitudinal study of the wellbeing of United States lawyers, they identify a 'specific, cost-effective strategy' for improving wellbeing as 'the provision of autonomy-supportive, rather than controlling, teaching, mentoring and work supervision'.[93] Clinic-based experiences, with their developmental focus and emphasis on supervision and collaboration, clearly have a valuable contribution to make to improving understanding of models of positive lawyering and reducing students' levels of stress and anxiety.[94]

A final characteristic of the well-rounded law graduate, not just a clinical graduate, is the degree of their ethical sophistication. Law schools must teach ethics and professional responsibility, but the extent to which such courses penetrate students' ethical consciousness is not well understood.[95] Arguably, almost no one emerges from an Australian law school with a real consciousness of ethical realities if they have not benefited from a clinic, but the truly resilient law graduate may be best developed through clinical experience of legal ethics, particularly that which exposes students to a thoroughly conceived ethics awareness program. Such programs can be summed up by the term *ethical infrastructure*; a concept that clinics are uniquely able to champion.

---

89   See Susan Brooks, 'Practicing (and teaching) therapeutic jurisprudence: importing social work principles and techniques into clinical legal education' (2004–05) 17 *St Thomas Law Review* 513; Marjorie Silver 'Supporting Attorneys' Personal Skills' (2009) 78 *Revisita Juridica Universidad de Puerto Rico* 147; and Ann Juergens, 'Practicing What We Teach: The Importance of Emotion and Community Connection in Law Work and Law Teaching' (2005) 11 *Clinical Law Review* 413.
90   Kennon Sheldon and Lawrence Krieger, 'Understanding the Negative Effects of Legal Education on Law Students: A Longitudinal Test of Self-Determination Theory' (2007) 33(6) *Personality and Social Psychology Bulletin* 883.
91   Richard Ryan and Edward Deci, cited at footnote 68.
92   Kennon Shelden and Lawrence Krieger, cited at footnote 90, 885.
93   Lawrence Krieger and Kennon Sheldon, 'What Makes Lawyers Happy?: Transcending the Anecdotes With Data From 6200 Lawyers' at perma.cc/8ZCT-HUW8.
94   See Chapter 6 of this book.
95   See the equivocal results of an investigation of students' ethical awareness in Adrian Evans and Josephine Palermo, 'Almost There: Empirical Insights into Clinical Method and Ethics Courses in Climbing the Hill towards Lawyers' Professionalism' (2008) 17 *Griffith Law Review* 252.

Ethical infrastructure

Although the culture of a clinic tends to be visible in the 'atmosphere' of the site after a short visit, there is a further intangible aspect to clinic that is harder to pin down but which is equally important to its reputation and sustainability. The ethical infrastructure, that is, the culture, attitudes and policies of the clinic to ethical practice, is critical to clinic sustainability and graduate resilience. We are not just talking about recognition of fiduciary obligations[96] and minimising the risk of client complaints, although these are very important. More fundamentally, does the clinic as a whole understand, recognise and deal with the need for each of its supervisors to reconcile their views on the appropriate balance of the clinic between these duties to clients and the more important duty to the administration of justice? The contrast in approach reflects a similar discussion in Chapter 5 below, concerning the technical skills versus law-in-context objectives of a clinical program. But the focus here is on legal ethics.

The debate is commonly summed up in the difference between zealous advocacy and responsible lawyering.[97] To take one example, the zealous advocate who is presented with a police prosecutor who forgets to tell a magistrate about the very significant prior convictions of their client, will commonly feel quite justified in staying silent when it comes to sentencing the client for his assault on his wife. The result can be that a violent man with a history of violence is returned to his family. But the responsible lawyer may take the view that such silence is too big a risk to the safety of that woman and will speak up to ensure the court has full information before it makes a decision. The professional conduct rules do not necessarily assist, because they typically support either perspective, depending on the circumstances. Inside a clinic, if one supervising solicitor has a zealous advocate approach and instructs their student to stay silent in a plea should this situation occur, then another supervisor who hears of this and takes the protective responsible lawyering view will likely become very upset, if not angry. If these jurisprudential differences are simply allowed to continue and are not resolved then, in an extreme case such as this, the ethical infrastructure

96   Lawyers are 'fiduciaries' (trustees) in the sense that clients place their trust and confidence in their lawyers to manage and protect property or money. This obligation is founded in equity, i.e. separate to any obligations under the lawyer–client retainer.
97   See e.g. Christine Parker, 'A Critical Morality for Lawyers: Four Approaches to Lawyers' Ethics' (2004) 30 *Monash Law Review* 49.

of the clinic will be compromised over time and the clinic grapevine will ensure that everyone knows. Students may begin to doubt the integrity of the learning process and, eventually, referring agencies, other practitioners and the law school will get to hear of the problems.

It is common in all legal practices for different views to be held as to the priority between these two perspectives, but they are particularly difficult in clinics because there tends to be a wider range of views than typically occurs in private legal practices. In addition to the primary divide between zealous advocacy and responsible lawyering, there are two other common categories of ethical preference that tend to resonate strongly for clinic supervisors: moral activism and the relationship of care. Moral activists tend to be public interest lawyers concerned to achieve substantive justice and law reform. They are more commonly found in the community legal centres that host clinics than in other legal practice settings; they may not think it is a lawyer's role to automatically support the adversarial justice system and will be content to apply whichever of zealous advocacy or responsible lawyering is necessary to achieve their goals as law reformers. On the other hand, lawyers who see the relationship of care as dominant (they are often family lawyers or those involved in the child welfare system) take a moral dialogue approach and consider the social and political role of lawyers to be irrelevant. They see their primary obligation as ensuring that their client(s), their colleagues, their family and even themselves, survive the legal system and legal practice.

Students need to recognise their clinic values in this four-part framework and, after a while, be able to identify their own preferences. Ideally, their exposure to this categorisation will be taught with coherence across the clinic. The clinic ought not just leave it to the law school's ethics classes. On the whole, these are still instructional in tone and too driven by adherence to a view that cases and conduct rules provide all that is needed to found good legal ethics.

To address again the question of resilience, the clinic needs to go back a step or two and accept the proposition that it, as an entity, needs to work through its fundamental values and ethical preferences. Obviously, this has to be done in the context of the whole of the clinical program, but there are several stages:

- Identifying and strengthening personal values among clinicians and students.[98]

- Accepting that there is such a thing as a corporate moral identity and that the clinic, just as a good law practice, needs to know what that identity is.

- Assessing whether the law school's dominant legal theory position, which is likely—but not always—to be generally positivist or associated with a 'thin' rule of law[99] is consistent with the directions set for students having regard to the clinic's moral identity.

- Setting down the clinic's views on its moral identity[100] in an accessible location. In the context of the discussion above about a court's awareness of a defendant's prior family violence, is it a clinic that believes always in getting the best result for each client regardless of the methods used (consequentialism), or does it, as an entity, think that the means to the end (that is, notions of fairness) are at least as important as the outcome and do not justify misleading the court about prior violence (Kantianism)? Or is there among the supervisors a significant discomfort with both these moral identities and a considered view that the strengthened character of each clinical supervisor is the best way to ensure moral behaviour in representing clients (virtue ethics)?[101]

- Identifying students' preferences for different lawyering types—in particular, dealing with the impact of the usually dominant zealous advocacy *versus* other lawyering models, recognising that all of these preferences are valid in certain contexts and that the key issue is to help individual students/supervisors understand their preferences with accessible scale tests,[102] in the context of the moral identity of the clinic and the wider clinical program.

---

98   For example, by using the resources in Christopher Peterson and Martin EP Seligman, *Character Strengths and Virtues: A Hand book and Classification* (2004) Oxford University Press, 130–32. This book contains a list of positive human strengths rather than a catalogue of deficits and disorders.

99   See, generally, Jeremy Bentham, *A Fragment on Government; or, A Comment on the Commentaries* (1823) W Pickering, 2nd ed; John Austin, *The Province of Jurisprudence Determined and the Uses of the Study of Jurisprudence* (1954) Weidenfeld and Nicholson; HLA Hart, *The Concept of Law* (1961) Clarendon Press; Joseph Raz, *The Authority of Law* (1979) Oxford University Press.

100   For example, those that engage well known general moral categories of consequentialism, Kantianism and virtue ethics. See Adrian Evans, *The Good Lawyer* (2014) Cambridge University Press.

101   Adrian Evans, cited at footnote 100, Chapters 3 and 4.

102   See e.g. Adrian Evans and Helen Forgasz, 'Framing Lawyers' Choices: Factor Analysis of a Psychological Scale to Self-Assess Lawyers' Ethical Preferences' (2013) 16 *Legal Ethics* 134.

Only after all of this work occurs can a clinic be said to have developed its ethical infrastructure, cemented its longer-term sustainability and contributed significantly to the growth of resilient legal professionals.

Clinical scholarship

Heavy teaching and service responsibilities have often made it challenging for clinicians to prioritise research scholarship in the way some other legal academics do. Chavkin used the image of Rumpelstiltskin spinning straw into gold when characterising the challenge for clinicians, facing expectations of a 'generally hostile academic community' to take on escalating teaching demands while also dealing with 'increasing collateral demands to participate in governance; to be the visible presence of the law school in the external legal community; and to produce scholarship'.[103] In Australia, as we noted above, much work remains to be done to foster clinic fluency within law schools.

The longstanding issue of managing these expectations has now become an imperative as those clinicians who are employed as academics are expected to improve both the quality and quantity of their research. There is little prospect that these expectations, faced by all academics, will moderate. Clinicians also face challenges regarding the merit and scope of their scholarship.[104] The 'odd one out' nature of clinical scholarship— 'writing outside mainstream legal disciplinary boundaries'—has seen such scholarship described as difficult to evaluate.[105] Clinicians also face unique

---

103 David Chavkin, 'Spinning Straw Into Gold: Exploring the Legacy of Bellow and Moulton' (2003) 10 *Clinical Law Review* 245, 247.
104 Neil Gold and Philip Plowden, 'Clinical Scholarship and the Development of the Global Clinical Movement' in Frank Bloch (ed), *The Global Clinical Movement: Educating Lawyers for Social Change* (2011) Oxford University Press, Chapter 21; Peter Joy, 'Clinical Scholarship: Improving the Practice of Law' (1996) 2(2) *Clinical Law Review* 385; and Peter Toll Hoffman, 'Clinical Scholarship and Skills Training' (1994) 1(1) *Clinical Law Review* 93. Bergman describes clinicians as 'strangers in a strange land', arguing that clinical education is 'increasingly out of synch with the worldview of many US legal academics' who come to law school with little experience or interest in legal practice: Paul Bergman, 'Reflections on US Clinical Education' (2003) 10(1) *International Journal of the Legal Profession* 109, 109–10.
105 Joseph Tomain and Robert Solimine, 'Skills Skepticism in the Postclinic World' (1990) 40 *Journal of Legal Education* 307, 312–13.

challenges in relation to the 'tension between the individual lawyer-professor's academic freedom and professional responsibility to clients and the law school's decision-making authority'.[106]

On the positive side, many clinicians have the capacity to contribute to multidisciplinary research as well as to research with the practising profession. Practice-related research may foster the further development of clinical programs, especially as universities intensify their research focus. In their analysis of the merit and potential of clinical scholarship, Gold and Plowden refer to the insular nature of much clinical scholarship and call for greater recognition of the shared nature of many of the concerns of the global clinical community.[107] They do not make a case for broader law-related research collaboration, let alone cross-disciplinary research. Grimes states: 'The client base provides a ready resource for legal research and socio-legal study, and generates related legal research, policy and reform initiatives.'[108]

As well, clinicians can contribute expertise related to client-centred models of legal practice, litigation processes, alternative dispute resolution and access to justice, emphasising the strengths and limitations of problem-solving approaches. Clinicians can also contribute to research projects involving academic colleagues, especially in areas well represented in clinical casework. For example, human rights, environmental law, family law, criminal law, migration law, discrimination law and alternative dispute resolution.

Conclusion

The importance of experiential education in law is being recognised in many countries.[109] Clinics have real potential to advance multiple objectives related to student learning, community service, professional engagement, research and policy development.[110] They also have a

106 Robert Kuehn and Peter Joy, 'Lawyering in the Academy: The Intersection of Academic Freedom and Professional Responsibility' (2009) 59 *Journal of Legal Education* 97, 99.

107 Neil Gold and Philip Plowden, cited at footnote 104, 320.

108 Richard Grimes, 'Reflections on Clinical Legal Education' (1995) 29(2) *Law Teacher* 169, 174.

109 Frank Bloch (ed), cited at footnote 104; William Sullivan, Anne Colby, Judith Welch Wegner, Lloyd Bond and Lee S Shulman, *Educating Lawyers: Preparation for the Profession of Law* (2007) Jossey Bass, Chapter 1; Roy Stuckey and others, *Best Practices for Legal Education: A Vision and a Road Map* (2007) Clinical Legal Education Association, 175.

110 Giddings (2013), Chapter 3.

distinctive capacity to provide a bridge between different groups interested in legal education—linking both law schools and law students to the practising profession, judiciary and government as well as connecting law schools with their local communities.[111]

Clinics face uncertain times, but it should be remembered that it was also in turbulent times that clinics emerged.[112] Clinics are now more broadly recognised and better understood by their law schools, but still have a long road to travel. The expectations placed on clinical programs by students, universities, regulators and the practising legal profession appear likely to continue to grow. Clinicians need to respond effectively to calls for them to offer intensive, morally accountable and constructive clinic experiences to increasing numbers of students.

This mixture of factors and expectations has led to a lack of effective arrangements to assist Australian LLB, JD and PLT students and junior lawyers undertaking supervised legal practice to make the best use of experiential learning opportunities. Clinical legal education has an important contribution to make in responding to this dilemma. Clinics provide important opportunities for linking law student learning to notions of professionalism. Few learning opportunities can be as powerful and immediate as collaborating with a skilful, ethical supervisor-practitioner, to advise and assist clients.

The greater use of clinical teaching methods in Australian law schools is yet to be matched by a strong understanding of the pedagogical choices required to make the most of this powerful teaching method. This lack of strong engagement with the pedagogy of clinical legal education was one catalyst for the *Best Practices* project, the results of which underpin much of this book.

---

111 Jeff Giddings and Jennifer Lyman, 'Bridging Different Interests: The Contributions of Clinics to Legal Education' in Frank Bloch (ed), cited at footnote 104, Chapter 15. See also Jeff Giddings, 'Two Way Traffic: The Scope for Clinics to Facilitate Law School Community Engagement' in Patrick Keyzer, Amy Kenworthy and Gail Wilson (eds), *Community Engagement in Contemporary Legal Education: Pro Bono, Clinical Legal Education and Service Learning* (2009) Halstead Press, 44–50. Fiona Cownie has characterised parties interested in legal education as stakeholders, identifying students, academics, the profession, feminists and the state. See Fiona Cownie (ed), *Stakeholders in the Law School* (2010) Hart Publishing, Chapter 1.
112 See Giddings (2013), Chapter 1, especially 8–10.

3

Australian clinical legal education: Models and definitions

Introduction

The term clinical legal education means different things to academics, legal practitioners and students. In our survey results for *Best Practices*, the data illustrate the variety of forms and models encompassed within this term. In particular, it is apparent that newer clinical legal education programs are often quite different from the community legal centre-based real client clinics developed in the 1970s and 1980s (see Chapter 5). To ground the process of formulating best practices in Australian clinical legal education and make the best practices as meaningful as possible across a range of endeavours, it was necessary when conducting the research to clearly define our nomenclature.

This is not a straightforward process. The definition of clinical legal education has been and remains contested. This is reflected in the different views expressed within the research group and more broadly in the international and domestic clinical community. The variety of clinical legal education endeavours across Australia indicates it is a dynamic pedagogy. New forms of clinical legal education continue to be developed, especially in relation to work-placement-type programs (called externships, internships or placements).[1] Additionally, there is a growing recognition that clinical legal education ideally occurs at all stages

---

1   For elaboration of these terms, see the section commencing at 'Terminology', in this chapter.

of a law degree and is integrated.[2] These factors warranted delineation between approaches while recognising that the categories are malleable. The categories of different forms of clinical legal education are based on the surveys we conducted and are relevant for the current Australian legal education environment.

In this chapter, we discuss and clarify key terms. We then focus on describing the emerging models of clinical legal education in Australia. We identify the merits of each model, and conclude by discussing the factors relevant to the choice of model. In discussing the merits of each model, we recognise that these are subjective considerations and can vary depending on the course goals, and on an individual's role within legal education as a full-time clinician, a traditional law academic, or a student.

What is clinical legal education?

A preliminary question is: what is clinical legal education? Put at its simplest, it is one method of learning and teaching law. However, the phrase has evolved in Australia over the last few decades and has different connotations.[3] In order to differentiate clinical legal education from simulated practical legal training, Campbell wrote in 1991 that the 'term "clinical legal education" should properly be used only to refer to programs where students act for real clients in the handling of their *real* legal problems'.[4] In 1999 Giddings commented that:

> [the] term clinical legal education has been used quite loosely in Australia … Students and practising lawyers tend to relate clinical legal education to work with real clients or to 'skills' … Other law teachers usually give clinical legal education a broader meaning, focusing on the use of teaching methods other than traditional lectures and seminars.[5]

---

2   Jeff Giddings, *Promoting Justice Through Clinical Legal Education* (2013) Justice Press, Chapter 2, 78–81 (cited hereafter as Giddings (2013)).

3   For discussion of the definition of clinical legal education in 1996, see Simon Rice and Graeme Coss, *A guide to implementing clinical teaching method in the law school curriculum* (1996) Centre for Legal Education, 9.

4   Susan Campbell, 'Blueprint for a Clinical Program' (1991) 9(2) *Journal of Professional Legal Education* 121, 122 (emphasis added).

5   Jeff Giddings, 'A Circle Game: Clinical Legal Education in Australia' (1999) 10(1) *Legal Education Review* 34, 35.

In the last two decades, clinical legal education has developed to encompass a variety of approaches, with the common element being 'real' experiences. Clinical legal education is a pedagogy that places students in real-life environments. It is a form of experiential learning where students learn by doing and then reflecting.[6] Experiential legal education takes many forms, including problem-solving, role plays, mooting, simulation and placements. Generally, experiential learning encompasses clinical legal education. It includes teaching about skills as well as the broader legal system. For students to get the most out of experiential learning there should also be feedback, reflection and application of new skills and ideas.[7]

In Australia, 'clinical legal education' generally refers to law school experiential learning that places students in the role of lawyers representing clients with legal questions or problems. The research data for *Best Practices* reveal a range of experiential learning, from clinical components in law courses, to externships in a wide variety of organisations, and to intensive live client experiences within a university-controlled legal practice. This last example usually involves students working with clients on their legal issues, under the direct supervision of academic staff.

Clinical legal education confronts law students with the realities, demands and compromises of legal practice. In so doing, it provides students with real-life reference points for learning the law. Clinical legal education also invites students to see the wider context and everyday realities of accessing an imperfect legal system, enabling them to integrate their learning of substantive law with the justice implications of its practical operation.[8]

Clinical legal pedagogy involves a system of reflection, self-critique and supervisory feedback (discussed in Chapters 6 and 7) by which law students learn how to learn from their experiences and observation and, at its most effective level, how to take personal responsibility for clients and their legal problems.

---

6   Hugh Brayne, Nigel Duncan and Richard Grimes, *Clinical Legal Education: Active Learning in Your Law School* (1998) Blackstone Press, 2; they state: 'Understanding through both doing and reflecting is at the centre of the clinical ethos', quoted in Giddings (2013), 3.
7   L Smith, 'Why clinical programs should embrace civic engagement, services learning and community based research' (2003–04) 10 *Clinical Law Review* 723, 725–27.
8   Adrian Evans, Anna Cody, Anna Copeland, Jeff Giddings, Mary Anne Noone, Simon Rice and Ebony Booth, *Best Practices: Australian Clinical Legal Education* (2013) Government of Australia, Office of Learning and Teaching, at perma.cc/2J6E-ZMQX.

Clinical legal education is normally intensive, one-on-one or small group in nature, and allows students to apply legal theory and develop lawyering skills to solve client legal problems. It relies on structured reflection to enable students to analyse the learning and insights they gain from their course. Favourable staff–student ratios (discussed in Chapter 9) and collaborative learning environments support a climate in which each student is motivated to improve and perform at their best. The personal responsibility of working with and being accountable to clients motivates students to perform to the best of their ability.[9]

With all the clinics, a key benefit is that students are responsible either for a client file or for a specific legal task such as research. 'The learning is deeper and more meaningful when a student is participating as a lawyer, rather than as an observer or assistant.'[10] Law students' legal work under supervision may include analysing client problems and giving legal advice; meeting with clients and witnesses to gather information; reviewing and preparing legal documents, such as contracts, wills, or legal briefs; negotiating with opposing parties or their lawyers; representing clients in administrative hearings, in court or before other tribunals in which the students have been granted a case-specific right of audience or the right to appear on behalf of a client; fact investigation; legal research for policy or law reform; and developing materials for community legal education and presenting a legal seminar.[11]

Working in a clinic is frequently the first time that students encounter clients who have been treated unfairly through the legal system. They have to communicate with them and form a professional relationship with these clients. This can cause them to question their own role as prospective lawyers and their role in providing access to justice for clients and improving the law and legal system to make it more just.

Clinical legal education might be considered a specific example of service learning. As we discussed in Chapter 2, service learning is a form of experiential learning that involves responding to humanitarian crises and focusing on community service, with students receiving little, if any, academic credit. Service learning is being actively promoted in a number

---

9   Adrian Evans and others, cited at footnote 8, 10; see also Chapter 7 of this book on 'reflection' and Chapter 6 of this book on 'supervision'.
10   Roy Stuckey and others, *Best Practices for Legal Education: A Vision and a Road Map* (2007) Clinical Legal Education Association, 190.
11   Adrian Evans and others, cited at footnote 8, 10.

of Australian universities and, as we pointed out, there is overlap between service learning and clinical legal education with differences in the voluntary nature of student contributions, the limited classroom component and the principal focus on service rather than student learning.[12] We also pointed out in Chapter 2 that clinical legal education is similar to practical legal training (PLT) courses[13] and work-integrated learning (WIL),[14] but that it is distinct in several respects. Both these approaches expose students to practical aspects of legal workplaces. Each approach also reinforces for students that a knowledge of legal theory is insufficient for legal practice and that their 'law school' impressions of what it is like to actually practise law will be expanded by time and a variety of experiences.[15]

An essential difference between clinical legal education and either PLT or WIL is that clinical legal education is an approach to integrating and strengthening the academic phase of legal education in the interests of students and clients. As we noted in Chapter 2, the emphasis in clinical legal education on meeting the diverse and complex needs (legal, emotional, systemic and therapeutic) of real clients, either individuals or organisations, places it well beyond the vocational focus of PLT and WIL, which can limit themselves to a 'how to' approach to practising law. Clinical legal education avoids any default concentration on apparently value-neutral practical skills (see Chapter 5) and is intended to develop a critical and analytical consciousness of law.[16]

---

12 Jeff Giddings, 'Two Way Traffic: The Scope for Clinics to Facilitate Law School Community Engagement' in P Keyser, A Kenworthy and G Wilson (eds), *Community Engagement in Contemporary Legal Education: Pro Bono, Clinical Legal Education and Service-Learning* (2009) Haltstead Press, 40; L Morin and S Waysdorf, 'The service-learning model in the law school curriculum: expanding opportunities for the ethical-social apprenticeship' (2011–12) 56 *New York Law School Law Review*; L Smith, cited at footnote 7, 723.

13 In Australia, a condition of admission to legal practice is that law graduates must complete a practical legal training component. For example, see *Legal Profession Uniform Admission Rules 2015* (NSW), r 6 (2).

14 See for example 'Work Integrated Learning' at www.flinders.edu.au/cilt/wil. Accessed 4 February 2017. Work-integrated learning (WIL) describes directed or supported educational activities that integrate theoretical learning with its application in the workplace.

15 WIL is a form of experiential learning. The Australian Collaborative Education Network (ACEN) lists the following forms of work-integrated learning: internships; cooperative education; work placements; industry-based learning; community-based learning; clinical rotations; sandwich year; and practical projects. See perma.cc/UY8L-HPWP. Accessed 9 July 2012.

16 Adrian Evans and others, cited at footnote 8, 11. For further discussion, see Chapter 5 of this book.

Similarly, clinical legal education is distinct from *pro bono publico* and student-run volunteer programs.[17] Such placements have limited educational objectives compared to clinical legal education, do not generally seek to develop students' normative awareness and do not set out to strengthen wider legal education and law reform curricula, although both can awaken and sustain graduates' civic consciousness once they are in practice.[18]

The role of simulations

The inclusion of simulated legal practice in the definition of clinical legal education is controversial. Students acting 'for real clients in the handling of their real legal problems' has been a point of differentiation from other forms of legal education and practical legal training for Australian clinicians. As Campbell illustrates above, Australian clinical legal education proponents have emphasised the 'real client' aspect of clinical legal education and purposefully excluded simulations from the definition (particularly to differentiate them from PLT programs).[19] In discussing our research for *Best Practices*, we found that we held different views on the status of simulation in the definition of clinical legal education but agreed on its importance in preparing students for the 'real client' experience.[20]

We agree on the value of simulations as a means of teaching students specific skills, such as negotiation or interviewing specifically in preparation for actual negotiation or interviewing, or generally doing legal work. Simulations are a form of experiential education; but we could not agree that student engagement in simulated legal practice be included in the definition of clinical legal education.

---

17   National Pro Bono Resource Centre, *Pro bono and clinical legal education programs in Australian law schools* (2004).

18   Although Nicolson would argue otherwise: D Nicolson, 'Learning in Justice: Ethical Education in an Extra-Curricular Law Clinic' in Michael Robertson, Lillian Corbin, Kieran Tranter and Francesca Bartlett (eds), *The Ethics Project in Legal Education* (2010) Routledge, 171.

19   Susan Campbell, cited at footnote 4, 122.

20   Roy Stuckey and others specifically include simulation within the definition of experiential education and recognise simulation-based courses for their value in developing professional skills: See Stuckey and others, cited at footnote 10, 181.

Understanding clinical legal education as a continuum in which simulations provide a valuable source of experience and learning for students provides a means of progressing the discussion.[21] Both simulations and 'real client' courses are valuable as a means of achieving specific learning goals with students. The ideal approach is an integrated one.[22]

An integrative approach to clinical legal education involves the use of simulations and case studies to prepare students for the responsibility of working with clients on real cases. It also involves drawing on real client experiences to inform the non-clinical law curriculum.[23] Students can best develop ethical awareness, judgment and proficiency in the application of professional skills through having 'repeated opportunities to perform the tasks to be learned or improved upon until they reach the desired level of proficiency'.[24] Clinical teaching methods and insights can be constructively integrated into classroom-based courses. Integration emphasises the client focus so important to both clinic-based learning and legal practice. The law and legal processes can be examined, analysed and critiqued within the framework of client concerns and interests. Short field placements can provide a primer for more intense clinical experiences later in a law program. The use of complementary clinical experiences, or components, in doctrinal courses enables students to acquire additional skills and enhance their understanding of the law as practised.[25] Integrative approaches will be most effective if they culminate in real client work enabling students to learn about the uncertain, dynamic nature of law-related professional practice.

---

21   James Moliterno, Plenary Presentation, *International Journal of Clinical Legal Education* Conference, Olomouc, Czech Republic, July 2014.

22   Giddings (2013), 113–14.

23   Kathy Mack refers to many of the benefits of clinical legal education relating to 'integration of different areas of law, integration of law and fact, synthesis of legal and non-legal materials and improved problem solving skills such as issue recognition, planning, strategy, tactics, analysis, synthesis and decision making. These are the sorts of "generic" skills which legal education must foster, since legal knowledge rapidly becomes outdated': Kathy Mack, 'Bringing Clinical Learning Into a Conventional Classroom' (1993) 4 *Legal Education Review* 89, 99.

24   Roy Stuckey and others, cited at footnote 10, 178.

25   L Smith, cited at footnote 7, 531. At 533, she further suggests linking 'simulation courses to live clinical work so that the simulations provide a framework for analysis, while the live work provides the richness of reality, additional practice, opportunities to learn from experience and experiences for contemplation'.

In a law degree, students would initially have simulated experiences and they use these as building blocks, or as a means to help them structure or scaffold their learning. This enables them to confidently and competently provide legal services to 'real clients' in a live client clinic or externship. Real clients have unexpected, unscripted issues and ways of dealing with legal problems and the 'real client' clinic provides a unique and rich learning environment for students. Clinicians recognise the importance of preparing students for real client interactions through simulations and, while some choose to include this within the definition of clinical legal education, others do not.

Distinguishing features of clinical legal education in Australia

In Australia, clinical legal education was established with dual goals: community service and educating law students.[26] A focus on access to justice and the need in the community for legal services triggered the early initiatives in clinical legal education.[27] Arising out of this, the connection between clinical legal education and Australian community legal centres has developed strongly, as we describe in detail in Chapter 5.[28]

Our research for *Best Practices* revealed a number of clear trends in Australian clinical legal education, among which are that:

• Australian clinical legal education still has a strong focus on service to the community;

• within the curriculum of a clinical legal education course there is usually discussion of law in context;

• students are engaged in a wide range of legal activities including individual case work, law reform, legal research and community legal education;

---

26   See Chapters 2 and 5 of this book; Jeff Giddings, 'Clinical Legal Education in Australia: A Historical Perspective' (2003) 3 *International Journal of Clinical Legal Education* 7; MA Noone, 'Australian Community Legal Centres – The University Connection' in Jeremy Cooper and Louise G Trubek (eds), *Educating for Justice: Social Values and Legal Education* (1997) Ashgate, 257.

27   Jeff Giddings, Roger Burridge, Shelley AM Gavigan, Catherine F Klein, 'The First Wave of Modern Clinical Legal Education: The United States, Britain, Canada, and Australia' in Frank Bloch (ed), *The Global Clinical Movement: Educating Lawyers for Social Justice* (2011) Oxford University Press, Chapter 1; and Frank Bloch and MA Noone, 'Legal Aid Origins of Clinical Legal Education' in Frank Bloch (ed), cited above, Chapter 10.

28   See Giddings (2013); and MA Noone, cited at footnote 26.

- most clinical legal education is located in not-for- profit organisations, community legal centres and legal aid organisations; and
- there is a significant growth in the number of work-placement-type programs (called externships or internships) across the country.[29]

Terminology

The data obtained from our *Best Practices* survey show a significant diversity of clinical legal education programs. It is apparent from the diversity that, in order to develop best practices in Australia, clarity around terms and a delineation of different models of clinical legal education are necessary.

What is 'clinic'?

In our experience, the word 'clinic' is used loosely and is often used to describe the actual site of the clinical legal education program, the legal practice or the clinical legal education course undertaken by students. Things happen 'at the clinic' or 'in the clinic'. The 'clinic' often refers to the physical legal practice or agency where students are undertaking their clinical legal education, and the simple word 'clinic' often refers to the clinical course.

What is a 'client'?

The variety of work performed in clinical legal education programs in Australia ranges across individual legal advice and representation, community legal education, policy and law reform work.[30] As a result, there are several meanings of 'client'. Doing 'legal work for the client' covers more than just legal work for individuals. The expression 'the client' can refer to one or more of:

- an individual (as a client of a live client clinic);
- groups of individuals with common interests or concerns;
- an organisation or group of organisations;

---

29   Adrian Evans and others, cited at footnote 8; and *Identifying Current Practices in Clinical Legal Education,* Regional Reports, cited in Chapter 1 at footnote 6.
30   *Identifying Current Practices in Clinical Legal Education,* Regional Reports, cited in Chapter 1 at footnote 6.

- a community (the client of a law reform or community development clinic or component within a clinical course); and

- the general beneficiaries of law reform or impact litigation.[31]

Models

Best Practices describes five models of clinical legal education,[32] developed from the survey data detailed in the Regional Reports and the distinguishing features of Australian clinical legal education outlined above. We acknowledge that other clinicians (especially from other countries and contexts) might prefer different models and criteria; however, we drew on our empirical data and our collective experience. With substantial diversity in the Australian clinical legal education environment, the identification of models is fraught. None is a discrete entity; there can be and is overlap. The models should be seen as a continuum and as complementary and, depending on the objectives of a course, there is significant scope for variations and hybrids of these clinical legal education models.[33] Our approach to categorisation focuses primarily on location and control of the learning environment.

In *Best Practices* we identified five models:

- in-house live client clinic;
- in-house live client clinic (some external funding);
- external live client clinic (agency clinic);
- externships (including internships and placements); and
- clinical components in other courses.[34]

In in-house live client clinical courses, law students work closely under the supervision of law school staff to provide legal assistance to clients or perform other legal tasks such as drafting law reform submissions, analysing legislation, mediating disputes, community legal education or other work done by lawyers. In external live client clinic (agency clinic), students work under the joint supervision of law school staff and agency staff. In externship courses, law students are placed in professional legal settings outside the law school where they work on real legal matters and

---

31   Adrian Evans and others, cited at footnote 8, 21.
32   Adrian Evans and others, cited at footnote 8.
33   Jeff Giddings, cited at footnote 5, 35.
34   Adrian Evans and others, cited at footnote 8, 20.

are primarily supervised by lawyers who are not law school staff. In all the above models, there is usually a classroom component in addition to the placement. In courses with clinical components, students assume lawyer roles in working with real clients, such as interviewing clients, drafting law reform submissions or other 'real' activities.

We recognise there may be other ways to classify clinical legal education models. There could also be a number of subcategories within the five models we have proposed. For example, a discussion about the legal aid origins of clinical legal education noted that legal aid–oriented law school clinics typically fall into one of three categories: the individual service model, a specialisation model or a community model.[35] Another approach to categorising focuses on the extent of legal representation the clinic engages in: full representation, partial representation, community lawyering orientation or community legal education (sometimes also called 'Street Law').[36] In the Australian context, especially in community legal centres where many clinical programs are based, the range of work can include all these aspects. Accordingly this categorisation would not be useful. The features of a clinic may change over time due to variations in funding, support from the university, withdrawal of host organisations and staffing issues. As well, some clinical legal education programs may combine a number of different models. At La Trobe and Griffith universities and the University of New South Wales, for example, there are live client clinics as well as externships and clinical legal education components.[37]

Another approach would classify clinics according to whether the law school or some other body has formal (legal) responsibility for client work and student supervision. This apparently straightforward subdivision would mean that there are just two types of clinics: those that the law school

---

35   Frank Bloch and MA Noone, cited at footnote 27, 158.
36   UK Centre for Legal Education, *What forms can clinic take?* at perma.cc/EM7T-MM7B. Accessed 2 September 2013. For discussion of Street Law, see Giddings (2013), 105–07; and www.streetlaw. org/en/home. Australian examples exist at Griffith University, the University of New England and the University of Melbourne: see *Identifying Current Practices in Clinical Legal Education, Regional Report: Queensland and Northern New South Wales*, 5, at perma.cc/257Z-6EMR.
37   *Identifying Current Practices in Clinical Legal Education, Regional Report: Victoria and Tasmania*, 5, at perma.cc/J562-X6GU; *Identifying Current Practices in Clinical Legal Education, Regional Report: New South Wales and Australian Capital Territory*, 5, at perma.cc/FU7X-5TNV; *Identifying Current Practices in Clinical Legal Education, Regional Report: Queensland and Northern New South Wales*, 5, at perma.cc/257Z-6EMR. See also Kingsford Legal Centre, *Australian Clinical Legal Education Guide 2014–2015,* Kingsford Legal Centre.

controls and those that it does not. However, this strict categorisation is not realistic or sufficiently subtle in the Australian context where many clinical programs are built on a partnership model with the legal services provider/agency. Specifically in our external live client clinic (agency clinic), the legal work may be the ultimate responsibility of the agency but law school staff act as supervisors and legal practitioners. They are formally responsible for student supervision. Additionally, it can never be said that an externship has full responsibility for student supervision. A law school never relinquishes its final say on the mark or credit that a student receives for the overall clinical course. The law school can therefore never fully divest itself of supervision in favor of an external agency. Therefore this classification is not helpful in the Australian context.

In this chapter we combine discussion of the models 'in-house live client clinic' and 'in-house live client clinic (some external funding)'. Keeping in mind our categorisation criteria of location and control of the learning environment, these two categories of clinic are fundamentally the same. The distinguishing feature is the funding source and this can vary from year to year. Other aspects of the models are similar so, to avoid repetition, the discussion is amalgamated.

In-house live client

'In-house live client clinics' are defined as being 'on campus, wholly or substantially funded and controlled by the law school for student education'. This is the dominant clinical program model in the United States. In this model, clinics may receive some external funding, as do the clinics at Kingsford Legal Centre, University of New South Wales (UNSW), or may not receive external funding, as at the Newcastle University Legal Centre.[38]

The oldest example of an in-house live client clinic without external funding in Australia is the Newcastle University Legal Centre. The clinic is situated on a city campus of the university and is dedicated to an integrated version of clinical legal education: students are offered the

---

38   *Identifying Current Practices in Clinical Legal Education, Regional Report: New South Wales and Australian Capital Territory*, at perma.cc/257Z-6EMR.

opportunity to be introduced to clinical legal education in their first year of study and, throughout their degree, students have further opportunities to study in the clinic.[39]

In 2011, the University of South Australia opened its in-house clinic wholly funded by the law school. At the time of our *Best Practices* survey, the University of South Australia Legal Advice clinic was physically situated within the law school. More recently, this clinic has received funding from external sources and now also provides services at various outreach locations.[40]

A key benefit of a wholly law school–controlled clinic is the substantial control of the clinical teaching. While an in-house live client clinic has additional functions, such as providing a legal service to students or the community, one of its primary goals is to teach students. The course goals determine the specific learning objectives for the program.

These joint aims, to provide both student learning and client service, can create a tension. However, to date, the Australian experience is that both aims can be accommodated.[41]

For example, in the Employment Law clinic at Kingsford Legal Centre, UNSW, students sometimes represent clients in conciliation hearings[42] at Fair Work Australia when clients are claiming they have been unfairly dismissed. While it could be argued that a client would be better represented by a lawyer, the level of representation is relatively high as students prepare thoroughly for their conciliation hearings and, in the process, they learn about interviewing clients, negotiation skills and dealing with informal tribunals. The student is accompanied in the conciliation hearing so that a clinical supervisor can contribute if there is a need for it, to ensure that a client's interests are not compromised. This example shows the balancing of both student learning goals and client interests being met together.

---

39   See *Identifying Current Practices in Clinical Legal Education, Regional Report: New South Wales and Australian Capital Territory*, at perma.cc/257Z-6EMR.
40   See University of South Australia Legal Advice Clinic Annual Report 2013, at perma.cc/J5BY-TNXS.
41   Judith Dickson, 'Clinical Legal Education in the 21st Century: Still Educating for Service?' (2000) 1 *International Journal of Clinical Legal Education* 33; Giddings (2013); Anna Cody, 'Clinical Programs in Community Legal Centres, The Australian Approach' (2011) 4 *Spanish Journal Education and Law Review*.
42   *Identifying Current Practices in Clinical Legal Education, Regional Report: New South Wales and Australian Capital Territory*, 11, at perma.cc/257Z-6EMR.

Analysis

There is a high degree of control by a faculty of law over an in-house clinical course. This means that the course can be specifically tailored to suit the learning goals in a course at any time and provides a level of flexibility to the faculty. As stated in the South Australian Regional Report, 'because our clinic is here within the cocoon of the law school we can control and look after them and keep tabs on them'.[43] In contrast, in an external live client clinic (agency clinic), for example, a student's learning has to be negotiated in the context of the external agency's priorities.

There is a range of approaches within in-house clinical courses. In some, the students' learning is paramount: 'A clinic is designed for a student experience. A community legal centre or a firm or any organisation has not been designed for the volunteers who come in.'[44] For some in-house clinics the focus is the students, and this clear prioritising means specific learning goals can be set and worked towards clearly. In others that are also community legal centres, there will be a shifting balance with constant attention on both student learning goals and client service.[45]

A benefit of this model, referred to in the Regional Reports, is that trained and experienced educators work with students. Clinical supervisors have experience teaching a range of diverse students. A core part of a clinician's job is to teach students. The in-house live client clinic has the advantage of being specifically established to teach students. There can be a strong and well-articulated link between practice experience and reflection. Another benefit referred to in the Regional Reports by interviewees is that students in in-house clinical courses are more likely to be given more responsibility.[46] Supervisors are accustomed to working with students in a supportive way to enable them to increasingly take more responsibility throughout a semester. In contrast, supervisors in an externship may feel less comfortable with giving students responsibility, even if they have formal (legal) authority to do so.

---

43 *Identifying Current Practices in Clinical Legal Education, Regional Report: South Australia*, 19, at perma.cc/3MPF-5U5A.

44 *Identifying Current Practices in Clinical Legal Education, Regional Report: South Australia*, 19, at perma.cc/3MPF-5U5A.

45 *Identifying Current Practices in Clinical Legal Education, Regional Report: New South Wales and Australian Capital Territory*, at perma.cc/257Z-6EMR.

46 *Identifying Current Practices in Clinical Legal Education, Regional Report: New South Wales and Australian Capital Territory*, at perma.cc/257Z-6EMR.

Another benefit of in-house live client clinics is the shared facilities and infrastructure, which offer some costs savings.[47] For example, the university may absorb some of the financial responsibilities for the clinical program, or provide human resources support to clinical staff, as discussed further in Chapter 9.

Another positive aspect of the in-house clinic is the more obvious integration of the clinical course within the law faculty. Clinics have sometimes been on the periphery of law teaching, but a clinic that is physically located within the law school gives the implicit message that it is an essential part of the law school's function, and provides a constant reminder of the connection of learning law with the practice of law. A further benefit of this model is that it is physically easy for students to gain access as the clinic is located where they study.

One of the disadvantages of an in-house clinic is that it can present a model of legal practice that a student is unlikely to encounter when they enter legal practice. Demand may be limited and the client numbers can usually be tightly controlled in order to ensure the educational experience. Students may gain the impression that they have unlimited time to devote to one particular case. In fact, one of the skills of legal practice is being able to allocate sufficient time to each client file, juggling the competing needs of clients, co-workers and other work priorities. If work is highly controlled, as it is more likely to be in an in-house live client clinic, then the hectic pace of legal practice is less likely to be found.

If an in-house clinic is the only model of clinic offered by a university, then our research for *Best Practices* shows that is more likely to be a clinic that provides legal services to disadvantaged clients.[48] An in-house clinic that is also serving the community is more likely to offer students a more intensely paced experience, akin to legal practice. However, an in-house clinic with a poverty law focus may not cater for the diversity of student interest. While many students are keen to learn about law in this

---

47   *Identifying Current Practices in Clinical Legal Education, Regional Report: Victoria and Tasmania,* at perma.cc/J562-X6GU.

48   This does not have to be the case, but if a law faculty is going to fund a legal practice for the purpose of teaching students, then this expense is more likely to be justified if it also fulfils the goals of community engagement. There are no examples of in-house clinics that do not provide legal services to either students or disadvantaged communities: see *Identifying Current Practices in Clinical Legal Education*, Regional Reports, cited in Chapter 1 at footnote 6.

environment, some may prefer to learn about other ways of practising law. Providing externships in a range of locations meets the needs of a greater variety of students.

One of the main disadvantages of in-house live client clinics is the cost of the model. In the current climate of constrained budgets, law schools are looking to expend their clinical programs in a cost-effective way. Establishing relatively expensive in-house live client clinics is not likely to be a growth area.

External live client clinic (agency clinics)

The distinguishing features of this model are that students are placed at an agency over which the university has limited control, often the subject of a memorandum of understanding, and a law school academic/legal practitioner provides the supervision of students onsite in the organisation. The model relies on a significant level of partnership and collaboration between the university and the agency. Longstanding clinical programs at La Trobe, Griffith, Monash and Murdoch universities and at ANU are external live client clinics.[49] The funding arrangements and the level of involvement in these clinics vary among the programs. One common and distinguishing aspect of this model is the involvement of law school staff onsite at the agency (away from the campus). Other agency staff are also often involved in the supervision of students, both formally and informally. In this type of clinic, supervisory control of students is a shared enterprise between the law school and the agency.

Analysis

In an agency clinic, students benefit from exposure to the realities of working in agencies like community legal centres. They experience the high levels of client demand and need, the challenge of insufficient resources, and the commitment of agency staff. Especially in a larger organisation, like a legal aid commission, students and academic staff get the opportunity to work and engage with a diverse range of legal practitioners.

---

49   Kingsford Legal Centre, *Clinical Legal Education Guide 2013–2014*, Kingsford Legal Centre.

In an agency clinic, the university will have limited responsibility for the running costs and infrastructure. The university will employ staff and often make a contribution to the agency, but the agency relies on external funding for the bulk of its support. Consequently, agency clinics are a less resource-intensive option for universities than in-house clinics.

Partnerships with local community agencies enhance the universities' community engagement profiles,[50] and agency clinics offer a positive way for universities to make a contribution to their communities.

Often, in agency clinics, the clinical legal education course operates only during university semesters, and the community agency is likely to take responsibility for any ongoing case commitments between semesters. Academics involved in such a program are likely to be able to focus on research and scholarship outside of semesters, as well as contribute to the teaching of other courses.[51]

In an agency clinic, the law school will have little direct control over the work of the agency and its staff. Although agency clinics usually have a memorandum of understanding that sets out details of student involvement and areas of work, the educational aspect of a program is often viewed by the agency as secondary. A tension between service and education is highlighted in an agency clinic,[52] so good working relationships between university staff and agency staff are therefore critical to the success of agency clinics. The maintenance of effective and productive relationships requires nurturing[53] and is often time-consuming.

As the university clinical staff are located at the agency clinic, they can become isolated from the law school. This can have implications both for the careers of the individuals involved and for the profile of clinical legal education within the university. At worst, the clinic and its staff can become marginalised. Time and energy is therefore needed to ensure the reputation and work of the clinical legal education program and its staff are recognised both by the law school and the broader university. This is an example of the same issue in all clinical models, as clinical teaching is distinct from traditional law teaching and frequently not understood by law faculties.

---

50   Jeff Giddings, cited at footnote 12, 40.
51   Giddings (2013), 104.
52   Judith Dickson, cited at footnote 41.
53   Giddings (2013), 104.

Externships (including internships and placements)

Our *Best Practices* survey revealed that the most significant growth in clinical legal education was in externship programs, also sometimes described as internships or placements.[54] From our research it is clear that these terms are used interchangeably and do not reflect substantial differences. In this book we use the word 'externships' to describe the form of clinical legal education where individual students are placed in an independent legal practice, community legal centre, government agency or not-for-profit organisation.

The distinguishing feature is that, unlike external live client clinics, everyday student supervision is the primary responsibility of the host organisation, although there may also be an academic supervisor who monitors the students' work. This form of education is not unique to law schools and is common in many other disciplines.[55] The pedagogy of externships is well developed in the United States.[56] However, externships have often been seen as a lesser form of clinical legal education in Australia and elsewhere, because frequently they are not rigorously designed with clearly defined learning outcomes. It is more likely that there will be variable learning outcomes in externships because the supervision varies from workplace to workplace. As the teaching of students is not an essential part of the student supervisors' role, there is a risk that student learning goals are of secondary importance to the functioning of the workplace.[57]

There is significant variability in this lower-cost clinical legal education model. Most externships programs involve students working for a day a week during the semester at the host organisation. However, this can vary, so that students work intensively for two or three weeks, particularly if the placement is overseas or interstate. Ideally, externship programs

---

54   Adrian Evans and others, cited at footnote 8.

55   The prevalence of this form of student experience and the experience of student exploitation prompted the Fair Work Ombudsman (with Rosemary Owens) to initiate a research project: see *Experience or Exploitation? The Nature, Prevalence and Regulation of Unpaid Work Experience, Internships and Trial Periods in Australia* (2013) Fair Work Ombudsman, Melbourne. As a consequence of the report's recommendations, the Fair Work Ombudsman has developed a range of material: see perma. cc/7JFA-WQ6J.

56   P Ogilvy, Leah Wortham, Lisa G Lerman and Alexis Anderson, *Learning From Practice: A Professional Development Text for Legal Externs* (2007) Thomson Reuters.

57   Giddings (2013), 89.

include a seminar program (often fortnightly) and an opportunity for students to come together and discuss their individual experiences in the larger group. For example, at La Trobe University, students in the course Public Interest Law Practice attend a fortnightly seminar and supervision session on campus. This enables students to learn about other student experiences and provides a supportive environment in which to discuss any issues or concerns.

Externship programs can be either generalist or specialist. For example, at Griffith Law School there is the Semester in Practice program; the University of Sydney offers an externship course focusing on social justice and at UNSW there are specialist externship programs (for example, the Hong Kong Refugee Law Clinic).[58]

Although this model enables law schools to provide diverse learning sites in a cost-effective way, the actual standard of any externship program will be dependent on available resources and skilled, sensitive relationship management. Universities do not have to cover the infrastructure costs of an externship program, but quality externships require ongoing training of supervisors, committed academic staff involvement and maintenance of the interpersonal relationships between law school and agency. The true cost of a good externship program should not be underestimated.

Analysis

The number of externship programs is increasing in Australian law schools because they are much less resource intensive than in-house clinic programs. They do not require establishing infrastructure and the clinical supervision is contracted out. The first Australian externship programs did not pay the host organisations for their participation in the programs. However, more recently, the establishment of some externship programs has involved the law schools paying the host organisations (often community legal centres) a fee.[59] As Giddings notes, '[t]he cost differential between externships

---

58 Kingsford Legal Centre, cited at footnote 49.
59 Discussion at presentation by Matilda Alexander, Andrea Perry-Petersen, James Farrell, Monica Taylor, Queensland Association of Independent Legal Services (QAILS), 'Outsourcing clinical legal education to community organisations: the good, the bad and the ugly' at 11th *International Journal of Clinical Legal Education* Conference and 12th Australian Clinical Legal Conference, Griffith University, Australia, July 2013.

and in-house clinics will be influenced by the resources the law school commits to supporting externship students',[60] but that differential will narrow if a trend for paying for externships continues.

The nature of the supervision arrangements in externships enables larger numbers of students to be given a clinical opportunity. For instance, Deakin Law School runs an externship program with over 30 partnerships.[61] This supervision aspect of externships also facilitates significant community engagement for the university. Externships also enable students based in regional campuses to participate in clinical legal education. Universities are less likely to establish in-house clinics in regional campuses where the number of students is fewer, although there may be opportunities to place students in local legal aid agencies, or to form partnerships with these organisations. In Bendigo, Victoria, La Trobe University offers an externship to second-year law students. This is beneficial for students' future job prospects and the university's relationship with the local legal profession.[62]

Externships are well suited to facilitate learning that involves an assessment of aspects of the justice system other than just legal practice. This wider perspective is particularly true for students who are placed with magistrates or judges, law reform agencies and government departments. Equally, externships can enable students to pursue their preferred areas of legal practice.

In the externship model, the law school has less control over the student learning experience as the supervision is primarily the responsibility of the host organisation. This delegation of supervisory responsibility by the law school to the host organisation may be formal under a memorandum of understanding, or informal. Ideally, the former will occur, but a *complete* delegation of responsibility is impossible where the student is receiving credit for their externship work. This is why we prefer to emphasise the collaborative reality of the supervisory environment rather than legal liability for supervision. Also, within a given clinical course, there is

---

60   Giddings (2013), 91.

61   *Identifying Current Practices in Clinical Legal Education, Regional Report: Victoria and Tasmania*, 4, at perma.cc/J562-X6GU; Adrian Evans and others, cited at footnote 8, 29.

62   Chris Casey and Judith Bennett, "'It really opened my eyes": The impact of a social justice focused, regional clinical legal education in attracting and retaining the next generation of lawyers in regional and rural settings: pilot findings' at 11th *International Journal of Clinical Legal Education* Conference and 12th Australian Clinical Legal Conference, Griffith University, Australia, July 2013.

a likelihood of significant variability in the work students are engaged to perform across different placement sites.[63] Accordingly, the overall quality and consistency of the externship program can be compromised.

Given that many externship placements in Australia are in community legal centres—which are severely under-resourced organisations—there is a risk that students will not receive appropriate levels of supervision. To counter these risks, supervisors should receive university-funded training and a supervision manual, and liaise with relevant university academics.[64] Another limitation of externships is that student responsibility for client work is reduced, because staff who are supervising students are accustomed to actually being responsible and performing the work themselves. Giving students responsibility for client files,[65] law reform submissions or other legal work is challenging and a different way of working from that with which placement supervisors may be familiar.

With the growing interest in developing externships, there is increased competition among law schools to obtain placements. A number of community legal centres in Queensland, for example, take students from a variety of law schools. With increased demand for placements and a static supply of placement sites, the need to obtain sufficient placement sites could mean less attention to the actual quality of the placement. However, increased competition among universities enables the host organisations to demand adequate resourcing from universities that could improve the quality.

A recent variation on the externship model is the creation of 'virtual clinics'. Utilising online communication, students work for an external organisation that is based overseas or interstate. The student remains in their local environment and works with the external organisation via online written, video or audio communication. They may have a designated supervisor in the external organisation and/or a supervisor in the home university. For instance, in the ANU course, The International Human Rights Clinic, students work with non-government organisations (NGOs) in the Pacific and Asian regions.[66] Because of the globalisation of

---

63   Giddings (2013), 89.

64   Adrian Evans and others, cited at footnote 8, 55–59; and see Chapter 6 of this book on 'supervision'.

65   Margaret Martin Barry, 'Practice Ready: Are we there yet?' (2012) *Boston College Journal of Law and Social Justice* 264.

66   Kingsford Community Legal Centre, cited at footnote 49.

legal practice and the increasing use of online technology to deliver legal services, especially to remote and rural areas of Australia, this mode of clinical legal education offers significant potential.

Clinical components in other courses

In *Best Practices* we described a clinical component as occurring when a substantive law course includes within its teaching and assessment a section that is clinical.[67] This can include interviewing clients and writing a reflective assignment,[68] participating in judicial mentoring (for example, accompanying a magistrate or judge in order to understand their work as a part of courses in criminal procedure, evidence, and family law and policy),[69] or working in a community legal centre for two weeks with a focus on family law.[70]

In the New South Wales (NSW) and Australian Capital Territory (ACT) Regional Reports, interviewees reported that specific skills such as interviewing, research, case evaluation and negotiation could all be incorporated into doctrinal law courses.[71] This is usually through a simulated approach to legal practice. For example, students may be asked to draft pleadings or conduct negotiations over specific scenarios.

The *Best Practices* research asked about the merits of an integrated approach to legal education, combining simulation, doctrinal teaching, clinical components and clinics. There is a range of views about whether any integration needs to occur in a linear form. Many responded that all approaches are useful for different purposes. One of the comments from the Regional Reports was that exposure to clinical methodology through a clinical component in a doctrinal subject may be difficult in law schools that do not have in-house live clinics. Interviewees expressed the view

---

67   Adrian Evans and others, cited at footnote 8, 20.

68   *Identifying Current Practices in Clinical Legal Education, Regional Report: New South Wales and Australian Capital Territory*, describing the Law, Lawyers and Society course with an interviewing component at Kingsford Legal Centre, at perma.cc/257Z-6EMR.

69   *Identifying Current Practices in Clinical Legal Education, Regional Report: Victoria and Tasmania*, at perma.cc/J562-X6GU.

70   *Identifying Current Practices in Clinical Legal Education, Regional Report: Western Australia and Northern Territory*, at perma.cc/4EDN-5SZG.

71   *Identifying Current Practices in Clinical Legal Education, Regional Report: New South Wales and Australian Capital Territory*, 20, at perma.cc/257Z-6EMR.

that '[i]t is not possible in the partnership external model'.[72] However, the approach taken by Charles Darwin University,[73] based in Darwin in the Northern Territory but with a clinical component in Albury-Wodonga (NSW and Victorian border), almost 4,000 kilometres away, suggests otherwise. In this course, students spend two weeks on site in Albury-Wodonga in a community legal centre family law practice where they learn client communication skills as well as substantive law.

Analysis

A clinical component has the benefit of providing a large number of students with a short, sharp experience of legal work that, with a reflective component, can be very effective. For many students, a clinical component in a course will be their first experience of law in practice or of real clients. It can be an affirming experience for students who are questioning what role they may play in the legal system, and it can bring academic learning to life through real legal issues faced by ordinary people in the community.

The logistics and administration required to provide large numbers of students with a clinical component is resource intensive. This can be taxing on the site where the clinical component is being provided[74] and requires a high level of administration in the course. Students' learning can be prioritised over client service[75] through a clinical component as the student will generally have more limited skills than if they were doing an entire clinical course, since they are there for a brief experience only.

---

72 *Identifying Current Practices in Clinical Legal Education, Regional Report: Queensland and Northern New South Wales*, 18, at perma.cc/257Z-6EMR.

73 *Identifying Current Practices in Clinical Legal Education, Regional Report: Western Australia and Northern Territory*, 5, at perma.cc/4EDN-5SZG.

74 Each semester Kingsford Legal Centre has to draw up rosters for up to 256 law students for separate advice clinics and ensure that they attend; *Identifying Current Practices in Clinical Legal Education, Regional Report: New South Wales and Australian Capital Territory*, at perma.cc/257Z-6EMR. See also, Anna Cody, 'What does legal ethics teaching gain, if anything, from including a clinical component?' (2015) 22(1) *International Journal of Clinical Legal Education* 1.

75 Two-week family law clinical component in Albury: *Identifying Current Practices in Clinical Legal Education, Regional Report: Western Australia and Northern Territory*, at perma.cc/257Z-6EMR.

Factors in choice of model

As discussed above, ideally, clinical legal education ought to be integrated throughout the law curriculum and a range of models will be used, including simulations, clinical components, externships, agency clinics and in-house clinics.[76] Currently, most universities have not adopted this approach. The choice of a clinical legal education model depends on a range of factors.[77] Although we discuss these factors discretely, they are not unrelated; each one affects another. The decision about which model of clinical legal education to adopt will be based on a combination of issues, including:

- learning objectives of the course;
- available resources, financial and physical;
- extent of control and supervision;
- potential partnerships/placements;
- types of legal work; and
- students' location and their numbers.

Learning objectives

The most important aspect of choosing a preferred model is matching the learning objectives of the course with the best model to facilitate those objectives.[78] The various models of clinical legal education offer different learning opportunities to students. In Chapter 4, 'Course design for clinical teaching', we discuss these issues more fully.

Extent of control and supervision

One of the key aspects of high-quality clinical legal education is the standard of supervision:[79] 'Close supervision is often described as a hallmark of clinical education.'[80] In any externship or external live client agency relationship, there is less control over the specific learning goals and

---

76   Giddings (2013), 80.
77   MA Noone, 'Planning a clinical legal education program: what are the issues?' (1994) 19(6) *Alternative Law Journal* 285.
78   See Chapter 4 of this book on 'course design'.
79   See Chapter 6 of this book.
80   Giddings (2013), 41.

supervision may not be as intensive.[81] The advantages of these as options for clinical legal education are that they are generally less expensive to establish for law schools, and also provide greater diversity in placement sites for students. Weighing up the degree of control that the law school wants with the cost of providing in-house clinics will be part of the decision-making in choosing the model.[82]

Available resources

Ideally, a staged approach, beginning with simulations and ending with a live client experience, enables students to scaffold their learning more effectively than in any other way. However, this is often seen as too resource intensive, and the choice of model is often limited by available funds. A law school will have to weigh up the specific educational objectives for students with the resources that are available. The resources needed to run a clinical legal education program include staff (academic, legal supervisors and administrative) and the costs of office infrastructure including information technology, rent, equipment and related expenses, which we discuss more fully in Chapter 9, 'Resourcing live client clinics'. As discussed above, establishing an in-house live client clinic is the most resource-intensive form of clinical legal education.[83] The benefits include the law school's ability to clearly shape and develop the educational experience it provides for its students with a high degree of control.

Potential partnerships/placements

Universities may have well-developed connections with the community and frequently see their role as reaching into and collaborating with the community. 'Community' can include student communities, local communities, the legal profession, the judiciary, the general public and even specific groupings within the general public and government agencies.[84] Universities and law schools may want to develop these relationships and

---

81   Liz Ryan Cole, 'Externships, A Special Focus to Help Understand and Advance Social Justice' in Frank Bloch (ed), cited at footnote 27, 327.
82   Giddings (2013), 82.
83   Giddings (2013), 99.
84   Neil Rees, 'How should law schools serve their communities?' (2001) 5 *University of Western Sydney Law Review* 111, 114, referred to in Giddings (2013), 42.

collaborations at particular points in time. These will in turn influence the decision about where to situate a clinical legal education program and how to develop it.

Another factor in deciding whether to develop an externship program is the diversity and opportunities of placement sites that might be available. Not all clinical legal education courses need to have learning objectives related to community or social justice. Placement opportunities may arise that give students the chance to develop their skills and reflection in another type of legal practice, such as commercial or sports law, or even internationally. Externships offer this last benefit and flexibility,[85] permitting international clinical courses to be offered that may be attractive to students.[86]

Types of legal work

A further factor related to facilitating learning objectives and making the most of placement opportunities is the type of legal work available. Some argue that students in in-house clinics are able to engage in a fuller range of work with greater responsibility and actual client representation.[87] However, in Australia diverse types of legal work with large levels of responsibility are practised throughout each of the types of clinical legal education. In clinical components, for example, students actually interview clients[88] and work on family law cases with a substantial degree of responsibility.[89] In externships, students may represent clients, draft law reform submissions or draft legislation, develop community legal education projects and provide legal advice, among many work possibilities.[90]

---

85 Liz Ryan Cole, cited at footnote 81, 328.
86 Liz Ryan Cole, cited at footnote 81, 329.
87 Roy Stuckey and others, cited at footnote 10, 191; Giddings (2013), 94.
88 *Identifying Current Practices in Clinical Legal Education, Regional Report: New South Wales and Australian Capital Territory*, 5 (Law, Lawyers and Society clinical component at UNSW), at perma.cc/257Z-6EMR.
89 *Identifying Current Practices in Clinical Legal Education, Regional Report: Western Australia and Northern Territory* (Charles Darwin University, Albury Wodonga Community Legal Centre), at perma.cc/257Z-6EMR.
90 Liz Ryan Cole, cited at footnote 81, 329.

Students' location and numbers

Another factor in choosing a clinical legal education model is the number of students that need to be accommodated within the program. If there is a law school commitment to provide a clinical legal education experience to all students—as is the case for Newcastle University, UNSW and the University of Western Sydney (UWS)[91]—and there are limited resources available, then the choice of model is also limited. For example, UWS gives students a five-day clinical exposure/component as it is committed to giving all law students some clinical experience.[92]

Another aspect of the 'student' factor is their location. Given the increase in online learning, the choice of clinical legal education program may be further limited. However, several universities in Australia are engaged in developing 'virtual' clinics and these may offer new opportunities to law schools.

Conclusion

In this chapter, we have clarified key terms and described the models of clinical legal education emerging in Australia. For each model we have identified both merits and some disadvantages. Finally, we have discussed a range of factors that need to be considered when choosing a model for clinical legal education.

---

91   *Identifying Current Practices in Clinical Legal Education, Regional Report: New South Wales and Australian Capital Territory*, 5, at perma.cc/257Z-6EMR.
92   *Identifying Current Practices in Clinical Legal Education, Regional Report: New South Wales and Australian Capital Territory*, 5, at perma.cc/257Z-6EMR.

4

Course design for clinical teaching

Introduction

In this chapter, we provide extensive detail to support an overall point: clinical course design is a complex, serious, pedagogical task that can too readily be overlooked or treated lightly. Many clinical courses are established with enthusiasm for innovative and novel legal education combined with public service provision. Although these can drive and sustain a clinical course for a while, there is a risk that longer-term sustainability and credibility will be compromised if the course is not designed and developed on a sound pedagogical basis.

Coverage

We first define course aims, or objects, and suggest a number of possible aims that a clinical course might pursue. We then spell out the nature and interrelationship of course aims and learning outcomes—often poorly understood—and point out the wide range of available outcomes for a clinical course. As we discuss, the model of clinic on which the course will be based should follow from the course design, although the excitement of establishing a clinical course often puts the choice of the model first. Once established, a clinical course must deal with issues such as student selection and course content, course timing and length, all of which we canvass in this chapter.

Naming a 'course'

Throughout this chapter, the term 'course' is used to refer to what is also called a 'subject', a 'unit' or a 'module'. A student will enrol in a number of law courses (or subjects or units or modules) in an academic semester or year, counting towards the award of a law degree. A course is, for example, assigned a code by the university administration, and is named according to its content (for example, Evidence, Contracts, Administrative Law, etc).

Course aims and learning outcomes

The fundamental importance of course aims

Course design does not start with the teaching method. The first question is: what are the aims (or 'goals') of the course? We use the terms 'aims' and 'goals' to describe the same thing, although a case can be made for giving them distinct meanings;[1] our point is to ensure that the larger aims or goals are established as a base for learning objectives. Only then is it possible to think about what teaching method will best meet those aims. As Stuckey reports Bellow saying in the United States over 40 years ago, 'clinical courses are only justified if they are accomplishing educational objectives that cannot be achieved by other, less expensive, methods of education'.[2]

There is often confusion over the nature and place of educational aims,[3] and enthusiasm for clinical teaching risks bypassing this basic issue ('Let's run a clinic!') or leads to reverse engineering ('We have a clinic! What will we do with it?'). In 2007, Stuckey reported the persistence of a phenomenon Bellow had complained of over 30 years earlier: 'a tendency, within clinical programs, to subordinate the question of what should be taught to the demands of what students are actually doing'.[4] Even though clinical

---

1   See e.g. M Le Brun and R Johnstone, *The Quiet Revolution: Improving Student Learning in Law* (1994) Law Book Co., 153.

2   Roy Stuckey, 'Teaching with Purpose: Defining and Achieving Desired Outcomes in Clinical Law Courses' (2006–07) 13 *Clinical Law Review* 807, 808.

3   Mary Jo Eyster, 'Designing and Teaching The Large Externship Clinic' (1998–99) 3 *Clinical Law Review* 347, 348.

4   Roy Stuckey, cited at footnote 2, 808.

legal education is a powerful teaching method, there must be educational rigour associated with it if it is to be taken seriously over time, and that rigour requires course design that starts with clearly stated course aims.[5]

It is fundamental to course design that the course aims are clearly articulated. Not only the teaching method, but topics, reading, and assessment (see Chapter 8) will be framed by—and be directed towards achieving—the course aims:

> proper evaluation and proper grading will only occur if the teacher and the student are aware of the clinic's goals and expectations, and if the teacher's recorded comments about their interventions and the student's performance are keyed to the goals and expectations that we have conveyed to students at the beginning of the clinic.[6]

Referring to an externship clinic in particular, Smith illustrates the planning process well:

> As the faculty member considers potential educational goals, she should compare the extern method with other available methods of instruction and ask whether a field placement (with a related academic component) is the best way to achieve those goals.[7]

Once established, the course aims will at least imply, if not mandate, an appropriate teaching method. Aims do need to be revisited periodically; an ongoing process rather than something engaged in once or sporadically.[8] A disincentive for continual review of educational aims, however, is the considerable investment that will have been made in the clinic: arrangements are not as easily put to one side as they can be for a standard course. But a review of educational aims should not be avoided for fear of discovering that the clinic is no longer an apt educational method. Rather, the review should be embraced as an opportunity to

---

5   See e.g. Jeff Giddings, *Promoting Justice Through Clinical Legal Education* (2013) Justice Press, Chapters 3 and 4 (cited hereafter as Giddings (2013)).

6   Wallace J Mlyniec, 'Where to Begin? Training New Teachers in the Art of Clinical Pedagogy' (2011–12) 18 *Clinical Law Review* 505, 577.

7   Linda F Smith, 'Designing An Extern Clinical Program: Or As You Sow, So Shall You Reap' (1998–99) 5 *Clinical Law Review* 527, 547.

8   Kimberly E O'Leary, 'Clinical Law Offices and Local Social Justice Strategies: Case Selection and Quality Assessment as an Integral Part of the Social Justice Agenda of Clinics' (2004–05) 11 *Clinical Law Review* 335, 339. See also Adrian Evans and Ross Hyams, 'Independent Evaluations of Clinical Legal Education Programs: Appropriate Objectives and Processes in an Australian Setting' (2008) 17 *Griffith Law Review* 52.

refine and redefine constituent parts of the clinic, such as those discussed below, ranging from student selection to case selection, and classroom content to methods of skills training.

Distinguishing learning outcomes

The aims (or 'goals') of a course have to be distinguished from the intended learning outcomes of the course. Outcomes, discussed further below, are more specific than aims, and describe what it is that a student will know or be able to do as a result of learning in the course. Only when aims and outcomes are established is it then possible to determine the appropriate model of clinic. Overall, the relationships among aims, outcomes and methods are simply illustrated:

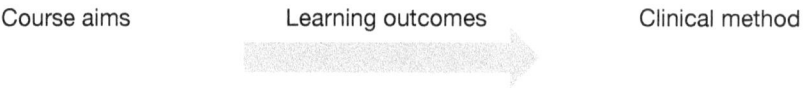

| Course aims | Learning outcomes | Clinical method |

Clinical course aims

Although Stuckey points out that '[a]ny subject can be taught using experiential education',[9] Hall and Kerrigan note that 'clinical legal education has its limits [and it is not] the best methodology for achieving all objectives of the law school'.[10] The challenge is 'to determine what lessons can be taught more effectively and efficiently using experiential education than through other methods of instruction'.[11] To make that assessment, it is necessary to know what it is that clinical teaching offers. To put it another way, what type of educational aims are well addressed by clinical teaching? If, as happens, a course is conceived of as a 'clinical course', before any course aims are first established, then a course must nevertheless be designed so that educational sense is made of the clinical experience in the context of the larger law curriculum.

---

9   Roy Stuckey and others, *Best Practices for Legal Education: A Vision and a Road Map* (2007) Clinical Legal Education Association, 168.

10   Jonny Hall and Kevin Kerrigan, 'Clinic and the wider law curriculum' (2011) 16 *International Journal of Clinical Legal Education* 25, 37.

11   Roy Stuckey, cited at footnote 2, 809; Roy Stuckey, 'Ensuring Basic Quality in Clinical Courses' (2000) 1 *International Journal of Clinical Legal Education* 47, 49.

As we discuss in Chapters 6 and 7, clinical legal education is characterised by supervision, reflection and student responsibility, with a focus on social justice issues (see Chapter 5). It operates intensively, in one-on-one or small group interactions, and allows students to apply legal theory and lawyering skills to solve legal problems that are real: students are in professional legal settings, working on real legal matters. Consistently with the 'spirit of inquiry' promoted by Dewey curriculum theory[12] and the power of experiential learning, the focus of clinical experience is to engage students with law as it operates, in context.[13] Although clinical legal education has a vocational context, its educational effectiveness depends on its dynamic relationship with the substantive, doctrinal curriculum.

Clinical legal education has, however, the capacity to address some of the shortcomings of the Dewey approach in which the teacher is in control of the classroom dynamic and of the opportunities for student inquiry. Taking a lead from the radical education theories of Paulo Freire, it is possible in clinical legal education to address the interests of the poor and, in so doing, to engage students in critiquing power structures and relations and their resulting injustices (see Chapter 5).[14]

With these distinctive features of clinical legal education in mind, it is apparent that the aims of some courses will be better supported by clinical legal education method than others.[15] Stuckey has proposed what he believes to be 'the five most important educational objectives that can be accomplished in clinical courses': developing problem solving skills; becoming more reflective about legal culture and lawyering roles; learning how to both behave and think like a lawyer; understanding the meaning of justice and lawyers' responsibility to strive to do justice; and discovering the human effects of the law.[16]

---

12   John Dewey, 'The educational situation (orig. Chicago, 1906)' (2002) 17(2) *Journal of Curriculum and Supervision*, 104, 119.
13   Adrian Evans, Anna Cody, Anna Copeland, Jeff Giddings, Mary Anne Noone, Simon Rice and Ebony Booth, *Best Practices: Australian Clinical Legal Education* (2013) Government of Australia, Office of Learning and Teaching, 15, at perma.cc/2J6E-ZMQX.
14   Paulo Freire, *Pedagogy of the Oppressed* (1970) Herder and Herder; and see e.g. Alan Singer and Michael Pezone, 'Education for Social Change: From Theory to Practice', at perma.cc/JKA9-B9UM.
15   Some examples are drawn from, but are not the same as, The Australian National University law courses.
16   Roy Stuckey, cited at footnote 11, 50–51. Similar goals are described for clinical education in Kenya: see TO Ojienda and M Oduor, 'Reflections on the Implementation of Clinical Legal Education in Moi University, Kenya' (2002) 2 *International Journal of Clinical Legal Education* 49, 57.

Stuckey does not offer evaluative criteria that support these as the 'most important' aims of clinical legal education. In listing possible aims, it is worth keeping in mind Failinger's caution that, in light of all that clinical legal education can achieve, aims should be modest: 'a small handful of realistic goals for many law students … or an ambitious set of goals for very few students'.[17] Goldfarb points out that it is exactly the large promise of clinical legal education that requires 'clinical teachers to abandon some portion of what ideally [they] strive to achieve'.[18]

Legal doctrine as a course aim?

It is common that a doctrinal course has as its aim that students will, for example, 'understand the core concepts and principles underpinning contracts/torts/criminal/public law, and to comment critically on the outcome and reasoning in cases'. Clinical method is not necessary to achieve these aims. However, the immediacy of the clinic can enable students to deepen their understanding of doctrine. Related aims may, for example, be for students to 'identify the considerations of policy that may underpin cases and legislation', 'to apply learned rules and principles to practice', 'to identify the practical implications of legislation', 'to understand current issues', and 'to identify weaknesses or gaps in the law'. For each of the related aims, an integrated clinical component to otherwise doctrinal courses would be apt.[19]

Legal theory as a course aim?

Some courses do not aim to focus on pure legal doctrine, the law as it relates to particular social issues or communities, or substantive law with practical contexts, but will aim instead to explore larger issues of law, legal theory, legal policy and the operation of law in society. Course aims might be, for example, for students to 'assess the adequacy of feminist legal theory as an explanation for aspects of the criminal justice system', or 'to evaluate the effectiveness of public legal services in meeting unmet legal need' and, in each case, clinical legal education will be an appropriate teaching method.

---

17   Marie A Failinger, 'A Home of its Own: The Role Of Poverty Law in Furthering Law Schools' Missions' (2007) 34 *Fordham Urban Law Journal* 1173, 1779–80.
18   Phyllis Goldfarb, 'Back To The Future Of Clinical Legal Education' (2012) 32 *Boston College Journal of Law and Social Justice* 279, 306.
19   See e.g. Jonny Hall and Kevin Kerrigan, cited at footnote 10, 25.

Legal and professional skills as a course aim?

Some courses on substantive law may have aims that are quite explicitly skills-based; aims with which clinical legal education is more obviously aligned. This skills/clinic alignment is deceptive, however, and needs to be kept in perspective. Although clinical legal education is an effective method for teaching skills—as shown by the experience in the United States in particular—its primary focus is more analytical and reflective than the vocational aim of 'how to' that characterises practical legal training (PLT) or work-integrated learning (WIL).[20] While legal practice skills are taught in clinical legal education and used for the delivery of legal services, they are at the same time subjected to analysis and reflection, and the apparently value-neutral nature of such skills are critiqued to develop in students a consciousness of the value-laden nature of legal practice (see Chapter 5 for a more detailed discussion of this).

Courses such as, for example, litigation, civil and criminal procedure, evidence, succession or corporations, address subject matter that relates closely to, or is often well illustrated by, legal practice requiring particular skills such as drafting, negotiation, advocacy and interviewing. A dispute resolution course, for example, has skills potential when it aims for students 'to appreciate the context of litigation practice and procedure' and 'to know the technical and strategic skills necessary to mediate a dispute and conduct litigation'.

Examples from the United States, where law is studied as a graduate degree with a strong vocational focus, tend to skew an appreciation of possible educational aims for clinic away from a broad range of possibilities towards preparation for legal practice.[21] For many early clinical programs '"clinical" … became synonymous with "skills-focused" education'.[22] However, in jurisdictions other than the United States, where law students are not necessarily as focused on an immediate legal career[23] and could be studying other disciplines in concurrent degree programs, clinical legal education can demonstrate its capacity to meet a much broader scope of educational

20   Adrian Evans and others, cited at footnote 13, 4–5.
21   See e.g. the warning to this effect for clinic in the United Kingdom, in Lydia Bleasdale-Hill and Paul Wragg, 'Models of Clinic and Their Value to Students, Universities and the Community in the post-2012 Era' (2013) 19 *International Journal of Clinical Legal Education* 257, 265.
22   Linda F Smith, cited at footnote 7, 530.
23   See e.g. Lydia Bleasdale-Hill and Paul Wragg, cited at footnote 21, 265, making the point for legal education in the United Kingdom.

aims. Since the early 2000s in Australia, however, this characterisation has been changing to an extent, with the growing popularity of graduate ('JD') law programs in which students have a more definite bent towards preparation for legal practice.

Where clinical legal education focuses on legal skills training, it should do so with a focus on 'students' development of a professional identity that contributes to a sense of purpose in their lives'.[24] Legal skills that are taught in a clinic's practice context include 'accepting and assuming responsibility for matters of great importance to real clients', 'improving problem-solving abilities', 'collaboration', 'discovering facts and figuring out how to turn them into admissible evidence', and 'traditional skills' such as 'interviewing, case planning, investigating facts, counselling, legal writing, witness examination, and oral argument'.[25] More broadly, clinical legal education is a teaching method that can meet aims of personal and professional development such as, for example, 'cross-cultural awareness', 'the role of emotions', 'creativity', 'exercising authority' and 'learning to learn'.[26] Clinical legal education can teach legal doctrine,[27] doctrinal analysis,[28] and policy perspective on doctrine,[29] and is a way of teaching legal professionalism, such as values and ethics,[30] promoting a willingness to engage in law reform and *pro bono* services,[31] and strengthening students' emotional awareness and sense of ethical behaviour.[32]

---

24   Leah Wortham, Catherine F Klein and Beryl Blaustone, 'Autonomy-Mastery-Purpose: Structuring Clinical Courses to Enhance these Critical Educational Goals' (2012) 17–18 *International Journal of Clinical Legal Education* 105, 113.

25   Philip G Schrag, 'Constructing A Clinic' (1996–97) 3 *Clinical Law Review* 175, 180–85; see also Peter Toll Hoffman, 'Clinical Scholarship and Skills Training' (1994) 1 *Clinical Law Review* 93; Special Edition *Clinical Law Review* (2001); Adam Babich, 'The Apolitical Clinic' (2004) 22 *Tulane Lawyer* 10.

26   Philip G Schrag, cited at footnote 25, 182, 184, 185.

27   Philip G Schrag, cited at footnote 25, 180.

28   Linda F Smith, cited at footnote 7, 531.

29   Linda F Smith, cited at footnote 7, 530.

30   Philip G Schrag, cited at footnote 25, 183–84; see L Curran, J Dickson and MA Noone, 'Pushing the Boundaries or Preserving the Status Quo? Designing Clinical Programs to Teach Law Students a Deep Understanding of Ethical Practice' (2005) 8 *International Journal of Clinical Legal Education* 104; Kevin Kerrigan, '"How do you *feel* about this client?" A commentary on the clinical model as a vehicle for teaching ethics to law students' (2007) *International Journal of Clinical Legal Education* 7, 37; Anna Cody, 'What does legal ethics teaching gain, if anything, from including a clinical component?' (2015) 22(1) *International Journal of Clinical Legal Education* 1.

31   Linda F Smith, cited at footnote 7, 530.

32   Anna Cody, cited at footnote 30.

Social justice as a course aim?

Perhaps the most pervasive educational aim for a clinical course, apart from skills training, and certainly the most distinctive, is to attune students to issues of social justice,[33] a course aim for students that is 'beyond being just practice ready'.[34] It is the contextual nature of clinical legal education, supported by supervision and reflection (see Chapters 6 and 7), which makes it particularly effective in focusing on lawyers' roles in achieving social justice (see Chapter 5).

There is a long and strong tradition in clinical legal education of aiming to inculcate social justice values that transcend mere legal service provision, and that 'produc[e] lawyers who will go on to change the nature and function of legal practice in the interests of more humane social values, and the advancement of the poor and disadvantaged'.[35] Such a conscious effort to promote social values may be warranted in light of research in Australia, which suggests that students who arrive at law school with '[a] desire to engage in social justice or public interest practice' lose that desire as they continue their studies,[36] and students in their final year of legal studies are least likely to agree that law has 'the power to bring about positive social change'.[37] Indeed, a tendency to cynicism has been observed among law students,[38] who may tend to be, at least, uninterested and 'ignorant about critical idealism and wider social perspectives'.[39]

33   See e.g. Jo Dubin, 'Clinical Design for Social Justice imperatives' (1980) 5 *Southern Methodist University Law Review* 1461; Jane H Aiken, 'The Clinical Mission of Justice Readiness' (2012) 32(2) *Boston College Journal of Law and Social Justice* 231; Stephen Wizner and Jane Aiken, 'Teaching and Doing: The Role of Law School Clinics in Enhancing Access to Justice' (2004) 73 *Fordham Law Review* 997; Margaret Martin Barry, Jon C Dubin and Peter A Joy, 'Clinical Education for This Millennium: The Third Wave' (2000) 7 *Clinical Law Review* 1; Shuvro Prosun Parker, 'Empowering the Underprivileged: The Social Justice Mission for Clinical Legal Education in India' (2013) 19 *International Journal of Clinical Legal Education* 321; Lydia Bleasdale-Hill and Paul Wragg, cited at footnote 21, 267 and the articles referred to therein at notes 29 and 30.
34   Jane H Aiken, cited at footnote 33, 232.
35   Jeremy Cooper and Louise Trubek (eds), *Educating for Justice: Social Values and Legal Education* (1997) Ashgate, 5; Frank Bloch and Mary Anne Noone, 'Legal Aid Origins of Clinical Legal Education' in Frank Bloch (ed), *The Global Clinical Movement: Educating Lawyers for Social Justice* (2011) Oxford University Press, 153.
36   Tamara Walsh, 'Putting Justice Back into Education' (2007) 17(1) *Legal Education Review* 119, 131.
37   Tamara Walsh, cited at footnote 36, 132.
38   Kim Economides, 'Cynical Legal Studies' in Jeremy Cooper and Louise Trubek (eds), cited at footnote 35, 26 and 29.
39   Kim Economides, cited at footnote 38, 26.

Many courses are concerned with the law as it relates to particular social justice issues, such as housing, social security and discrimination law, or to particular communities such as Indigenous peoples, poor people,[40] women, children and refugees. These issue-specific courses are very contextual, and clinical legal education would be an effective method for meeting course aims that students will, for example, 'understand domestic legal issues affecting Indigenous peoples', or 'assess the effectiveness of legal remedies for human rights violations against Indigenous peoples'.

Public service as a course aim?

Most forms of clinical legal education in Australia bring with them their own necessary aim, that of providing legal services to a section of the public.[41] This is a separate process that means 'understand[ing] the legal needs of the community and of the population the clinic hopes to help',[42] and brings with it the perennial dilemma in clinical legal education of how to meet the related but often competing goals of student education and client service: 'sensitivity to the balance between student needs and client needs must be considered at every decision-making juncture',[43] although in Reed's view 'the traditional emphasis [is] placed on the service goal rather than the educational goal'.[44] As we noted in Chapter 3, the Australian experience is that the joint aims of providing both student learning and client service can be accommodated.[45]

---

40   See e.g. Marie A Failinger, cited at footnote 17, 1173; Lois Johnson and Louise Trubek, 'Developing a Poverty Law Course: A Case Study' (1992) 42 *Journal of Urban and Contemporary Law* 185.

41   Philip G Schrag, cited at footnote 25, 180.

42   Kimberly E O'Leary, cited at footnote 8, 342; and see Shuvro Prosun Parker, cited at footnote 33, 322–23.

43   Kimberly E O'Leary, cited at footnote 8, 339.

44   Stephen F Reed, 'Clinical Legal Education At A Generational Crossroads: A Self-Focused Self-Study Of Self' (2010) 17(1) *Clinical Law Review* 243, 249.

45   Judith Dickson, 'Clinical Legal Education in the 21st Century: Still Educating for Service?' (2000) 1 *International Journal of Clinical Legal Education* 33; Giddings (2013); Anna Cody, 'Clinical Programs in Community Legal Centres, The Australian Approach' (2011) 4 *Spanish Journal Education and Law Review*.

Legal policy and law reform as a course aim?

A clinical course that aims to attune students to issues of social justice is likely to incorporate advocacy for changes to law and policy as a complementary course aim. It has been argued for some time that there is, in fact, an ethical obligation on legal education, and perhaps clinical legal education in particular, to pursue changes to law and policy in the public interest.[46] A 'law reform' aim complements aims of teaching both doctrine and professional skills: doctrine, simply because a conventional critical analysis of law should generate options for reform; and professional skills because conventional lawyers' skills of research, drafting, negotiation and advocacy are necessary for effective law reform.

Student wellbeing and engagement as a course aim?

Increasing attention is being paid to law students' mental health and wellbeing.[47] The dissonance between students' justice aspirations and the actual law curriculum, noted above, is a significant factor in students' distress, as is the intensely competitive nature of law school.[48] Complementing, say, the social values and social justice aims mentioned above, a clinical course can aim to meet a student's aspirations to work for justice, and can promote a collaborative and supportive work environment. An explicit aim of wellbeing may be particularly important for students from other cultural or legal traditions, such as Indigenous students,[49] who risk feeling quite alienated from any real sense of law's role in society.

---

46   See e.g. Stephen Wizner, 'The Law School Clinic: Legal Education in the Interests of Justice' (2001–02) 70 *Fordham Law Review* 1929; Sameer M Ashar, 'Law Clinics and Collective Mobilization' (2008) 14 *Clinical Law Review* 355; Donald Nicolson, 'Calling, Character and Clinical Legal Education: A Cradle to Grave Approach to Inculcating a Love for Justice' (2013) 16(1) *Legal Ethics* 36.

47   See e.g. Massimiliano Tani and Prue Vines, 'Law Students' Attitudes to Education: Pointers to Depression in the Legal Academy and the Profession?' (2009) 19 *Legal Education Review* 3; Molly O'Brien, Stephen Tang and Kath Hall, 'No time to lose: Negative impact on law student wellbeing may begin in year one' (2011) 2(12) *International Journal of the First Year in Higher Education* 49; Molly O'Brien, 'Connecting Law Student Wellbeing to Social Justice, Problem-Solving and Human Emotions' (2014) 14(1) *QUT Law Review* 52.

48   See e.g. Molly Townes O'Brien, Stephen Tang, and Kath Hall, 'Changing our Thinking: Empirical Research on Law Student Wellbeing, Thinking Styles and the Law Curriculum' (2011) 21 *Legal Education Review* 149, citing Nancy J Soonpaa, 'Stress in Law Students: A Comparative Study of First-Year, Second-Year, and Third-Year Students' (2004) 36 *Connecticut Law Review* 353.

49   Anna Cody and Sue Green, 'Clinical legal education and Indigenous legal education: What's the connection?' (2007) 11 *International Journal of Clinical Legal Education* 51.

Student aims?

In addition to teacher-determined aims, a clinic can aim to meet students' own goals. While these will often be the same as the standard goals, they will sometimes be more personal,[50] which may be difficult to incorporate into a planned curriculum other than through the reflective element of clinical legal education, and which risks seeing students' 'career placement goals [being] elevated above educational goals'.[51]

A conflict 'between the student's individual ambitions and the larger social aims of the clinic'[52] may have to be resolved. The student is on notice for the clinic, as for any conventional course, of the intended aims and will have to reconcile their own aims with those of the course they have chosen, thereby 'resisting' student-led design.[53] More constructively (but requiring more work), '[c]ooperative learning theory posits that the role of the professor is to engage in "the spirit of mutuality" of learning between students and instructors',[54] such that 'clinic students themselves can determine the subject matter and the political focus of their lawyering tasks'.[55] However, this does carry the risk that 'inexperienced law students' motivation and excitement to tackle a social problem might lead to overly ambitious projects that could in turn lead to considerable frustration during implementation'.[56]

Clinical learning outcomes

The aims of a clinical course are, effectively, a statement by the law school of why it is offering the course. From a different perspective, 'learning outcomes' are a statement by the law school of what a student will be able to show they have learnt from a course:

---

50   Philip G Schrag, cited at footnote 25, 185–86; and on the 'novelty of relying on students to dictate the goals of an academic program', see Mary Jo Eyster, cited at footnote 3, 354–58.

51   Linda F Smith, cited at footnote 7, 537.

52   Lydia Bleasdale-Hill and Paul Wragg, cited at footnote 21, 266.

53   Lydia Bleasdale-Hill and Paul Wragg, cited at footnote 21, 266.

54   William Wesley Patton, 'Getting Back to the Sandbox' (2011) 16 *International Journal of Clinical Legal Education* 96, 103–04, citing Fran Quigley, 'Seizing The Disorienting Moment: Adult Learning Theory And The Teaching Of Social Justice In Law School Clinics' (1995) 2 *Clinical Law Review* 37, 58–59.

55   William Wesley Patton, cited at footnote 54, 104.

56   William Wesley Patton, cited at footnote 54, 114.

Simply put, learning outcomes are the skills and knowledge which it is intended that students should be able to demonstrate by the time the assessment processes for the course have been completed. The intention of learning outcomes is to give students more idea of what is expected of them during the course they are undertaking ... objectives state what the teacher plans to achieve, outcomes state what it is that the student should achieve.[57]

Learning outcomes are central to course design; they affect 'course content, practical experience and assessment'.[58] As a matter of best practice, a clinical course is 'designed to promote specified student learning outcomes'. Materials, class time and activities are directed towards achieving the learning outcomes, casework is selected to support them, academic and practical content is designed to support them, assessment tasks align with them, and infrastructure investment is defined by what is necessary to achieve them.[59] Literature on clinical legal education supports the central role of learning outcomes: they 'provide the framework for ... teaching and methodology',[60] they are 'important in the choice of suitable clinical models'[61] and they are the focus of an assessment regime. 'The main purpose of assessments in educational institutions is to discover if students have achieved the learning outcomes of the course studied.'[62]

Even if statements of learning outcomes do not encompass everything a student might learn in the course, they 'force us to think more carefully about what we believe are the most important purposes of our courses and guide us in designing the delivery of the promised outcomes'.[63] Learning outcomes may not, however, be wholly at the discretion of the teacher,

57 The Learning Institute, *Good Practice Guide on Writing Aims and Learning Outcomes* (2011) Queen Mary, University of London, 4.
58 Adrian Evans and others, cited at footnote 13, 48.
59 Adrian Evans and others, cited at footnote 13, throughout.
60 Rachel Spencer, 'Holding up the Mirror: A Theoretical and Practical Analysis of the Role of Reflection in Clinical Legal Education' (2012) 17–18 *International Journal of Clinical Legal Education* 181, 186.
61 See Giddings (2013).
62 Roy Stuckey, 'Can We Assess What We Purport to Teach in Clinical Law Courses' (2006) 9 *International Journal of Clinical Legal Education* 9, 10.
63 Roy Stuckey and others, cited at footnote 9, 199–200.

and may have to be articulated so as to conform to externally imposed outcomes required by, for example, the Australian Threshold Learning Outcomes (TLOs) for Law.[64]

Terminology for learning outcomes

In drafting learning outcomes there is an important difference between merely describing what a student will have learnt and stating what a student will be able to do to show what they have learnt:

> useful learning outcomes are those which describe what the typical student will be able to do by the time the course has been completed, and which can be assessed to measure to what extent students have achieved these outcomes ... a less useful outcome would describe the understanding that students are expected to have developed, whereas a more useful one would outline how they can articulate, or demonstrate this.[65]

Useful learning outcomes incorporate verbs that suggest activity on the part of the student. The Centre for University Teaching at Flinders University, for example, suggests verbs to follow the statement 'On successful completion of this (assignment/topic/course) students should be able to':

> analyse, apply, appreciate, classify, collaborate, compare, compute, conduct, contrast, define, direct, derive, designate, demonstrate, discuss, display, evaluate, explain, identify, infer, integrate, interpret, justify, list, name, organise, outline, report, respond, solicit, state, synthesise.

The Australian TLOs for Law specify, in relation to 'Thinking Skills' for example, that graduates 'will be able to identify ... articulate ... apply ... generate ... engage in ... and think creatively ...'.[66]

Clinical legal education scholarship often sets out learning outcomes of the 'less useful' type, such as: 'I want my students to be able to ...'; 'I want my students to understand ...'; 'I want my students to learn the

64 Sally Kift, Mark Israel and Rachael Field, *Learning and Teaching Academic Standards Project: Bachelor of Laws Learning and Teaching Academic Standards Statement December 2010* (11 February 2011) Australian Learning and Teaching Council, at perma.cc/RP3A-PWRQ. See also e.g. James Marson, Adam Wilson and Mark Van Hoorebeek, 'The Necessity of Clinical Legal Education in University Law Schools: A UK Perspective' (2005) 7 *International Journal of Clinical Legal Education* 29, 32, discussing learning outcomes required by the United Kingdom Quality Assurance Agency for Higher Education.
65 The Learning Institute, cited at footnote 57, 8.
66 Sally Kift, Mark Israel and Rachael Field, cited at footnote 64.

doctrine of …'.[67] These are not invalid, but they are less useful because it is difficult for both teacher and student to measure progress towards achieving them, and they are less amenable to assessment. More useful clinical learning outcomes are, for example: 'On completion of this course, students should be able to: explain … reflect … evaluate … identify … articulate … discuss … demonstrate …',[68] and 'Students should be able to plan … develop … organise …'.[69]

In *Best Practices* we proposed the following possible learning outcomes for clinical legal education:[70]

> Upon the completion of a clinical course, the clinical student will demonstrate:
>
> > critical analyses of legal concepts through reflective practice
> >
> > an ability to work collaboratively
> >
> > an ability to practise 'lawyering' skills
> >
> > developed interpersonal skills, emotional intelligence and self-awareness of their own cognitive abilities and values
> >
> > a developing ability to 'learn from experience'
> >
> > an understanding of continuing professional development and a desire for life-long self-learning
> >
> > an understanding, and appropriate use, of the dispute resolution continuum (negotiation, mediation, collaboration, arbitration and litigation)
> >
> > an awareness of lawyering as a professional role in the context of wider society (including the imperatives of corporate social responsibility, social justice and the provision of legal services to those unable to afford them) and of the importance of professional relationships

---

67 Carolyn Grose, 'Beyond Skills Training, Revisited: The Clinical Education Spiral' (2012–13) 19 *Clinical Law Review* 489, 503.

68 Rachel Spencer, cited at footnote 60, 186.

69 Cath Sylvester, Jonny Hall and Elaine Hall, 'Problem-Based Learning and Clinical Legal Education: What can Clinical Educators Learn from PBL' (2004) 4 *International Journal of Clinical Legal Education* 39, 58–59.

70 Adrian Evans and others, cited at footnote 13.

a developing personal sense of responsibility, resilience, confidence, self-esteem and, particularly, judgment

a consciousness of multi-disciplinary approaches to clients' dilemmas – including recognition of the non-legal aspects of clients' problems

a developing preference for an ethical approach and an understanding of the impact of that preference in exercising professional judgment

a consolidated body of substantive legal knowledge, and knowledge of professional conduct rules and ethical practice, and

an awareness of the social issues of justice, power and disadvantage and an ability to critically analyse entrenched issues of justice in the legal system.

Whether, on completion of a clinical course, a student can in fact demonstrate these learning outcomes, is a matter for assessment (see Chapter 8).

Choosing the type of clinic

As we said above, it is only after the course aims and outcomes are established that the appropriate model of clinic can be determined. In Chapter 3, we discussed the different possible models of clinic. Most of the possible learning outcomes that are mentioned above as best practice[71] are achievable in all of the models. A good reason to distinguish among the models is the degree of control that a law school can exercise over the clinic. Both in-house and external live client clinics have students working with clients under supervision, but the greater control that a law school can exercise over the work done by an in-house clinic gives scope for pursuing a wide range of learning outcomes. For an external live client clinic, the organisational goals of the agency can limit the range of possible learning outcomes, and so an agency should be selected with those constraints in mind. This is so to an even greater extent for externships, where the learning outcomes are achievable only within the bounds of the placement agency's own, independent goals, which places greater emphasis on the complementary content of the classroom, discussed

---

71   Adrian Evans and others, cited at footnote 13.

below. Differently from any of these models, a substantive law course that has clinical components to it will have its own intended learning outcomes—often knowledge of doctrine—and the clinical method has been chosen within the established aims of that course.

When deciding on the type of clinic that will best achieve the intended learning outcomes, significant considerations are the nature of the work that the students will do, the practice methods that are used, the social contexts in which the work is done, and the issues that are commonly addressed. These are considerations that the law school will have in mind when deciding whether it needs to exercise more or less control over the clinic and, so, whether to work with an in-house clinic, an external clinic or a placement agency for externships (see Chapter 3).[72] Eyster makes the point clearly, in relation to a placement clinic:

> [T]he availability of particular placement opportunities should not completely govern the structure of the clinic. Rather, goals should be established for the program, and curricular decisions (including size; seminar topics and format; nature of placements; faculty involvement in supervision; and other factors) should derive from those goals … It simply does not make sense to decide where to place students, what to teach in the seminar, whether and how to train and supervise field instructors, without first having a clear understanding of the goals of the program.[73]

Consider, for example, a learning outcome that 'the student will demonstrate an understanding, and appropriate use, of the dispute resolution continuum'.[74] The externship model allows the flexibility of choosing a range of placement sites whose work offers a student the opportunity to engage with a continuum of dispute resolution mechanisms, in areas of debt, employment or family law rather than, say, criminal law or domestic violence protection, and the opportunity for students to learn from other student experiences about dispute resolution. Consider another possible learning outcome: that a student will demonstrate 'an awareness of: lawyering as a professional role in the context of wider society; the imperatives of corporate social responsibility, social justice, and the provision of legal services to those unable to afford them; and the importance of professional relationships'.[75] For this outcome, the student

---

72   See e.g. Philip G Schrag, cited at footnote 25, 191–92, who makes this goal-oriented point in the more specific context of case selection in a legal practice clinic.

73   Mary Jo Eyster, cited at footnote 3, 352.

74   Adrian Evans and others, cited at footnote 13.

75   Adrian Evans and others, cited at footnote 13.

needs to be exposed to something other than conventional legal practice. Many externships with private or public legal practices will not offer the diversity of practice methods, contexts and issues required for this learning outcome, while an association with a community legal centre—whether in an in-house clinic, external clinic or externship—is likely to do so.

Selecting students

Student demand for clinic often outstrips available places, necessitating the invidious task of selecting (and excluding) students. It is good practice to ensure that the selection process for students is administered by the university, not by the teacher, in a transparent and non-discriminatory manner, subject only to prerequisites that are clearly articulated.[76] Within these process requirements, there is a wide diversity of methods, ranging from ballot to interview, as we note below. Few of the accounts of methods for student selection say anything about the criteria, and few of the possible criteria have any real relationship with what a clinic will expect of a student. After an overview of the many possible methods for student selection, we examine possible valid criteria.

Processes for selection

A national survey of clinic selection methods reports the many ways that students can be selected in Australia:[77] ballot, priority of application, preference to final- or penultimate-year students, academic merit, 'suitability' to meet a clinic site's needs, student interest and desire, experience, prerequisite subjects, social justice experience, previous volunteering, level of other commitments, and previous academic conduct. Methods used elsewhere include a simple sign-up sheet, a lottery, criteria-based selection, written applications, essays,[78] volunteer contributions,[79] interviews[80] and grade-point averages.[81]

---

76 Adrian Evans and others, cited at footnote 13, 51.
77 *Identifying Current Practices in Clinical Legal Education*, Regional Reports, cited in Chapter 1 at footnote 6; Adrian Evans and others, cited at footnote 13.
78 Frank Dignan, 'Bridging the Academic/Vocational Divide: The Creation of a Law Clinic in an Academic Law School' (2011) 16 *International Journal of Clinical Legal Education* 75, 80.
79 Lawrence Donnelly, 'Irish Clinical Legal Education *Ab Initio*: Challenges and Opportunities' (2008) 13 *International Journal of Clinical Legal Education* 56, 61.
80 Maureen E Laflin, 'Toward the Making of Good Lawyers: How an Appellate Clinic Satisfies the Professional Objectives of the MacCrate Report' (1997–98) 33 *Gonzaga Law Review* 1, 11.
81 Philip G Schrag, cited at footnote 25, 210.

Frustratingly, these accounts describe mere processes, and no account is given of the criteria that are applied to make those processes useful. A wide range of considerations are, notoriously, taken into account when selecting students for clinic but none is obviously valid for clinical legal education generally, and the most that can be said is that some, in some circumstances, may be a rational basis for selection and exclusion.

Common criteria for selection

It may be thought that, because of the particular demands of clinical legal education, students are more or less 'suitable' to participate, having regard to, for example, prior experience in legal practice, levels of emotional maturity, or their having reached a later stage in the law degree program. In fact, the extent to which a student needs to 'know law', or to demonstrate 'maturity', will vary according to the aims of the course, the model of clinic and the type of work that is done. Bleasdale-Hill and Wragg (who usefully distinguish the vocationally oriented nature of clinical legal education in the United States) discuss student selection considerations that arise, in their case, in the United Kingdom, and that are true for similar legal education systems such as that in Australia.[82] They express some sympathy for a view that preference could be given to students with a stated intention to practise law, but note that there is 'a certain degree of speculation' in saying that such students are more likely to show commitment to the clinic, and they see no reason why those who do not wish to become lawyers should not be able to apply.

Care should be taken to not assume that a clinic student, in order to work and learn under supervision, needs either a practice-level command of legal principles or familiarity and comfort with challenging practice issues. Although the partnering organisation might seek students who have some prior 'real world' experience, less experienced students can benefit more from the closely supervised and supported nature of clinical legal education. The partnering organisation will, understandably, be concerned to ensure that its service provision is not unduly compromised by the inability of clinic students to do what is needed. Reference here to 'unduly' indicates an acceptance that clinic students may adversely affect service delivery to some degree, but within tolerable limits having regard to the joint goals of service and education (and, of course, clinic students

---

82 Lydia Bleasdale-Hill and Paul Wragg, cited at footnote 21, 265–66.

can have a positive effect on service delivery too). We noted in Chapter 3 that good working relationships between university staff and the staff of a partnering organisation are critical to address the tension between service and education.

Clinics will often avoid the hard task of seriously considering what, if any, prior knowledge or experience is actually needed, both to achieve the learning outcomes and meet the needs of a partnering organisation. The common proxy for a real or perceived need for previous experience is to give priority to later- or final-year students, avoiding a serious analysis of what is actually required to engage successfully with the course. One risk generated by this approach is that the clinic experience is more easily (and misleadingly) characterised as an exercise in work-readiness, putting undue emphasis on 'practice preparation'. Another is that students have no opportunity to approach other law courses through the critical reflective lens they acquire in clinical legal education.[83] Although there is a view that for younger, less practice-focused students, clinical legal education is inappropriate altogether,[84] another view is that first-year students will benefit from clinical methodology, particularly first-year Indigenous students who may be at risk of withdrawing from their legal studies.[85]

In second semester of their first year, Aboriginal and Torres Strait Islander students at the University of New South Wales (UNSW), for example, learn basic interviewing skills and have the opportunity to interview clients at the in-house clinic. In their second or third year, all law students attend the in-house clinic for a class on interviewing skills, participate in a client advice session and write a reflective assignment.

Valid criteria for selection

There are two pedagogically sound considerations for admission into a clinic: the student's capacity to achieve the intended learning outcomes; and the service requirements of an external agency. As Massey and Rosenbaum put it: 'Client needs and pedagogical objectives drive

---

83   HL Packer, T Ehrlich and S Pepper, *New Directions in Legal Education* (1972) Carnegie Foundation for the Advancement of Teaching/McGraw-Hill, 41; and see CLEPR 'Clinical Education: The Student Perspective' (1974) 7(1) *Clinical Legal Education PR Newsletter* 5–6.

84   Rodney J Uphoff, 'Why In-House Live Client Clinics Won't Work in Romania: Confessions of a Clinician Educator' (1999–2000) 6 *Clinical Law Review* 315.

85   Anna Cody and Sue Green, cited at footnote 49.

the criteria for determining student enrollment in clinics.'[86] At times, adherence to these considerations will be compromised by external factors, such as expectations of a placement site, requirements imposed by the funder of a program and obligations imposed by the law school (for example, to final year students). However, we put those to one side in this analysis, except for issues of affirmative action and accommodating disability, which we address below.

The first consideration for admission into a clinic—the student's capacity to achieve the intended learning outcomes—will raise very few barriers to participation in a clinic. Achieving new doctrinal knowledge may, as in any law course, require prior knowledge of foundational concepts, and in a specialist clinic preference could be given to students with a demonstrated commitment to working in that particular field.[87] Other likely intended learning outcomes for a clinic can be achieved by any law student, to some degree. Only if a learning outcome is pitched at a level of demonstrating 'advanced' or 'sophisticated' ability, for example, is there a reason to enrol students with an existing level of ability. For example, 'at Monash University, admission into [the clinical course] Advanced Professional Practice generally requires satisfactory completion of Professional Practice', and the Griffith University course Advanced Family Law Clinic requires students to have completed the classroom-based family law course.[88] A clinic in which students will represent clients in court may have minimum expectations of students, but those expectations need to be clearly set out and closely tied to what is actually required of well-supervised students.[89]

The more influential consideration in setting prerequisites for clinic enrolment is the service requirements of an external agency, relevant for all models of clinic apart from the rare, fully in-house live client clinic, and the relatively uncommon occurrence of clinical components in doctrinal courses. For an external (or 'agency') live client clinic, and for the widely used externship model, a clinical course must operate within the operational imperatives of the partnering organisation. This may,

---

86 Patricia A Massey and Stephen A Rosenbaum, 'Disability Matters: Toward a Law School Clinical Model for Serving Youth with Special Education Needs' (2004–05) *Clinical Law Review* 271, 318.

87 See e.g. admission requirements for the various specialist clinics described in Patricia A Massey and Stephen A Rosenbaum, cited at footnote 86, 318–21.

88 Adrian Evans and others, cited at footnote 13, 13.

89 See e.g. Susan Campbell, 'A Student Right of Audience – Implications of Law Students Appearing in Court' (2004) 4 *International Journal of Clinical Legal Education* 22, 38.

although not necessarily, result in the need for minimum requirements for students on matters such as legal knowledge, legal practice skills, or familiarity with social issues or particular communities.

As we observed in Chapter 3, there can be a tension between the intended learning outcomes and an agency's service requirements. Addressing that tension in the context of clinic course design, Chavkin says:

> In designing a clinic to maximize service to a client community, selection of a student would necessarily be based on the anticipated ability of that student to provide legal services to clinic clients. Students with poor skills and/or a lack of political commitment to serving low-income clients would be discouraged or prevented from enrolling.
>
> By contrast, if the goal were to maximize educational benefits for students, to ensure that all students develop the skills and values necessary to be responsible and effective lawyers before they graduate, we would target clinic enrollment on the very students with the poorest skills and/or with the lowest level of commitment to serving under-represented populations. We would depend on the effectiveness of clinical methodology to transform the skills and values of these students and to ensure that clinic clients receive legal representation consistent with professional standards.[90]

The recommended best practice for clinical student selection in Australia is set out in this way:

> The process of student selection conforms to the university's regulations (in consultation with external agencies if relevant). The selection process is transparent and non-discriminatory. The prerequisites for selection are clearly articulated. The reasons for choosing particular methods of selection (which can include ballot, interview, stage of study or completion of a prior clinic) are articulated. There is no presumption that access to CLE courses and clinical experiences should be limited to later-year students.[91]

What needs to be added to this is that any prerequisites for selection, and any hurdles such as stage of study, completion of a prior clinic or being limited to later-year students, are in place only because they are necessary for the intended learning outcomes to be achievable, to ensure equity in students' opportunities to undertake clinical course and, if required, to meet the service requirements of an external agency.

---

90   David F Chavkin, 'Spinning Straw into Gold: Exploring the Legacy of Bellow and Moulton' (2003) 10(1) *Clinical Law Review* 245, 266.

91   Adrian Evans and others, cited at footnote 13, 13.

Few of the usual processes for selecting clinic students can be justified as general rules. Each of them may be justifiable according to these considerations in particular circumstances. There is, for example, no necessary connection between a student's prior academic performance and their ability to meet a clinic's intended learning outcomes, or between a student's prior 'social justice experience' and the service requirements of an external agency. Each clinical course needs to establish—and to be able to defend, when challenged by unsuccessful applicants—selection criteria that are relevant to the work, the intended learning outcomes of the clinic and the situation of the law school.

When no particular factors exclude a student and a clinic is open to all applicants, two methods of selection are commonly used, both relying on arbitrariness in place of evaluation against criteria. A more equitable system for 'neutral' student selection than 'first-come, first-served' is a ballot or lottery, 'a randomized selection process that gives every student an equal chance for selection'.[92] It is described in *Best Practices* as 'a process of random selection from all eligible students who express interest'.[93]

Actively promoting the opportunity to enrol

The social justice focus of clinical legal education, particularly in Australia (see Chapter 5), invites students to examine issues of social inequality. Student selection for a clinic is an opportunity for the clinic itself to demonstrate a commitment to redressing inequality, 'serving as a model for promoting diversity in law practice'.[94] We noted above that selection processes must be transparent and non-discriminatory, but they can go further, and can actively promote access to the clinic for students from socioeconomic groups that are under-represented among lawyers and law students. A clinic can promote opportunities for people—such as people with disabilities and people with carer's responsibilities—whose participation requires reasonable adjustments to be made. Rather than waiting for a person to bring issues of accessibility to a clinic's attention, the clinic can take anticipatory measures to ensure that it is accessible.

---

92   David F Chavkin, cited at footnote 90, 267; see e.g. a description of student selection by lottery in the George Washington Small Business Law Clinic: Susan R Jones, 'Small Business and Community Economic Development: Transactional Lawyering for Social Change and Economic Justice' (1997–98) 4 *Clinical Law Review* 195, 208.

93   Adrian Evans and others, cited at footnote 13, 14.

94   Frances Gibson, 'The Convention on the Rights of Persons with Disabilities: The Response of the Clinic' (2011) 16 *International Journal of Clinical Legal Education* 11, 21.

Such measures could include flexible work hours and attendance requirements, audio-visual and other aids, adaptation of premises and workspaces and choosing accessible externship sites, waiving enrolment prerequisites, and adjusting assessment requirements.[95]

Gibson points out that '[i]t can be difficult for people with a disability to get into law schools, complete studies and get jobs as lawyers'.[96] She suggests:

> Clinical staff can assist law school colleagues to experience and understand issues about disability through seminar programs on the issue, encouraging students with and without disabilities to present aspects of their work relating to disability rights, to encourage sessions at university level to be run for staff on disability issues and through collaboration on research on legal issues that incorporate issues of disability.[97]

Teaching in the classroom

It is best practice for a clinic to have a classroom component: 'Each clinic includes classes that enable students as a group to examine the broader context of law and the legal system.'[98] In fact, the classroom component is a significant point of distinction between a clinical externship and a work internship in, for example, WIL. Our *Best Practices* research shows that most but not all clinics in Australia have a classroom component,[99] although Shrag reported in 1996 that a classroom component 'is not a universal practice' in the United States.[100]

Consistently with all other aspects of a clinic, '[t]he goal of the classroom component is of course inextricably linked to the overall goals of the program'.[101] In addition to any doctrinal content, and practice skills development,[102] the classroom educates students in reflective practice, legal ethics, and the practice skills necessary to

---

95 See, e.g. Sande L Buhai, 'Practice Makes Perfect: Reasonable Accommodation of Law Students with Disabilities in Clinical Placements' (1999) 36 *San Diego Law Review* 137, 167–71.

96 Frances Gibson, cited at footnote 94, 17.

97 Frances Gibson, cited at footnote 94, 18.

98 Adrian Evans and others, cited at footnote 13, 54.

99 *Identifying Current Practices in Clinical Legal Education*, Regional Reports, cited in Chapter 1 at footnote 6; Adrian Evans and others, cited at footnote 13.

100 Philip G Schrag, cited at footnote 25, 236, note 110.

101 Mary Jo Eyster, cited at footnote 3, 354.

102 Mary Jo Eyster, cited at footnote 3, 350.

ensure a good quality of legal service to the client. The classroom is a structured environment in which students can place their experience in the context of academic reading, and share reflections on their clinical experience. Indeed, if nothing else, the classroom component is a way to help students reflect, to 'assess, optimize and build upon the placement experience'.[103] But enthusiasm for class is not necessarily shared by clinic students. Coss warns of '[s]tudent resistance to a classroom component', because '[h]aving their impatience to practice satisfied by the externship experience, [students] then resent the return to the classroom'.[104]

Conduct of the class

Classes for in-house and external live client clinics can be conducted for a single cohort of students, largely sharing a common clinical experience. In contrast, students in a class for an externship clinic are likely to be placed in a variety of different environments, creating both the opportunity for comparative experiences and the challenge of finding common ground. Although a class of externship students can be divided into 'groups with common experiences',[105] Coss points out that '[t]his has the disadvantage of losing the shared experiences of group discussions, where the very diversity of the settings is the enhancement'.[106]

The actual conduct of classes in a clinic course needs to be considered carefully. Noting that 'creating a classroom where there is active student engagement is the aspirational clinic seminar model', Louis confesses that 'when I started ... I was focused so much on what I needed to tell the students that I had very little time to absorb andragogical methodology'. In other words, teaching a clinic class is different.[107]

Students' expectations of both dynamic interaction and responsible participation have important implications for the conduct of classes in a clinic course. A clinical teacher ought not, for example, enter the

---

103 Margaret Barry, 'Clinical Legal Education in the Law University: Goals and Challenges' (2007) 11 *International Journal of Clinical Legal Education* 27, 37, note 48.

104 Graeme Coss, 'Field Placement (Externship) – A Valuable Application of Clinical Education?' (1993) 4(1) *Legal Education Review* 29, 48, citing J Motley, 'Self-Directed Learning and the Out-of-House Placement' (1989) 19 *New Mexico Law Review* 211, 227.

105 Graeme Coss, cited at footnote 104, 48, citing H Rose, 'Legal Externships: Can They Be Valuable Clinical Experiences for Law Students?' (1987) 12 *Nova Law Review* 95, 109.

106 Graeme Coss, cited at footnote 104, 48.

107 C Benjie Louis, 'Reflections upon Transitions: An Essay on Learning How to Teach after Practicing Law' (2012) 17–18(2) *International Journal of Clinical Legal Education* 227, 230.

classroom in 'the teacher's cloak', representing the conventional approach to legal education in which '[s]uppression of the emotional and intellectual integrity of the pupil is the result [of an authoritarian pedagogy]; their freedom is repressed and the growth of their own personalities is stunted'.[108] Rather, a clinical teacher needs to approach the classroom as a facilitator of students' learning,[109] both respecting the experience they are getting and nurturing their capacity for reflection: '[t]he professor acts as ... tutor, rather than as someone who is professing at or dictating to the student'.[110] Students can take greater responsibility for their learning and participate in a respectful and trusting relationship with their supervisor.

Apart from the role played by the teacher, the classroom activity itself needs to be dynamic, characterised by discussion, small group work, and simulations for skills development: 'the class work is designed to further the application of the concepts, do group work,[111] and provide an opportunity for students to share challenges and solve problems through discussion and case rounds. Collaboration is encouraged'.[112] Citing Ledvinka,[113] James[114] and Maughan and Webb,[115] Spencer describes 'a number of practical ideas that clinical teachers can employ':

> the classroom can be arranged to encourage reflection by avoiding placement of the teacher in the 'power' role at the front; my own experience confirms that in a circle is best ... [in lecture theatres] asking the students to sit in the front few rows is helpful, especially if the teacher can join them, or at least avoid being above or detached from them (such as behind a lectern or desk) ... Small group or pair discussions provide opportunities for peer and self-assessment and also encourage discussion amongst less extroverted students who prefer not to speak frankly about personal experiences in front of a larger group.[116]

---

108 Robert Schehr, 'The Lord Speaks through Me: Moving beyond Conventional Law School Pedagogy and the Reasons for Doing So' (2009) 14 *International Journal of Clinical Legal Education* 9, 23, citing Joseph Ratner, *Intelligence in the Modern World: John Dewey's Philosophy* (1939) Modern Library, 623.
109 Georgina Ledvinka, 'Reflection and assessment in clinical legal education: Do you see what I see?' (2006) 9 *International Journal of Clinical Legal Education* 29, 36.
110 Leah Wortham, Catherine F Klein and Beryl Blaustone, cited at footnote 24, 125.
111 See e.g. RN Lacousiere, 'A Group Method in Clinical Legal Education' (1980) 30 *Journal of Legal Education* 563.
112 Leah Wortham, Catherine F Klein and Beryl Blaustone, cited at footnote 24, 125.
113 Georgina Ledvinka, cited at footnote 109.
114 Colin James, 'Seeing Things As We Are. Emotional Intelligence and Clinical Legal Education' (2005) 8 *International Journal of Clinical Legal Education* 123.
115 C Maughan, and J Webb, 'Taking Reflection Seriously: How was it for us?' in C Maughan and J Webb (eds), *Teaching Lawyers' Skills* (1996) Butterworths.
116 Rachel Spencer, cited at footnote 60, 195.

Literature

Students should be expected to read, analyse and use academic, professional and practical material,[117] and it is considered good practice that '[t]he readings for the clinical course encourage a broad, critical and contextual analysis of law'.[118] Students' resistance to reading materials, reported by Shrag,[119] may be particular to the skills-focused practice-oriented nature of clinical legal education in the United States, but even in that environment academic literature should be the basis of students' critical analysis of their work. As an example, Smith points out that 'jurisprudence … can become alive as an applied skill as well as an inquiry into legal theory when the jurisprudence discussions are linked to [for example] judicial internships'.[120]

Quoting Andrew Goldsmith, Cooper and Trubek say:

> it is only through the fusion of [sociolegal] scholarship and practice that law students can learn to appreciate 'the full complexity of the lawyer's social role, including responsibility to clients, others, and oneself through empirical and conceptual understanding of what lawyering in society involves'.[121]

This approach to clinical legal education assumes that a learning goal is indeed 'to appreciate the full complexity of the lawyer's social role'. That is indeed a valid assumption for clinical legal education in Australia, which is to a very large extent an exercise in exploring issues of social justice (see Chapter 5). It should not be hard, therefore, for clinicians in Australia to 'transcend the theory-practice rhetoric',[122] and to give a theoretical underpinning to clinical teaching, even in its practice-oriented skills aspects.

---

117 Adrian Evans and others, cited at footnote 13, 51.
118 Adrian Evans and others, cited at footnote 13, 54.
119 Philip G Schrag, cited at footnote 25, 239.
120 Linda F Smith, cited at footnote 7, 547–48.
121 J Cooper and LG Trubek (eds), cited at footnote 35, 6, quoting Andrew Goldsmith, 'An Unruly Conjunction? Social Thought and Legal Action in Clinical Legal Education' (1993) 43 *Journal of Legal Education* 415.
122 Eric Mills Holmes, 'Education for Competent Lawyering – Case Method in a Functional Context' (1976) 76 *Columbia Law Review* 535, 562; and see Amy D Ronner, 'Some In-House Appellate Litigation Clinic's Lessons in Professional Responsibility: Musical Stories of Candor and the Sandbag' (1995–96) 45(3) *American University Law Review* 859, 860–62, especially the references at note 5.

The 'law-in-context' focus of clinical legal education in Australia requires students to read and engage with literature about law and society. Ideas and manifestations of poverty, for example, are many and complex, and have to be understood by students if—as is often the case—a clinic is addressing legal causes of, and responses to, needs arising from poverty.[123] In any context, clinical legal education confronts students with challenging and problematic aspects of law in practice, inviting the most basic interrogation of issues of law and morality through, for example, theories of natural law and positivism, and deontology and consequentialism.

At the same time, students in clinical legal education are examining the roles of lawyers, and a critical analysis requires perspectives informed by, for example, philosophy, psychology and sociology.[124] In relation to legal ethics (see Chapter 6), for example, 'professional responsibility can be approached as an exploration of philosophy which would be as theoretical as any other part of law school. Starting the inquiry into these issues from [clinic] performance ... arguably strengthens the possibility of meaningful theoretical discussion'.[125]

Timing, scheduling and course credit

Length and scheduling of a clinical course

The experiential nature of clinical activity militates against periods of short engagement. A range of respondents to our *Best Practices* research emphasised that there is a necessary minimum period to ensure that the clinical experience has meaning for the student. Depending on how the clinical course is structured, this minimum is generally put at a block of five consecutive days, or a day a week over a semester.[126] However, there

---

123 See e.g. Rose Voyvodic, 'Considerable Promise and Troublesome Aspects: Theory and Methodology of Clinical Legal Education' (2001) 20 *Windsor Yearbook of Access to Justice* 111, 118–19.

124 Mark Spiegel, 'Theory and Practice in Legal Education: An Essay on Clinical Education' (1986–87) 34 *UCLA Law Review* 577, 593–94.

125 Mark Spiegel, cited at footnote 124, 592.

126 See the account of 'minimum effective time periods for good clinical programs' in *Identifying Current Practices in Clinical Legal Education*, Regional Reports for Victoria and Tasmania, South Australia, Queensland and Northern New South Wales, Western Australia and Northern Territory, and New South Wales and Australian Capital Territory, cited in Chapter 1 at footnote 6.

are views that in a live client clinic 'even one day can impact on a student', while an externship requires 'minimum two days a week for minimum 20 days for continuity and intensity'.[127]

It was apparent from our *Best Practices* research that the usual level of student commitment over a full semester is at least one half day a week, and more usually one or two days, sometimes expressed in terms of hours (for example, six hours a week, 15 hours a week).[128] We discuss below the implications this has for the value of course credit. Subject to our above view that it is best practice to run a clinical course over a semester, a clinical course with limited learning objectives can be structured to be offered in a block of days: daily for two weeks, for example, rather than one day a week for 12 weeks. This is especially the case for courses offered over a summer or winter break.

In the discussion above about student selection, we noted a view that it is preferable to schedule a clinical course later in a law degree program so that students have more maturity and knowledge. But, as we said there, the extent to which a student needs to 'know law' or to demonstrate 'maturity' will vary according to the aims and learning outcomes of the clinic. It is therefore quite feasible to operate a clinic for first-year students, while a clinic with a specialist focus may have to be offered only to students who have studied particular prerequisite courses.

Course credit value

As a matter of fairness to the students, the credit weighting of a clinical course can be approached in the same way as would be the case for a conventional course. In a conventional law course there is usually a tariff of a number of hours a week—say 10—that a student is expected to spend on class attendance, reading and preparation. That same tariff can be met by a clinical course that requires, say, one day's attendance each

---

127 See the account of 'minimum effective time periods for good clinical programs' in *Identifying Current Practices in Clinical Legal Education, Regional Report: New South Wales and Australian Capital Territory*, at perma.cc/257Z-6EMR.

128 See the accounts of 'hours per week students spend on clinical tasks' and 'how much academic credit do students receive' in *Identifying Current Practices in Clinical Legal Education*, Regional Reports for Victoria and Tasmania, Queensland and Northern New South Wales, Western Australia and Northern Territory, and New South Wales and Australian Capital Territory, cited in Chapter 1 at footnote 6.

week as well as a classroom component. Clinics requiring more intensive attendance, or running for longer than a normal semester, can be weighted accordingly, perhaps being offered for double credits.

Our *Best Practices* research showed that clinics in Australia commonly take this approach, broadly equating hours spent in a live client clinic or an externship with the student hours expected for a conventional law course.[129]

Conclusion

The excitement of establishing and operating a clinical course can distract from the need for rigorous course design. A clinical course is a sophisticated exercise in legal pedagogy, and the tension between education on the one hand and client service on the other will be best managed if educational design is considered and entrenched. As we described above, this requires clearly stated aims and associated learning outcomes, which will determine such essential aspects as the clinic model, the classroom content, and student selection criteria.

---

129 See the account of 'hours per week students spend on clinical tasks' in *Identifying Current Practices in Clinical Legal Education*, Regional Reports for Victoria and Tasmania, South Australia, Queensland and Northern New South Wales, Western Australia and Northern Territory, and New South Wales and Australian Capital Territory, cited in Chapter 1 at footnote 6.

5

Teaching social justice in clinics

Introduction

Clinical legal education in Australia has many connections with social justice. In this chapter, we explore the longstanding relationship between clinical programs and community legal centres and how it has influenced the teaching of various aspects of social justice goals in Australian clinical courses. We explain how situating clinical courses in community legal centres gives a particular context to teaching legal ethics and challenges concepts of value-neutral, objective lawyering, and how teaching lawyering skills in community legal centres highlights the legal skills required in a social justice setting. We look at how the community legal centre context focuses on 'access to justice' as one understanding of social justice, and at other connections between social justice and clinical legal education such as multidisciplinary practices, community engagement, working on law reform, community legal education and community development. We examine the implications of the growth in clinical externship courses in Australia for the connections to social justice issues; while the growth in externships has built on the strong tradition of social justice goals in clinical courses in Australia, it has also diversified clinical courses into areas not explicitly related to social justice. We point out that through classroom discussion and readings the relationship between the legal system and social justice can be explored even in externship courses that are not explicitly 'justice-related'.

The idea of 'social justice' in law

Although the term 'social justice' is widely used, it is usually undefined. It is a contested concept, meaning different things to different people. It may be that '[a]t the present time it is almost unthinkable to be against the idea of social justice',[1] but that same idea was notoriously dismissed by Hayek as having 'no meaning whatsoever'.[2] A generally accepted meaning of social justice is a state of fairness and equity,[3] and of 'inclusion' or even 'justice in general',[4] although ideas of what is fair will play out differently for different disciplines and in different circumstances. Buettner-Schmidt and Lobo's research leads them to conclude that although there are 'differences among and within the various disciplines about the uses of social justice … the goal of obtaining social justice, that is, attaining fairness and equity, appeared to be similar in each discipline'.[5]

The term 'social justice' has a long history.[6] However, more recently, especially after Rawls' seminal *A Theory of Justice*,[7] a general, contemporary idea of social justice usually entails the provision to all people of basic human needs including income, housing, education and health care; equal enjoyment of human rights including non-discrimination, freedom of expression and movement, the right to liberty and the right to live free from violence; and some redistribution of resources to maximise the position of the worst-off.

An idea of social justice along these lines is comfortably accepted in Australia as a legitimate progressive social policy position, contested by conservative commentators. This level of acceptance is quite different from the position in the United States, where social justice is often seen as code for socialism and as antithetical to classical liberal ideas of individual

---

1   Brendan Edgeworth, 'From Plato to NATO: Law and Social Justice in Historical Context' (2012) 35(2) *University of New South Wales Law Journal* 417.
2   FA Hayek, *The Mirage of Social Justice*, Vol 2 of *Law, Legislation and Liberty* (1976) University of Chicago Press, xii, 33, cited in Andrew Lister, 'The "Mirage" of Social Justice: Hayek Against (and for) Rawls' (2013) 25(3–4) *Critical Review* 409, 410.
3   See e.g. Belinda Carpenter and Matthew Ball, *Justice in Society* (2012) The Federation Press.
4   Brendan Edgeworth, cited at footnote 1.
5   K Buettner-Schmidt and ML Lobo, 'Social justice: A concept analysis' (2012) 68(4) *Journal of Advanced Nursing* 948, 953.
6   See Brendan Edgeworth, cited at footnote 1.
7   John Rawls, *A Theory of Justice* (1971) Harvard University Press.

liberty.[8] Even so, the idea of social justice is an accepted goal of many professional disciplines in the United States, such as nursing, public health, law and economics.[9]

In their multidisciplinary research on the issue, Buettner-Schmidt and Lobo found that in the discipline of law, the social justice emphasis is on 'empowerment [of under-represented minority groups], a just ordering of society and [a process of] remedying of oppression'.[10] This is an apt description of the concerns of community legal centres in Australia, and suggests what some of the content of a clinical legal education course might be in a community legal centre environment.

In fact, in clinical legal education (and the legal education curriculum more generally) the idea of social justice is often narrowed to a specifically legal characterisation of 'access to justice'.

'Access to justice'

Access to justice is usually seen by lawyers as access to the legal system (the so-called 'justice' system). In this sense, the fair and effective operation of the legal system is itself 'justice'[11]—'[t]he purpose of court proceedings is to do justice according to law'[12]—and so access to justice is concerned with the extent to which people understand the law, are able to get legal advice and representation, and are able to make or defend a claim. More narrowly still, access to justice can be seen simply as 'making it easier for people to solve disputes'.[13]

In contrast, in their daily practice, community legal centres focus on 'access to justice' as an aspect of social justice. Access to justice is multifaceted, and can be a measure of the extent to which 'justice' is done by law in a range of ways, such as punitive retribution, victim recognition, wealth redistribution, loss compensation and rights vindication. But law

8   See e.g. John Bowman, *Socialism in America* (2005) iUniverse, 116; Sovereignty Education and Defense Ministry, *Socialism: The New American Civil Religion* (2014) Google eBook, 207–12.
9   K Buettner-Schmidt and ML Lobo, cited at footnote 5, 950–52.
10   K Buettner-Schmidt and ML Lobo, cited at footnote 5, 952, 953.
11   See e.g. Elizabeth Ellis, *Principles and Practice of Australian Law* (2013) Thomson Reuters, 3rd ed, Chapter 5; Attorney-General's Department, *Access to Justice Taskforce, A Strategic Framework for Access to Justice in the Federal Civil Justice System: A Guide for Future Action* (September 2009).
12   *Giannarelli v Wraith* [1988] HCA 52; (1988) 165 CLR 543, per Brennan J at 578.
13   Productivity Commission, *Access to Justice Arrangements*, Draft Report Overview (April 2004), 3.

can, of course, be used to advance social causes both progressive and conservative, and 'access to justice' can have a strong political dimension to it that, as we explain below, can be problematic in some clinics.[14]

More broadly, access to justice can have a meaning that is removed from a necessary connection with law: 'access to justice is not just a matter of bringing cases to a font of official justice, but of enhancing the justice quality of the relations and transactions in which people are engaged'.[15] This takes the idea of justice away from an exclusively legal context, and addresses issues of justice in 'primary institutional locations of [people's] activity—home, neighborhood, workplace, business setting and so on'.[16]

As we note below when discussing social justice practice in clinics, ideas of social justice and access to justice tend to overlap or conflate. While some precision might be expected when designing learning outcomes of a clinical course (see Chapter 4), it is perhaps sufficient to say that clinical practice is an opportunity for students to analyse and reflect on the relationship between law and these various ideas of access to justice and social justice, and the part that lawyers play.

Clinical legal education and social justice

Clinical legal education in Australia was imbued from the outset with an ethic of social justice,[17] as courses were established by law schools whose critical approach to legal education explored the intersections of law and social justice.[18] Early clinical teachers and academics in Australia shared a progressive vision of legal education, and saw:

---

14   See e.g. Peter Joy, 'Political Interference in Clinical Programs: Lessons from the U.S. Experience' (2005) 8 *International Journal of Clinical Legal Education* 83; Peter Joy, 'Government Interference with Law School Clinics and Access to Justice: When Is There a Legal Remedy?' (2011) 61 *Case Western Reserve Law Review* 1087.

15   Marc Galanter, 'Justice in Many Rooms' in Mauro Cappelletti (ed), *Access to Justice and the Welfare State* (1981) Sijtoff, 147, 161.

16   Marc Galanter, cited at footnote 15, 161–62.

17   Frank Bloch and Mary Anne Noone, 'Legal Aid Origins of Clinical Legal Education' in Frank Bloch (ed), *The Global Clinical Movement: Educating Lawyers for Social Justice* (2011) Oxford University Press, 153.

18   See Jeff Giddings, *Promoting Justice through Clinical Legal Education* (2013) Justice Press, Chapters 6 (Monash) and 7 (UNSW) (cited hereafter as Giddings (2013)).

a social, political and moral agenda in … teaching, an agenda that exposes students to the maldistribution of wealth, power and rights in society, and that seeks to inculcate in them a sense of their own ability and responsibility for using law to challenge injustice by assisting the poor and the powerless.[19]

Within this legal education environment the Australian clinical movement has, since the beginning, been closely linked to community legal centres.

The 1960s and 1970s were times of questioning social hierarchies in Australia, the United States, the United Kingdom and in Europe.[20] As Neal has observed, '[s]omething big happened to public consciousness about law and power in the 1970s. Somehow law got caught up in a broader social upheaval about equality and poverty and the scales that masked the power embedded in legal relations fell away'.[21] In the new law schools this was reflected in a critical approach to legal education in both the curriculum and extra curricula activities. The University of New South Wales (UNSW) Law School and its staff and students were associated with the Australian Legal Workers' Group, the Prisoners' Action Group and the Feminist Legal Action Group and, in its curriculum, UNSW offered courses in poverty law, social security and housing.[22] Its staff and students established and staffed Redfern Legal Centre.[23] Monash University was similarly exploring new ways of teaching law and was well connected to community legal centres in Victoria, particularly in the founding of Springvale Legal Service.[24] And '[t]he founders of the Legal Studies Department at La Trobe University wanted to focus on law as a social institution and to make the power associated with legal knowledge widely available not only to its students but also to a wider public'.[25]

19   Stephen Wizner, 'Beyond Skills Training' (2001) 7 *Clinical Law Review* 327, 331.
20   See, generally, e.g. Adam Jamrozik, Cathy Boland and Robert Urquhart, *Social Change and Cultural Transformation in Australia* (1995) Cambridge University Press.
21   David Neal, 'Law and Power – livin in the 70s' (2013) 29(2) *Law in Context* 99, 103.
22   Marion Dixon, *Thirty Up: The Story of the UNSW Law School 1971–2001* (2001) UNSW Faculty of Law.
23   David Nichols, *From the Roundabout to the Roundhouse – 25 years of Kingsford Legal Centre* (2006) UNSW Faculty of Law, 8.
24   Simon Smith, 'Clinical Legal Education: the Case of Springvale Legal Service' in David Neal (ed), *On Tap, Not on Top: Legal Centres in Australia 1972–1982* (1984) Legal Service Bulletin Cooperative, 49; see also Kerry Greenwood, *It Seemed Like a Good Idea at the Time: a history of Springvale Legal Service 1973–1994* (1994) Springvale Legal Service.
25   David Neal, cited at footnote 21, 104.

This early commitment to social justice among emerging law schools in the 1970s has persisted and 'social justice'–designated projects, activities and positions exist at a number of law schools in Australia.[26]

Clinical legal education and community legal centres

Just as clinical legal education in the United States had its origins 'in the fight against poverty, injustice and under-representation of minority interests in the legal process',[27] so clinics in Australia have always been in 'a symbiotic relationship [with] legal aid agencies, in particular community legal centres … with a deep commitment to access to justice'.[28] Founders of the clinical movement in Australia[29] had previously worked in and with community legal centres (independent, non-profit legal services),[30] and the first clinical programs were established as 'live client clinics' in a community legal centre setting. Monash University collaborated with Springvale Community Aid and Advice Bureau in 1973,[31] and then established the clinic in 1975. La Trobe University explored the use of paralegal students in client service from the mid-1970s and, in 1978, arising from the Henderson Commission of Poverty,[32] it funded

26 For example, law reform and social justice activities at the ANU College of Law; the Social Justice Project at UNSW Law Faculty; the Social Justice Program at Sydney University Law School; the social justice major in the law degree at Macquarie Law School; the Law and Social Justice research grouping at the TC Beirne Law School at the University of Queensland; social justice elective courses at Notre Dame Law School; the *Journal of Law and Social Justice* ('Public Space') at the University of Technology, Sydney; the Social Justice/Public Interest Clinic at Newcastle University Law School.

27 J Cooper and LG Trubek, 'Social Values from Law School to Practice: an Introductory Essay' in Jeremy Cooper and Louise Trubek (eds), *Educating for Justice: Social Values and Legal Education* (1997) Ashgate, 1 at 5.

28 Giddings (2013), 323–24.

29 Giddings (2013), 324.

30 See Mary Anne Noone, 'Community legal centres: Autonomous and alternative' in Mary Anne Noone and Steven Tomsen, *Lawyers in Conflict: Australian Lawyers and Legal Aid* (2006) The Federation Press; see also National Association of Community Legal Centres Australia (NACLC): 'Community Legal Centres (CLCs) are independently operating not-for-profit, community-based organisations that provide legal services to the public, focusing on the disadvantaged and people with special needs', at perma.cc/5UN3-HSQY.

31 Jeff Giddings, 'Two Way Traffic: the Scope for Clinics to Facilitate Law School Community Engagement' in Patrick Keyzer, Amy Kenworthy and Gail S Wilson (eds), *Community Engagement in Contemporary Legal Education: Pro bono, Clinical Legal Education and Service-Learning* (2009) Halstead Press, 40, citing Simon Smith, cited at footnote 24, 49; see also Kerry Greenwood, cited at footnote 24.

32 Australian Government Commission of Inquiry into Poverty, *Poverty in Australia: first main report* (April 1975) Australian Government Publishing Service.

a lecturer/solicitor position to establish West Heidelberg Community Legal Service as a clinic.[33] UNSW established its first clinic as a community legal centre, Kingsford Legal Centre, in 1981.[34]

Community legal centres 'are committed to striving for equitable access to the legal system and justice, and the equal protection of human rights'.[35] Three essential aspects of community legal centre work are the provision of legal advice and the conduct of casework for disadvantaged clients and communities, the provision of community legal education, and the promotion of law and policy reform. Community legal centres work in legal areas that affect disadvantaged people in the community,[36] and their advice and casework in civil law is mostly in the areas of tenancy, credit and debt, administrative law, social security, family law, and family/ domestic violence, all areas of work that have an affinity with issues of social justice.[37]

The claim by community legal centres that they work for equitable access to the legal system and to improve social justice has not gone unchallenged. Rich has criticised community legal centres for being overly focused on individual casework and advice.[38] Rich argues that they should adopt a 'law and organising' model that seeks the transformation of clients' lives, rather than dealing with their individual legal problems, and she advocates the importance of law reform work that is linked to social justice. This critique is significant and has caused many to question the role of community legal centres.[39] Nevertheless, a recurring theme in our research into the operation of clinical programs in Australia has been the reference to 'social justice' as a touchstone or guiding principle

---

33 David Neal, cited at footnote 21, 123.

34 Giddings (2013), Chapters 6 and 7.

35 See www.naclc.org.au. Accessed 27 February 2014.

36 National Association of Community Legal Centres Australia (NACLC) *Annual Report 2012/13* (2013), 13, at perma.cc/9W9H-76KL.

37 Mary Anne Noone, 'The Activist Origins of Australian Community Legal Centres' (2001) 19 *Law in Context* 128; T Ellis, 'Human Rights and Social Justice: A frontline perspective from a Community Legal Centre' (1996) 3(4) *ELaw Journal*, at perma.cc/DTE6-TJYM.

38 Nicole Rich, *Reclaiming Community Legal Centres: Maximising our potential so we can help our clients realise theirs* (2009) Victoria Law Foundation Community Legal Centre Fellowship 2007–08 Final Report, Consumer Action Law Centre.

39 Peter Noble, 'The Future of Community Legal Centres' (2012) 37(1) *Alternative Law Journal* 22; Simon Rice, 'Are CLCs Finished?' (2012) 37(1) *Alternative Law Journal* 16; Paula O'Brien, 'Changing Public Interest Law: Overcoming the law's barriers to social change lawyering' (2011) 36(2) *Alternative Law Journal* 82.

for designing clinics,[40] establishing course learning outcomes,[41] selecting clinical supervisors,[42] selecting casework,[43] and student selection.[44] Engaging in law reform work to improve the law or legal system for disadvantaged communities is also a significant aspect of various law schools' clinical offerings.[45]

Working with other professions

A significant beneficial legacy in Australia of co-locating clinics with community legal centres is the exposure clinic students get to the multidisciplinary practice that characterises many centres. Since the outset, community legal centres have recognised that clients rarely have only a legal problem, and that their legal problems commonly arise from other social issues, such as poverty and related problems of housing, unemployment, debt, literacy, health and domestic violence.[46] As a result, a 'legal' client actually needs support and intervention from a range of other professional services including social workers, counsellors,

---

40   *Identifying Current Practices in Clinical Legal Education, Regional Report: Victoria and Tasmania,* 11, at perma.cc/J562-X6GU.

41   *Identifying Current Practices in Clinical Legal Education, Regional Report: New South Wales and Australian Capital Territory,* 13, 15 (at perma.cc/FU7X-5TNV); *Identifying Current Practices in Clinical Legal Education, Regional Report: Queensland and Northern New South Wales,* 10, 13, 19 (at perma.cc/257Z-6EMR); *Identifying Current Practices in Clinical Legal Education, Regional Report: South Australia,* 17 (at perma.cc/3MPF-5U5A); *Identifying Current Practices in Clinical Legal Education, Regional Report: Victoria and Tasmania,* 16, 18 (at perma.cc/J562-X6GU).

42   *Identifying Current Practices in Clinical Legal Education, Regional Report: New South Wales and Australian Capital Territory,* 8, 24 (at perma.cc/FU7X-5TNV); *Identifying Current Practices in Clinical Legal Education, Regional Report: Queensland and Northern New South Wales,* 7 (at perma.cc/257Z-6EMR); *Identifying Current Practices in Clinical Legal Education, Regional Report: South Australia,* 7–8 (at perma.cc/3MPF-5U5A); *Identifying Current Practices in Clinical Legal Education, Regional Report: Victoria and Tasmania,* 19 (at perma.cc/J562-X6GU).

43   *Identifying Current Practices in Clinical Legal Education, Regional Report: New South Wales and Australian Capital Territory,* 29, at perma.cc/FU7X-5TNV.

44   *Identifying Current Practices in Clinical Legal Education, Regional Report: South Australia,* 23, at perma.cc/3MPF-5U5A.

45   *Identifying Current Practices in Clinical Legal Education, Regional Report: Victoria and Tasmania,* 10 (at perma.cc/J562-X6GU); *Identifying Current Practices in Clinical Legal Education, Regional Report: South Australia,* 10 (at perma.cc/3MPF-5U5A); *Identifying Current Practices in Clinical Legal Education, Regional Report: New South Wales and Australian Capital Territory,* 15 (at perma.cc/FU7X-5TNV); *Identifying Current Practices in Clinical Legal Education, Regional Report: Queensland and Northern New South Wales,* 13 (at perma.cc/257Z-6EMR).

46   Mary Anne Noone, 'Key Features of Integrated Legal Services: lessons from West Heidelberg Community Legal Service' (2012) 37(1) *Alternative Law Journal* 26.

and therapists.[47] These complementary services are sometimes available within and as part of a community legal centre or are available from co-located social services or by referral to other services.

The opportunity to work with professionals and students in those other disciplines characterises many of the community legal centres in which clinical courses are located.[48] The Southern Communities Advocacy Legal and Education Service (SCALES), for example, hosts the Murdoch University legal clinic, which focuses on refugee and immigration law and frequently works with social workers and torture and trauma counsellors.[49] The degree of multidisciplinary practice varies from agency to agency—at one end of the scale two professionals can address a client's needs cooperatively but, essentially, independently (commonly the case in community legal centres) while, at the other end, two professionals can address a client's needs in close collaboration, consciously working together in a joint enterprise to understand and meet the client's needs.

Multidisciplinary clinics

A multidisciplinary practice creates the opportunity for a multidisciplinary clinic where students of different disciplines can share a clinical experience. For a period, the UNSW clinic at Kingsford Legal Centre operated a multidisciplinary clinic, employing a social work academic who supervised social work students on placement alongside law students, in a shared clinic experience.[50]

A substantial current example is the multidisciplinary clinic at the Monash-Oakleigh Legal Service, comprising supervisors and students from the Faculties of Law, Medicine, Business and Economics and Arts.[51] Hyams and Gertner wrote that '[b]y focusing on assisting low income clients/patients and meeting their needs in a fully coordinated manner,

---

47   Liz Curran, 'University law clinics and their value in undertaking client-centred law reform to provide a voice for their client's experiences' (2007) 12 *International Journal of Clinical Legal Education* 105.

48   See Ross Hyams and Fay Gertner, 'Multidisciplinary clinics – broadening the outlook of clinical learning' (2012) 17 *International Journal of Clinical Legal Education* 35.

49   See Anna Copeland, 'Clinical Legal Education within a Community Legal Centre Context' (2003) 10(3) *Murdoch University Electronic Journal of Law* 25; Giddings (2013), Chapter 9.

50   Giddings (2013), 226–27.

51   *Identifying Current Practices in Clinical Legal Education, Regional Report: Victoria and Tasmania*, 5, at perma.cc/J562-X6GU.

academic staff and students involved in the practice would deliver "whole of person" services to the community on a permanent basis'.[52] The multidisciplinary clinic has concentrated on refining its cross-disciplinary supervision and student debriefing protocols to ensure that the objective of a 'whole of person' service is not dissipated by competing priorities among supervisors or student despair that can accompany their recognition of the enormity of a 'whole person' life in disarray. When handled correctly, these experiences make not just law but also medical, social work and finance students acutely aware of the justice dimensions of their professionalism.

A multidisciplinary clinic offers students a powerful counter to conventional legal education, which both explicitly and unconsciously promotes Lopez's idea of 'regnant lawyering'—a form of lawyering that assumes the centrality of the lawyer to the process rather than placing the client's vision and needs at the centre.[53] One of the key learnings that law students take away from working with another discipline is that an issue can be addressed in many ways, not only through law, and that other ways of dealing with problems may be more effective than a purely legal approach.

In a multidisciplinary clinic, students receive a strong message that teamwork is key to effective work. Law students commonly work with social work or other professionals to help the client resolve their issues, working not in an isolated and individual way, but collaborating in a team. This shows students another way to practise law, in stark contrast to the conventional model of legal practice, which focuses on an individual lawyer representing an individual client.

Differing professional rules and ethical understandings among professional disciplines also provide rich ground for law students to discuss the role of lawyers. A multidisciplinary clinic enables students to see that, unlike lawyers' professional conduct rules, the conduct rules of other disciplines recognise social justice as an explicit ethical responsibility.[54]

---

52 Ross Hyams and Fay Gertner, cited at footnote 48, 35.

53 Gerard Lopez, *Rebellious Lawyering: One Chicano's Vision of Progressive Law Practice* (1992) Westview Press, 24.

54 Australian Association of Social Workers, *Code of Ethics*, 1.1 Commitment and aims; and see Margaret Castles 'Possibilities for Multidisciplinary Collaboration in Clinical Practice: Practical Ethical Implications for Lawyers and Clients' (2008) 34(1) *Monash University Law Review* 116.

The opportunity for law students to collaborate with a range of skilled professionals reinforces the message that a client is a 'whole person', not a combination of problems, and that law is not the only means through which to address clients' issues. Multidisciplinary approaches are inherently related to social justice purposes as they challenge each discipline's view of its own centrality in resolving issues, and encourage students to think broadly about their role as future lawyers.

Growth in clinical externship courses

As we discussed in Chapters 1 and 3, externships are an area of growth in clinical legal education. Our *Best Practices* research project found that of all the universities in Australia who have clinical legal education courses, over half of those courses are externships.[55] Many externship placement sites are community legal centres, maintaining the historical relationship with clinical legal education.[56]

Externships have also grown through partnerships with a wide range of public legal agencies other than community legal centres.[57] Different course aims and learning outcomes have taken many of these externships away from a social justice orientation, and place students with agencies that provide clinical legal experience but do not engage in social justice–oriented activity. Even so, any externship placement course can aim to give students the opportunity to critically examine law and lawyers from a social justice perspective, in a concurrent classroom component supported by readings and discussion, and in reflective practice.

---

55   See Chapter 3 of this book.

56   *Identifying Current Practices in Clinical Legal Education, Regional Report: Queensland and Northern New South Wales*, 5, 6 (at perma.cc/257Z-6EMR); *Identifying Current Practices in Clinical Legal Education, Regional Report: Western Australia and Northern Territory*, 5 (at perma.cc/4EDN-5SZG).

57   *Identifying Current Practices in Clinical Legal Education*, Regional Reports for Victoria and Tasmania, New South Wales and Australian Capital Territory, Queensland and Northern New South Wales, Western Australia and Northern Territory, and South Australia, cited in Chapter 1 at footnote 6.

International externships

Working internationally, for example, through clinical externships with non-government organisations (NGOs), offers students an opportunity to engage in a wider range of social justice issues than might be available to them domestically, and to experience diverse ways of working with community and within the law.

International opportunities can be complicated by issues of interruption to studies, insurance, risk, expense and, related to expense, equity of student access. Although students can and do travel overseas for a clinical externship in another country,[58] communications technology such as email, voice-over-internet protocol (VOIP) and internet video services mean that an NGO in another country can conduct remote supervision of clinical students who remain 'at home' while working on research and writing projects for the externship.[59] Clinical courses that have 'placed' students as clinical interns in this way have been offered at ANU[60] and QUT,[61] working with NGOs in Vietnam, Thailand, Laos and Swaziland.[62]

The practice of social justice in clinics

Clinics commonly have 'access to justice' course aims and related learning outcomes. At the same time, community legal centres, where many clinical courses operate, have a broad social justice mission. But, as discussed above, the idea of social justice lacks precision. Its place in law, or as a goal of the operation and practice of law, is further complicated by a legal focus on 'access to justice', a term that itself has various meanings.

---

58   For example, the Hong Kong Refugee Law Clinic, UNSW, where students are trained before leaving Australia and then interview and represent asylum seekers in Hong Kong in applications to the United Nations High Commission for Refugees.

59   *Identifying Current Practices in Clinical Legal Education*, Regional Reports for Queensland and Northern New South Wales (QUT), New South Wales and Australian Capital Territory (UNSW and ANU), and Victoria and Tasmania (La Trobe), cited in Chapter 1 at footnote 6.

60   *Identifying Current Practices in Clinical Legal Education, Regional Report: New South Wales and Australian Capital Territory*, 6, at perma.cc/FU7X-5TNV.

61   *Identifying Current Practices in Clinical Legal Education, Regional Report: Queensland and Northern New South Wales*, 5, at perma.cc/257Z-6EMR.

62   See Bruce Lasky, Simon Rice, Tina Cockburn, Wendy Morrish, 'The use of virtual law programs to support access to justice education' (2011) Presentation to the 6th Conference of the Global Alliance for Justice Education, Valencia, at www.gaje.org/conferences/6th-worldwide-conference. Accessed 4 February 2017.

In both clinics and community legal centres, concrete aspects of social justice and access to justice are often not directly addressed and these concepts tend to overlap or conflate.

As we discuss in the following sections, a community legal centre environment enables analysis of and reflection on justice issues in a wide variety of ways. Clinical courses often focus on specific areas of law and legal practice, on skills development, and on ways of working professionally, such as in a multidisciplinary clinic. Giddings points out that '[c]linics have pursued social justice objectives by working well beyond the traditional service delivery model of advice and representation for individual clients',[63] and in the following section we canvass some of the different ways that clinics can pursue social justice goals.

Skills development

Clinical legal education is clearly an effective means of teaching lawyering skills.[64] The question in a clinical course is not whether to teach skills or something else, but whether to teach something more about skills and examine what a lawyer can do with those skills.[65] One thing a lawyer can aspire to do with their legal skills is pursue social justice; there is a nexus between legal skills and social justice, such that 'the skills development and social justice dimensions of clinical legal education [share] a strong unifying justification'.[66]

Skills are not value-neutral. Reference is commonly made to teaching 'just skills', which suggests that skills are taught in a vacuum. An entire account of 'best practices for legal education', for example, characterises the teaching of skills as merely an exercise in professional competence, with no critical component.[67] Teaching 'just skills' ignores the potential

---

63 Giddings (2013), 63.

64 See e.g. William M Sullivan, Anne Colby, Judith Welch Wegner, Lloyd Bond and Lee S Shulman, *Educating Lawyers: Preparation for the Profession of Law* (2007) Jossey-Bass.

65 See e.g. Amy Ruth Tobol, 'Integrating Social Justice Values into the Teaching of Legal Research and Writing: Reflections from the Field' in Jeremy Cooper and Louise Trubek (eds), cited at footnote 27, 88.

66 Giddings (2013), 62, citing Frank Bloch and MRK Prasad, 'Institutionalising a Social Justice Mission for Clinical Legal Education: Cross-National Currents from India and the United States' (2006) 13 *Clinical Law Review* 165, 171.

67 Roy Stuckey and others, *Best Practices for Legal Education: A Vision and a Road Map* (2007) Clinical Legal Education Association.

to explore the implications of a lawyer's use (or not) of a legal skill in a particular circumstance, and fails to appreciate that the way a skill is used reflects the lawyer's own values (perhaps unconsciously) about the client and the legal matter.

In teaching interviewing skills, for example, clinical legal educators will often emphasise a client-centred approach. The importance of listening to the client and treating them as a person, not just as a legal problem, is stressed, reflecting social justice values such as people's dignity and right to equality. Teaching interviewing skills will also frequently focus on developing students' awareness of their preconceptions about clients, leading easily into a discussion about stereotypical views the student may have,[68] and 'the effects of race, class and … gender on the interaction between lawyer and client'.[69]

At its most complex and analytical, skills teaching can be seen as truly complementary to a clinic's social justice mission, enabling students to 'suspend judgment, to communicate and listen across differences and to explore solutions creatively'.[70]

Although critical perspectives on lawyering—for example, on exercising power, mediating law's differential impact, and promoting reform—are available for any area of law, a critical perspective is more likely to be taken in a clinic involved in work that is explicitly concerned with exactly those aspects of lawyering. Conversely, critical perspectives may be less likely to arise in a clinic whose work implicitly accepts and relies on the established relations of law and power in society.

Class content and readings

The classroom component of a clinical course complements the teaching and learning occurring in the clinic's legal practice (see Chapter 4), and frequently focuses on legal theory and concepts of justice, on skills

---

68   See e.g. Paul R Tremblay, 'Interviewing and Counseling across Cultures: Heuristics and Biases' (2002–03) 9 *Clinical Law Review* 373.

69   Michelle Jacobs, 'People from the footnotes: The missing element in client-centered counselling' (1997) 27 *Golden Gate University Law Review* 345, 346.

70   Antoinette Sedillo Lopez, 'Learning through Service in a Clinical Setting: The Effect of Specialization on Social Justice and Skills Training' (2000–01) 7 *Clinical Law Review* 307, 322; and see Susan Bryant, 'The Five Habits: Building Cross-Culture Competence in Lawyers' (2001–02) 8 *Clinical Law Review* 33.

development and on areas of law relevant to community lawyering such as the legal aid system, housing law, employment law, debt and family law. Practice skills such as working with cultural competency, interviewing, negotiation, advocacy, and doing effective law reform work are taught in ways that specifically relate to disadvantaged client groups, emphasising the centrality of the client. Teaching plain English drafting, for example, both improves conventional lawyer communication, and addresses one of the demands of 'access to justice as access to law' discussed above.

Legal ethics

A clinic in a social justice setting, such as a community legal centre, offers a rich opportunity for the study of legal ethics, professional responsibility and models of lawyering. For many years, for example, the La Trobe University legal ethics course offered this opportunity through its external, live client clinical course in successive partnerships with a Victoria Legal Aid office and West Heidelberg Community Legal Service.[71] In these clinics, La Trobe students interviewed, advised, and represented clients using clinical tools of supervision and reflection that '[encourage] students to critically analyse the law of lawyering including the various codes of practice and their rationales within a framework of access to justice issues, a client centred approach and a recognition of the public role of a legal practitioner'.[72] To the same end, UNSW incorporates a clinical component within the mandatory ethics course, enabling all law degree students to interview clients and then reflect on the role of lawyers and the capacity of law as a vehicle to achieve justice.[73]

Clinics provide the opportunity for students to reflect on the standard conception of a lawyer as a value-neutral, partisan and adversarial advocate for their client, and to actively consider other ethical approaches

---

71 Mary Anne Noone, Judith Dickson and Liz Curran, 'Pushing the Boundaries or Preserving the Status Quo? Designing Clinical Programs to Teach Law Students a Deep Understanding of Ethical Practice' (2005) 8 *International Journal of Clinical Legal Education* 104; Kingsford Legal Centre, *Guide to clinical legal education courses in Australian universities, 2011–2012*, UNSW Faculty of Law; Judith Dickson, '25 Years of Clinical Legal Education at La Trobe University' (2004) 29(1) *Alternative Law Journal* 41; Liz Curran, 'Innovations in an Australian Clinical Legal Education Program: Students Making a Difference in Generating Positive Change' (2004) 5 *International Journal of Clinical Legal Education* 162.

72 Mary Anne Noone, Judith Dickson and Liz Curran, cited at footnote 71.

73 Anna Cody, 'What does legal ethics teaching gain, if anything, from including a clinical component? (2015) 22(1) *International Journal of Clinical Legal Education* 1.

to lawyering, such as responsible lawyering, moral activist lawyering, and an ethic of care.[74] Clinic cases in social justice settings such as community legal centres are an excellent vehicle for alternative perspectives such as these, enabling students to explore their values and to ask themselves broader ethical questions about their part, as lawyers, in improving access to justice and working to achieve social equality. Curran, Dickson and Noone, for example, describe their use in a clinic of ethical lawyering paradigms, drawing on the work of Parker and Evans to encourage students to reflect on the different approaches that a lawyer can take in lawyer–client relations: the zealous advocate (for one of the parties), the responsible lawyer (for a just outcome within the legal system), the moral activist (for a morally just outcome) and an ethic of care (for the parties' wellbeing).[75] Analysing ethical frameworks enables students to understand moral activist lawyering, or 'cause lawyering',[76] and how it contributes to law's pursuit of social justice goals.[77]

In these social justice settings, a clinic invites students to see that lawyers have agency. That is, the students have opportunity and responsibility, in contrast to the implicit lesson of conventional legal education that can encourage students:

> to think like lawyers by adopting an emotionally remote, morally neutral approach to human problems and social issues, distancing themselves from the sentiments and suffering of others, avoiding emotional engagement with clients and their causes, and withholding moral judgment.[78]

Ethical discussions in a clinic setting can illustrate to students that lawyers, rather than being mere instruments of neutral positivist law, have choices about the clients they serve, the cases they take, the positions they adopt and about how they relate to clients, communities and causes.

---

74   Christine Parker and Adrian Evans, *Inside Lawyers' Ethics* (2014) Cambridge University Press, 2nd ed, Chapter 2.
75   Christine Parker and Adrian Evans, cited at footnote 74, Chapters 2 and 11.
76   See e.g. Margareth Etienne, 'The Ethics of Cause Lawyering: An Empirical Examination of Criminal Defense Lawyers as Cause Lawyers' (2005) 95(4) *Journal of Criminal Law and Criminology* 1195; Deborah J Cantrell, 'Sensational Reports: The Ethical Duty of Cause Lawyers to be Competent in Public Advocacy' (2007) 30 *Hamline Law Review* 567.
77   Christine Parker and Adrian Evans, cited at footnote 74, Chapter 2.
78   Jane Aiken, 'The Clinical Mission of Justice Readiness' (2012) *Boston College Journal of Law and Social Justice* 231.

Clinical legal education encourages students to reflect critically on both the influence on their work of stereotypical assumptions about clients and on their personal reactions to their clients. These views can influence how they perform their legal work and the decisions they make about actions to take in a legal case. For example, a student might assume when working with a client with an intellectual disability who wants to make a power of attorney, that they do not have the capacity to execute this type of legal document. Challenging this assumption provides an opportunity to explore concepts of disability, legal capacity, and the role of the lawyer. Models of client empowerment, and the assumption of 'inability' when working with clients with disability,[79] can be discussed immediately with students. This experience is an opportunity for students to reflect on client-centredness in legal practice.

Part of a supervisor's role in helping students to envisage themselves as lawyers is to model types of lawyering. One such model is 'community lawyering'. Cody says that '[c]ommunity lawyering seeks to improve the daily lives of community members', and is defined as 'lawyering for both individuals and communities, aware of how power may influence the relationships between lawyer and client and responsive to the needs of communities'.[80] Community lawyering often involves a partnership between lawyers and communities to achieve structural or real change in their lives; it may involve, but goes beyond, individual claims.[81] Modelling community lawyering in clinics provides career options to students.

The continuing connections between many clinics and community legal centres mitigates to an extent the 'waning of student commitment to the public interest'[82] and students' cynicism about practising law for justice.[83]

---

79   On the assumption of 'inability', see Bruce Arnold, Patricia Easteal, Simon Easteal and Simon Rice, 'It just doesn't ADD Up: ADHD/ADD, the Workplace and Discrimination' (2010) 34(2) *Melbourne University Law Review* 359.

80   Anna Cody, 'Clinical programs in community legal centres, the Australian approach' (2011) 4 *Education and Law Review* 4; and see Nicole Rich, cited at footnote 38; Karen Tokarz, Nancy Cook, Susan Brooks and Brenda Bratton Blum, 'Conversations on "Community Lawyering": The Newest (Oldest) Wave in Clinical Legal Education' (2008) 28 *Washington University Journal of Law and Policy* 359.

81   Muneer Ahmad, 'Interpreting Communities: Lawyering Across Language Difference' (2007) 54 *UCLA Law Review* 999.

82   Adrienne Stone, 'Women, Law School and Student Commitment to the Public Interest' in Jeremy Cooper and Louise Trubek (eds), cited at footnote 27, 60.

83   Kim Economides, 'Cynical Legal Studies' in Jeremy Cooper and Louise Trubek (eds), cited at footnote 27, 26 at 29.

A clinical legal education experience helps counter any tendency that law students may have to be uninterested and 'ignorant about critical idealism and wider social perspectives'.[84]

The modelling of approaches to lawyering by supervisors raises the issue of a clinic's own ethical approach to teaching, and the opportunity to practise transformative ethics.[85] Transformative ethics promote:

> perspective transformation ... the process of becoming critically aware of how and why our assumptions have come to constrain the way we perceive, understand and feel about our world; changing these structures of habitual expectation to make possible a more inclusive, discriminating, and integrating perspective; and finally, making choices or otherwise acting upon these new understandings.[86]

If students' assumptions and judgments are to be challenged, then it is essential for a clinic to adopt an explicit ethic of perspective transformation. An effective clinic challenges students' willingness to apply legal rules to neatly stated problems, dispassionately and without regard to personal values. Engaging in perspective transformation through systematic reflection enables students to make constructive use of the opportunity that a clinic gives them to question their ways of looking at the world and to open themselves to alternatives.

As with any legal practice, a clinic operates within the formal, prescribed framework of professional ethics, and therefore presents regular opportunities to consider the apparently strict and clear ethical duties set out in legal profession practice rules.[87] A pedagogical advantage

---

84   Kim Economides, cited at footnote 83, 26; see also T Walsh, 'Putting Justice Back into Legal Education' (2007) 17(1) *Legal Education Review* 119, and the growing literature on engaging students' interest in the context of concerns about student mental health and wellbeing—e.g. Massimiliano Tani and Prue Vines, 'Law Students' Attitudes to Education: Pointers to Depression in the Legal Academy and the Profession?' (2009) 19 *Legal Education Review* 3; Molly O'Brien, Stephen Tang and Kath Hall, 'No time to lose: Negative impact on law student wellbeing may begin in year one' (2011) 2(12) *International Journal of the First Year in Higher Education* 49; Molly O'Brien, 'Connecting Law Student Wellbeing to Social Justice, Problem-Solving and Human Emotions' (2014) 14(1) *QUT Law Review* 52.

85   Kevin Kerrigan, '"How do you feel about this client?" – A commentary on the clinical model as a vehicle for teaching ethics to law students' (2007) 11 *International Journal of Clinical Legal Education* 7.

86   Jack Mezirow, *Transformative Dimensions of Adult Learning* (1991) Wiley, 167, quoted in Kevin Kerrigan, cited at footnote 85.

87   See e.g. Law Council of Australia, *Australian Solicitors Conduct Rules 2011*.

that a clinic has over the classroom in teaching ethics is that the ethical issues are neither abstract nor clear cut: they relate to a real client, giving them authenticity, immediacy, complexity and variability. A pedagogical advantage that a clinic has over legal practice in teaching ethics is that the spontaneous ethical issue—or the unnoticed one—is more easily identified and managed in a safe and supportive environment, in discussion with peers and supervisors.[88]

Of the prescribed ethics rules of legal practice, those concerning confidentiality and conflict of interest often arise in a clinic. Difficult issues concerning client confidentiality, for example, frequently arise in a community legal centre or legal aid practice where a lawyer may be told of possible harm to a child.[89] In a case where a client describes a violent family relationship, possibly exposing children to seeing and hearing violence, students and their supervisors must consider the limits of the duty of confidentiality and the possible harm that might follow when they respect that duty.[90] This responsibility can be discussed alongside models of client empowerment in domestic violence,[91] incorporating feminist perspectives of social change and, in the process, encouraging students to more confidently explore the permissive exceptions to confidentiality that apply in most conduct rules.[92] This process not only challenges students to gain a deeper understanding of the gendered nature of domestic violence, but also encourages them to critique ethical and legal duties from feminist perspectives. The social justice dimension of this arises when, for example, students explore how law commonly reflects the values of dominant groups and may or may not incorporate women's needs. Students can

---

88   Mary Anne Noone, Judith Dickson and Liz Curran, cited at footnote 71; Anna Cody, cited at footnote 73.
89   Rule 9.2.4 *Australian Solicitors Conduct Rules 2011* states that 'the solicitor [may] disclose the information for the sole purpose of avoiding the probable commission of a serious criminal offence'. In *Attorney-General (NT) v Kearney* (1985) 158 CLR 500, the High Court of Australia held, more widely than cases of crime and fraud, that 'anything that might be described as a fraud on justice' would not fall under legal professional privilege.
90   Rule 9.2.5 *Australian Solicitors Conduct Rules 2011* allows a lawyer to breach client confidentially 'for the purpose of preventing imminent serious physical harm to the client or to another person'.
91   H Douglas and R Fitzgerald, 'Legal Processes and Gendered Violence: Cross-applications for Domestic Violence Protection Orders' (2013) 36(1) *University of New South Wales Law Journal* 56–87; H Douglas, 'Battered Women's Experiences of the Criminal Justice System: Decentring the Law' (2012) 20(2) *Feminist Legal Studies* 121–34.
92   See e.g. Rule 9 *Australian Solicitors Conduct Rules 2011*.

see that law and perceptions of 'justice' are not synonymous; they are encouraged to recognise that law is value laden and that it frequently reflects the needs and values of the powerful in the community.[93]

Justice issues in individual client clinics

When a clinic operates in a community legal centre setting, it is in the nature of the work that issues of access to justice arise daily, with almost every client who comes in the door. As a result, clinics offer students a powerful opportunity to analyse the 'justice' dimensions of law, ranging from the relationship between law and the perceived justice of its effect, to a lawyer's ethical obligations to achieve what a client wants as a 'just' result, to systemic questions about access to law and legal services. These are especially rich opportunities for reflective practice (see Chapter 7).

Students who work with poor and disadvantaged clients learn some of the issues these people face. As well as seeing individual problems, students can begin to see that a person's legal problem may be a product of external factors, such as poverty.[94] Students are frequently taught to solve complex problems, as the issues that clients present are multilayered and are rarely solely 'legal', as we discussed in relation to multidisciplinary clinics above.

Questions of the relationship between law and justice arise, for example, in public housing cases where the housing department, the community and various residents will each have their own—and often very different—idea of what a 'just' outcome will be. As well as reflecting on these differences, students can consider the role of the lawyer and related ethical issues, such as reconciling their own values with what their client wants as a 'just' result. For example, a client who is unhappy with the loud use of television by a public housing neighbour may want their neighbour to be evicted or transferred. Giving advice to the client will involve explaining the law and its limitations for dealing with neighbour disputes in public housing

---

93   H Douglas and R Fitzgerald, cited at footnote 91; Zoe Rathus, 'Shifting Language and Meaning Between Social Science and the Law: Defining Family Violence' (2013) 3(1) *University of New South Wales Law Journal* 359; H Douglas, cited at footnote 91; J Stubbs, 'Relations of Domination and Subordination: Challenges for Restorative Justice in Responding to Domestic Violence' (2010) 16(2) *University of New South Wales Law Journal* 970–86; J Stubbs, 'Gendered violence and restorative justice' in A Heydon, L Gelsthorpe, V Kingi and A Morris (eds), *A Restorative Approach to Family Violence: Changing Tack* (2014) Ashgate.

94   Juliet Brodie, 'Little Cases on the Middle Ground: Teaching Social Justice Lawyering in Neighbourhood-Based Community Lawyering Clinics' (2009) 15 *Clinical Law Review* 333.

estates. Debriefing with a student afterwards would involve a discussion of the role of public housing, how it is organised and its scarcity, the number of people living with mental illness and psychiatric disability in public housing, and the justice of a remedy that sees the eviction of a mentally ill public housing tenant. Different understandings of justice and social justice are inherent in ethical paradigms of lawyering raised by the scenario, discussed above.

The role of a clinic as a service provider will itself raise systemic questions about access to justice, for example, about available alternative services (private, public, legal and non-legal), about accessibility (geography, physical, cultural, language, etc) and about public policy (state funding, professional oversight, etc). Within the work of a clinic based in a community legal centre or legal aid organisation, questions of access to justice attach to almost every client, inviting students to reflect on, for example, why the legal needs of a client and a community are not being met, or how they can be better met.

Justice issues in dispute resolution clinical courses

Particular clinical courses can examine more explicitly 'how' the legal system resolves disputes. Concepts of justice are, for example, explored in clinical dispute resolution courses where the practice of mediation or forms of dispute resolution other than litigation offer a means of critiquing courts as a legal dispute resolution mechanism. These clinical courses enable students to question adversarial approaches to dispute resolution that are reinforced in their legal studies through a case method of teaching. Macquarie University, for example, involves students in family dispute resolution mediation in a clinical course it runs with Macquarie Legal Centre.[95] Clinical courses at Griffith University involve a partnership with the Department of Justice that provides students with opportunities to complete a placement with Queensland's major mediation service provider. Complemented by a focused classroom component (see Chapter 4), a clinical placement such as this enables

---

95   Anna Cody and Frances Gibson, 'Dispute Resolution and Experiential Learning' in Michael Legg, *The Future of Dispute Resolution* (2013) LexisNexis, Chapter 25; and see *Identifying Current Practices in Clinical Legal Education, Regional Report: New South Wales and Australian Capital Territory*, 6, at perma.cc/FU7X-5TNV.

exploration of ways in which power is used within negotiation and mediation.[96] At the same time, the students' observation of the different role of a mediator is an opportunity for the perspective transformation we discussed above. The mediation process offers a critical perspective on both the conventional ethical paradigm of adversarial lawyering and the 'just' operation of law and legal processes.

Justice issues in community engagement clinics

Clinical courses that do not have individuals as clients present students with a different approach to issues of lawyers, law and social justice. Different forms of community engagement enable students to see the systemic problems, legal and non-legal, in a community, and encourage them to analyse systemic issues as well as address the needs of a client.[97] Such clinics focus on community legal education, community development and law reform, each of which is discussed below.

It has been argued that a one-to-one individual client experience is essential for a student to have a 'transformative'[98] experience, to encounter that 'disorienting moment'[99] that can, with supervision and good reflective practice, fundamentally shift a student's perception of the law and legal system. There is, however, no empirical research that compares approaches in a controlled manner, and no way currently to prove or disprove this assertion. Whatever the merits of seeking the disorienting moment, community engagement offers something else to students: they work at a systemic level, focusing on larger issues that affect an individual and working for a different type of legal response. This is as valid and

---

96   *Identifying Current Practices in Clinical Legal Education, Regional Report: Queensland and Northern New South Wales*, 5, at perma.cc/257Z-6EMR.

97   *Identifying Current Practices in Clinical Legal Education, Regional Report: Queensland and Northern New South Wales*, 5 (Street Law clinic at Griffith University), at perma.cc/257Z-6EMR; *Identifying Current Practices in Clinical Legal Education, Regional Report: New South Wales and Australian Capital Territory*, 6 (Family Law Community Education clinic at UNSW), at perma.cc/ FU7X-5TNV; *Identifying Current Practices in Clinical Legal Education, Regional Report: Victoria and Tasmania*, 5 (Law Reform Community Development clinic at Monash University), at perma.cc/J562-X6GU.

98   Jane Aiken, cited at footnote 78, 238–41.

99   Fran Quigley, 'Seizing the Disorienting Moment: Adult Learning Theory and the Teaching of Social Justice in Law School Clinics' (1995) 2 *Clinical Law Review* 37, 50.

important a means for achieving the 'law-in-context' goal of clinical legal education, enabling students to analyse and critique law from the perspective of disadvantaged clients and communities.[100]

Community legal education

A distinctive feature of community legal centres is their commitment to community legal education as a means of promoting access to justice. Through plain language materials and active engagement with the community, community legal education aims to empower people so they can engage effectively with the law that affects them.[101] Community legal education enables law students to understand how a lawyer can 'journey with the community':

> This journey has to involve the community really getting a sense of who they are, in the sense of beginning to understand their own power. In working with community, the wisdom or the knowledge of the lawyer does not outweigh the wisdom and knowledge of the community, about itself especially ...[102]

Community legal education, as a dimension of a clinic, offers students an opportunity to examine the way law affects people and how they can respond, and to think critically about the different ways that a lawyer can work to promote access to justice. Students in the UNSW clinic at Kingsford Legal Centre, for example, run family law community

---

100 Anna Cody and Annie Pettitt, 'Our rights, our voices: a methodology for engaging women in human rights discourse' (April 2007) 43 *Just Policy*, VCOSS; Jim Ife, *Human Rights from Below, Achieving Rights through Community Development* (2009) Cambridge University Press; Jim Ife, *Community Development: Community based alternatives in an age of globalisation* (2006) Pearson, 3rd ed.

101 See e.g. Sue Bruce, Elsje Van Moorst and Sophia Panagiotidis, 'Community Legal Education: Access to Justice' (1992) 17(6) *Alternative Law Journal* 278; Mark Rix, 'Community legal centres and *pro bono* work: for the public good?' (2003) 28(5) *Alternative Law Journal* 238, 240.

102 William P Quigley, 'Reflections of Community Organizers: lawyering for empowerment for Community Organizations' (1995) 21 *Ohio Northern University Law Review* 455, quoted in Margaret Martin Barry, A Rachel Camp, Margaret E Johnson, Catherine F Klein and Lisa V Martin, 'Teaching Social Justice Lawyering: Systematically including Community Legal Education in Law School Clinics' (2012) 18(2) *Clinical Law Review* 401, 406.

education workshops, collaborating with community agencies to develop topics and then designing and delivering workshops to community workers and community members.[103]

An aspect of community legal education is the increasingly popular 'Street Law'[104] activity that has been popularised in clinics in India,[105] South Africa,[106] Thailand,[107] the United States[108] and the United Kingdom.[109] 'Street Law' focuses on teaching practical legal skills to people in the community through workshops and active classes. In the 'Street Law' course at Griffith University, for example, law students teach high school students about areas of law identified (in consultation with school students and teachers) as being of interest to the high school students.[110]

Community development

Community development work is different from community legal education in that it empowers and supports local communities to improve their own 'social, economic, and material conditions',[111] through action, advocacy, education and, if necessary, litigation. Monash University, for

---

103 *Identifying Current Practices in Clinical Legal Education, Regional Report: New South Wales and Australian Capital Territory*, 6, at perma.cc/FU7X-5TNV; other examples of clinical students working in community legal education are the Clinical Youth Law Program at ANU, the Clinical Legal Education courses at La Trobe University and the Legal Clinic at QUT: see Kingsford Legal Centre, *Guide to clinical legal education courses in Australian universities* (2014) UNSW Faculty of Law.

104 See www.streetlaw.org; note that the different URL www.streetlaw.org.au is for a homelessness legal service in the Australian Capital Territory.

105 Ajay Pandey and Sheena Shukkur, 'Legal Literacy Projects Clinical Experiences of Empowering the Poor in India', in Frank Bloch (ed), cited at footnote 17, 241.

106 R Grimes, D McQuoid-Mason, J O'Brien and J Zimmer, 'Street Law and Social Justice education', in Frank Bloch (ed), cited at footnote 17, 225.

107 B Lasky and MRK Prasad, 'The Clinical Movement in Southeast Asia and India, A Comparative Perspective and Lessons to be Learned', in Frank Bloch (ed), cited at footnote 17, 42.

108 R Grimes, D McQuoid-Mason, J O'Brien and J Zimmer, cited at footnote 106.

109 Richard Grimes, 'Legal Literacy, community empowerment and law schools – some lessons from a working model in the UK' (2003) 37(3) *The Law Teacher* 273.

110 *Identifying Current Practices in Clinical Legal Education, Regional Report: Queensland and Northern New South Wales*, 5, at perma.cc/257Z-6EMR; other examples of clinical students working in 'Street Law' programs are at Griffith University, La Trobe University, the University of New England and the University of Melbourne: see Kingsford Legal Centre, *Guide to clinical legal education courses in Australian universities* (2014) UNSW Faculty of Law. See also Brian Simpson, *Taking Street Law to Regional and Rural Towns* (2010) University of New England.

111 See e.g. Daniel S Shah, 'Lawyering for Empowerment: Community Development and Social Change' (1999) 6 *Clinical Law Review* 217, 218.

example, runs a course in 'Law Reform and Community Development'[112] in which students work with groups in the community on an issue or problem they have in common, and focus on law reform activities and community development strategies.

Law reform

With the growth in clinical externships, many universities offering clinical courses include the option of clinical externships at policy agencies, including law reform commissions.[113] While law reform work is not always aimed directly at improving the lives of disadvantaged communities and their access to justice, many of the approaches to law reform do have that as one of their goals; a clinic may be law reform–focused, but we cannot assume that it has specific social justice goals. An externship at a law reform commission is a good way of teaching students the processes of law reform, because it allows students a close-up view of how policy is developed, of the choices a government must make, and of the ways in which law reform issues are prioritised.[114] At the same time, there is considerable value in integrating law reform activity with individual client work[115] and community development.

Conclusion

There is a profound and longstanding connection between Australian clinical legal education and social justice. Unlike in the United States, there is in Australia no dichotomy between teaching social justice and teaching skills in clinics. This integration is a significant positive characteristic of Australian clinics, creating many opportunities for teaching students about lawyering towards social justice. A diverse range of clinics teach ideas, values, skills and ethics of justice, through individual client work, specialist clinics, and innovative models such as multidisciplinary and

---

112 *Identifying Current Practices in Clinical Legal Education, Regional Report: Victoria and Tasmania*, 5, at perma.cc/J562-X6GU.

113 UNSW and Sydney University both offer internships at law reform commissions; *Identifying Current Practices in Clinical Legal Education, Regional Report: New South Wales and Australian Capital Territory*, 6, at perma.cc/FU7X-5TNV.

114 Les McCrimmon and Ed Santow, 'Justice Education, Law Reform and the clinical method' in Frank Bloch (ed), cited at footnote 17, 211, 214–16.

115 See e.g. Liz Curran, cited at footnote 47.

international clinics, and through community engagement. As externships grow in number, the explicit connection between clinical legal education and social justice may fall away, in which case focus on clinical learning objectives becomes increasingly important. Class content and reading, and supervision and reflection, are essential to ensure that social justice aspects of law and the legal system remain integral to clinical teaching.

6

The importance of effective supervision

Introduction

In this chapter, we address the central role of effective supervision in enabling law students to make the most of the learning opportunities presented by clinic-based experiences.[1] Clinical methods will not achieve their potential without effective supervision tailored to each student and to the particular objectives set for the clinical experience. Supervision also needs to address the legal and related needs of the clients served by the clinic, ensuring their interests are safeguarded and advanced. External placement arrangements raise particular supervision issues in terms of balancing the needs of the host organisation, its clients and the participating students.

A range of difficulties is likely to be generated by inadequate student supervision. Without clear guidance and support, students will struggle to appreciate the complexities and practicalities of the environment in which they are working. Clients may suffer, with students failing to gather key information and address all of the legal issues. Students may also suffer if they are dealing with particularly challenging matters. Students will not

---

1   This chapter draws extensively on research undertaken by Jeff Giddings as part of his PhD study, 'Influential Factors in the Sustainability of Clinical Legal Education Programs'. See also Jeff Giddings, *Promoting Justice Through Clinical Legal Education* (2013) Justice Press (cited hereafter as Giddings (2013)). It also draws on the Effective Law Student Supervision Project: see www.griffith.edu.au/criminology-law/effective-law-student-supervision-project and perma.cc/G2JQ-RB4P.

be able to learn so readily as they would from the example of an effective supervisor, and may adopt poor practices without recognising the need to change their approach. Without clear and supportive supervision, students may not benefit from receiving feedback and are unlikely to develop reflective practices. The confidence that builds from being effectively supported and appropriately challenged is critical to clinic students.

While the clinical legal education literature emphasises the importance of effective supervision, there is a need to further deepen the shared understanding of what supervision practices support the achievement of particular learning objectives. Our *Best Practices* research revealed a genuine interest among both in-house and external supervisors for practical insights about how to make their supervision efforts as constructive as possible for all involved. The project also revealed that supervision arrangements are often underdeveloped, relying on untested assumptions about the effectiveness of legal practice supervision models in clinic contexts.[2]

Supervision appears to be the issue most in need of close attention. Those involved in clinical programs acknowledged the limits of their knowledge of how to make the most effective use of clinic-based student learning. The recognition of the importance of quality supervision needs to be matched by a greater focus on what that means and how it can be fostered. Quality controls of supervision are limited.

Our research identified differences in the ways externship programs are constructed with 'what we might think of as the essential features of the clinical method—supervision, responsibility and reflection' being 'present to different degrees, and at times … absent'.[3] Student supervisors describe 'varying understanding of teaching concepts such as problem based learning, scaffolding for student learning and student responsibility and autonomy', and all supervisors said that 'the client or service needs will trump student or pedagogical needs'.[4] We found that:

---

2   *Identifying Current Practices in Clinical Legal Education Regional Report: Queensland and Northern New South Wales*, 26–27, at perma.cc/257Z-6EMR.

3   *Identifying Current Practices in Clinical Legal Education: Regional Report: New South Wales and Australian Capital Territory*, 33, at perma.cc/FU7X-5TNV.

4   *Identifying Current Practices in Clinical Legal Education: Regional Report: Western Australia and Northern Territory*, 16, at perma.cc/4EDN-5SZG.

a significant area where most law schools seem to have a clear quality deficit concerns training of clinical supervisors, in either live client or externship/placement contexts. As far as we can tell, there is currently no requirement for such supervisors to hold a higher education certificate or equivalent.[5]

Our survey of staff involved in Australian clinical programs showed clear recognition of the need for effective supervision, while also demonstrating a lack of clarity about the processes that would best be used to improve supervision standards. With the student and other workloads that some supervisors are expected to carry, it is unrealistic to expect in-depth supervision tailored to each student. If programs rely on external supervisors, then the law school needs to prioritise preparing and resourcing them effectively. This is especially so when the supervisor is involved in the student assessment process. While most programs provide supervisors with written guidelines, it was acknowledged in the survey responses that a deeper form of ongoing engagement and professional development is required for supervisors to understand and promote consistent practices.[6] We found that '[t]here was a clear desire for supervisors to have access to their own supervision and support' and that 'such supervision should include training in education theories and skills as well as ongoing professional development in their area of law. There also seemed to be a desire for more opportunities to discuss and to workshop supervision and clinical practice generally'.[7]

Further, our survey revealed innovative practices involving senior in-house clinic students mentoring junior students involved in a preliminary placement. Law schools involved in external placement programs identified the need for administrative support to enable placements to work effectively. However, there appears to be limited law school recognition of the resource implications for community organisations of supervising students. Building strong relationships with the organisations that are hosting students is recognised as important to the ongoing functioning of placement programs. Our research confirmed

---

5   *Identifying Current Practices in Clinical Legal Education: Regional Report: Victoria and Tasmania*, 28, at perma.cc/J562-X6GU.
6   *Identifying Current Practices in Clinical Legal Education: Regional Report: New South Wales and Australian Capital Territory*, at perma.cc/FU7X-5TNV, 19, 24–36; and *Identifying Current Practices in Clinical Legal Education: Regional Report: South Australia*, 26, at website cited at perma.cc/3VFN-3BWK.
7   *Identifying Current Practices in Clinical Legal Education: Regional Report: Western Australia and Northern Territory*, 18, at perma.cc/4EDN-5SZG.

that it will be important for the partners to develop realistic expectations of what can be achieved through such partnerships and the need to adequately support and resource such collaborations.[8] It also emphasised the benefits of strong relationships in supporting student learning in externship programs.[9]

The supervision terrain is uneven by reason of the diversity of clinical arrangements in place—different models, different objectives, different students and different sites. Online supervision can add further variation to the mix. Clinical supervision involves responsibility for client work being shared to some degree with the student for the purpose of student learning. Chavkin emphasises that the process involves supervision rather than direction: 'Students need to invest in the quality of their decisions and this process is facilitated by having supervisors help students reflect on their experiences and not by displacing students as the lawyers for their clients.'[10] This clearly distinguishes the clinic setting from other legal practices where supervisors delegate work to less senior lawyers and paralegals, largely because of pressure of business and to maximise fee generation. The legal work required by a client can almost always be done more quickly and more effectively by an experienced lawyer than by a student.[11]

In their review of the substantial literature on supervision in health-related disciplines, Kilminster and Jolly describe clinical supervision as a 'complex activity, occurring in a variety of settings, [with] various definitions, functions and modes of delivery'.[12] The literature on legal professional supervision is relatively underdeveloped, focusing on risk management with limited attention paid to other aspects. Greater attention should be

---

8   *Identifying Current Practices in Clinical Legal Education, Regional Report: Queensland and Northern New South Wales*, 24, at perma.cc/257Z-6EMR.
9   *Identifying Current Practices in Clinical Legal Education, Regional Report: Victoria and Tasmania*, 25, which refers to the benefits of strong relationships in supporting student learning in externship programs, at perma.cc/J562-X6GU.
10   David Chavkin, 'Experiential Learning: A Critical Element of Legal Education in China (and Elsewhere)' (2009) 22(3) *Pacific McGeorge Global Business and Development Law Journal* 3, 17.
11   See David Chavkin, 'Spinning Straw Into Gold: Exploring the Legacy of Bellow and Moulton' (2003) 10 *Clinical Law Review* 245, 257–58.
12   For a comprehensive cross-disciplinary review of the clinical supervision literature, see SM Kilminster and BC Jolly, 'Effective Supervision in Clinical Practice Settings: A Literature Review' (2000) 34 *Medical Education* 827, 828. Despite supervision practices in medicine being considerably further developed than in law, Kilminster and Jolly contend that there are no adequate theoretical accounts of supervision in medicine. Their review included databases covering medicine, health care, nursing, education, social work and psychology.

paid to practices that will assist in fostering awareness of ethical and client-focused practices, fostering resilience, enhancing quality and promoting work practices that are sustainable in the long term.

This chapter considers the changing dynamics of supervision in law firms and the key supervision issues facing clinical programs. The chapter also considers the potential for clinical programs to foster 'reciprocal professional development', which addresses the reciprocal nature of supervision arrangements and the potential for clinic students to learn from the experience of others.[13] If clinical programs are to consolidate their foothold in the legal academy, then they need to articulate the benefits supervisors can draw from their work with students. This is particularly so for external placement arrangements, discussed in Chapter 3. Students involved in external placements can also benefit from group sessions that allow them to share and make sense of their respective experiences, identifying common experiences and points of difference. Having considered the professional and educational contexts in which clinical supervision takes place, we then provide practical guidance and support for supervisors, students and those responsible for clinical programs to make their efforts as constructive as possible. We set out both principles and practices designed to foster best practices in clinical supervision.

Supporting and challenging students through supervision

Effective clinical supervision is not a straightforward process. It relies on an elusive set of skills from both education and legal practice. The nature and style of supervision required depends on the students involved, what they have already learnt, and what they are expected to learn from the particular experiences in question. If the learning objectives for a clinic are general in nature, and relate to the students' developing an understanding of the dynamics of law-related processes and workplaces, then the

---

13   The concept of reciprocal professional development is being examined as part of an Australian Office for Learning and Teaching National Teaching Fellowship, awarded to Jeff Giddings to assist Australian legal education providers to make informed choices about the design and delivery of experiential learning opportunities, and to enhance the supervision of law students in practice contexts by focusing on the dynamic that enables both students and their practitioner teachers to benefit from the collaborative nature of practice-based learning. See www.olt.gov.au/olt-national-teaching-fellow-jeffrey-giddings and www.griffith.edu.au/criminology-law/effective-law-student-supervision-project.

supervision the student receives will be particularly important. Without effective supervision, the richness of real client clinic environments in particular is unlikely to be harnessed effectively. Students may well fail to appreciate what they are experiencing unless their supervisor guides and fosters such appreciation. Students also require feedback about their performances, both in terms of 'what conduct is inappropriate (and requires avoidance) and what conduct is acceptable (and deserves repeating)'.[14] Stuckey and others refer to the theory of 'frustrated non-reward'—that the lack of reward where reward is expected has an 'adverse effect much like punishment'—and suggest that this 'places a heavy burden on the clinician to give effective feedback and to reinforce good performance'.[15] The expertise, roles and priorities of the supervisor are likely to vary considerably among different clinical models.

Developing an environment in which students feel both suitably supported and challenged is a key aspect of the work of supervisors. Barry refers to the risks involved in clinical supervision as including the:

> risk of destroying confidence in the very attempt of building it. The risk of allowing creative tension to dissolve into hostility. The risk of permitting clinic precepts of social justice, commitment and professionalism to deconstruct into alienation, intolerance and mediocre performance.[16]

Developing such an environment is also what makes clinical teaching more expensive than lecture- and seminar-based teaching methods. Efforts by law schools to cut the cost of providing clinical experiences have often focused on limiting direct supervision and having each supervisor responsible for greater numbers of students. Others have involved increased reliance on placements in external organisations with supervisors whose principal responsibility is not student learning. While the move to external placements raises supervision challenges, it also presents law schools with opportunities to offer students a broader range of placement options and the ability to engage with the practising profession, providing professional development for external supervisors.[17]

---

14   Roy Stuckey and others, *Best Practices for Legal Education: A Vision and a Road Map* (2007) Clinical Legal Education Association, 175.

15   Roy Stuckey and others, cited at footnote 14.

16   Margaret Martin Barry, 'Clinical Supervision: Walking That Fine Line' (1995) 2(1) *Clinical Law Review* 137, 138.

17   See Chapter 3 of this book for discussion of external placements.

It is important to consider how law students can most constructively share and learn from their respective placement experiences through the classroom component of their studies. As is the case in other forms of experiential education, clinicians take a purposeful approach to teaching students how to learn from their experience. Issues related to the training of external supervisors need to be addressed along with the roles that can best be played by mentoring and coaching arrangements. Clinical supervisors can make an important contribution by preparing students to approach supervision in a constructive manner. Ryan Cole and Wortham have helpfully provided guidance to students on how they can learn from supervision.[18] They note the need for clinical legal education students to develop their ability to 'be a good supervisee': anticipating supervisor questions, understanding when to seek clarification and recognising when to exercise greater autonomy.

Supervision in legal workplaces

Supervision arrangements and practices in legal workplaces can influence clinic student supervision in a range of ways. We noted in Chapter 2 that there is growing reliance on external supervisors working with students. Legal practitioners tend to begin supervising students with little in the way of training and guidance and are often guided in their approach by their own experiences of workplace supervision.

Given the importance of supervision in modern legal practice, it is surprising that the literature on legal professional supervision more generally is underdeveloped, focusing on risk management dimensions.[19] While risk management is a key consideration, other important supervision dimensions include:

- enhancing quality—accuracy, timeliness, value for money, ethical soundness, suitability for task;
- mentoring junior staff;
- fostering awareness of ethical and client-focused practices;

---

18   Liz Ryan Cole and Leah Wortham, 'Learning From Practice' in JP Ogilvy, Leah Wortham and Lisa Lerman, *Learning From Practice* (2007) West Academic, 2nd ed, Chapter 3.
19   Jeff Giddings and Michael McNamara, 'Preparing Future Generations of Lawyers for Legal Practice: What's Supervision Got to Do With It?' (2014) 37(3) *University of New South Wales Law Journal* 1225.

- identifying and supporting staff who develop a mental illness;
- fostering resilience;
- promoting work practices that are sustainable in the long term; and
- fostering critical analysis of the law and the legal system.

The structures used by law firms to manage their work and meet their professional responsibilities have always been underpinned by supervision arrangements.[20] Partners and senior lawyers take responsibility for the work of junior and trainee lawyers as well as paralegals. There is an ongoing expectation that law graduates will do a lot of their practical learning once they start work, yet the supervision that is crucial in supporting new and inexperienced practitioners appears to be increasingly difficult to secure.

As we noted in Chapter 2, the numbers of law schools and law students have both grown significantly since the Dawkins reforms of the late 1980s; in 1987 there were 12 law schools in Australia and in 2015 there were 40.[21] Those law schools are graduating students in much greater numbers. There have also been dramatic changes in the professional training required of law graduates prior to admission to legal practice. Across Australia, the traditional articles of clerkship have been replaced with practical legal training (PLT) programs (offered by law schools or private providers) and workplace traineeships.[22] While these PLT programs provide considerable educational advantages, the placement experiences offered to students vary considerably in terms of duration and nature and have not been effectively integrated with other program components. The opportunities for law graduates to participate in a closely supervised transition to professional practice have reduced.[23]

---

20 Jeff Giddings and Michael McNamara, cited at footnote 19.

21 David Barker, 'An Avalanche of Law Schools, 1989–2013' (2013) 6 *Journal of the Australasian Law Teachers Association* 153; Richard Johnstone and Sumitra Vignaendra, *Learning Outcomes and Curriculum Development in Law: A Report Commissioned by the Australian Universities Teaching Committee* (2003); David Weisbrot, *Australian Lawyers* (1990) Longman Professional, Chapter 5; Jeff Giddings, 'Clinical Legal Education in Australia: A Historical Perspective' (2003) 3(1) *International Journal of Clinical Legal Education* 7. The website of the Council of Australian Law Deans lists 36 member law schools: see www.cald.asn.au.

22 Allan Chay and Frances Gibson, 'Clinical Legal Education and Practical Legal Training' in Sally Kift, Michelle Sanson, Jill Cowley and Penelope Watson (eds), *Excellence and Innovation in Legal Education* (2011) LexisNexis Butterworths, Chapter 18.

23 Jeff Giddings and Michael McNamara, cited at footnote 19, 1229–31.

The emergence of national law firms and, over the past decade, the internationalisation and the digitisation of legal practice, have further challenged the traditional supervisory structures. Dramatic increases in the size of law firms have meant that supervision has become more important than ever, yet close supervision is less readily available to law graduates. Some law graduates seek to enter their chosen profession with little in the way of direct experience of legal work. These changes make clinical supervision practices increasingly important in shaping the expectations of law graduates entering the legal profession.

While experiential learning opportunities have become more prominent in some law schools, the pedagogy informing these programs requires further development. As our *Best Practices* research revealed, the models used vary considerably, as do the supervision processes.[24] Despite this greater prominence, many Australian law students remain unable to access clinical programs because of the high staff–student ratios required for practice-based learning. In an effort to reduce costs, some law schools have relied on unpaid external supervision. While external placements have great potential to provide students with excellent learning opportunities, this requires careful structuring in terms of the supervision arrangements and the classroom component linked to the placement.[25]

Clinical programs and their academics involved in supervision (whether directly supervising students or managing other supervisors) can make a significant contribution by developing their understanding of how effective supervision underpins learning in the clinic, and implementing more effective practices. This can set the scene for promoting best practices in the supervision of law graduates once they leave the clinic environment.

---

24 *Identifying Current Practices in Clinical Legal Education: Regional Report: Western Australia and Northern Territory*, 16, states that supervisors possess 'varying understanding of teaching concepts such as problem based learning, scaffolding for student learning and student responsibility and autonomy', at perma.cc/4EDN-5SZG. *Identifying Current Practices in Clinical Legal Education, Regional Report: Queensland and Northern New South Wales*, 24, states: 'Quality control of supervision is limited. Assumptions are made as to the suitability of law offices and law-related organisations to effectively supervise students.' at perma.cc/257Z-6EMR. *Identifying Current Practices in Clinical Legal Education, Regional Report: South Australia*, 26, states: 'It was acknowledged that not all supervisors (in externships) are interested in pedagogy or able to give appropriate feedback. There was no regular supervision training.', at perma.cc/3VFN-3BWK.
25 Linda Smith, 'Designing an Extern Clinical Program: or as You Sow, so Shall You Reap' (1999) 5(2) *Clinical Law Review* 527; Jeff Giddings, 'Two Way Traffic: The Scope for Clinics to Facilitate Law School Community Engagement' in Patrick Keyzer, Amy Kenworthy and Gail Wilson (eds), *Community Engagement in Contemporary Legal Education: Pro Bono, Clinical Legal Education and Service Learning* (2009) Halstead Press, 40.

How supervision underpins learning in the clinic

Student supervision is a hallmark of clinical legal education. It should be understood as directly related to the design and implementation of objectives for a clinical course. Close supervision of students is significant in providing the scaffolding that enables novices to further develop their professional skills:

> By making explicit important features of good performance through various conceptual models and representations, teachers can guide the learner in mastering complex knowledge by small steps. These devices of representation serve as scaffolds (in the language of learning theorists) to support efforts at improved performance.[26]

Quigley refers to insights from Schön, Dewey and Brookfield in identifying that the clinic setting facilitates experiential learning because it provides structured opportunities to learn by reflecting on the experience provided.[27] The relationship between a student and their supervisor is central to structuring the learning process. The process can challenge students because they are required to 'begin to practice before they know everything … a difficult and scary process that requires honest and searching inquiry about paths taken and mistakes made'.[28] Reflective practice is also considered central to professional development in other disciplines, although 'total reliance on reflection may not always be appropriate in supervision because beginners need direction'.[29] Quigley states: 'Adults' capacity for self-direction is dependent on their ability to be self-aware and to reflect on the implications of their experiences for future action.'[30]

---

26   William Sullivan, Anne Colby, Judith Welch Wegner, Lloyd Bond, and Lee S Shulman, *Educating Lawyers: Preparation for the Profession of Law* (2007) Jossey Bass, 27.

27   Fran Quigley, 'Seizing the Disorienting Moment: Adult Learning Theory and the Teaching of Social Justice in Law School Clinics' (1995) 2 *Clinical Law Review* 37, 50. See also the discussion in Chapter 7 of this book on reflective practice.

28   Susan Bryant and Elliot Milstein, 'Rounds: A "Signature Pedagogy" For Clinical Education?' (2007) 14 *Clinical Law Review* 195–215.

29   SM Kilminster and BC Jolly, cited at footnote 12, 831, referring to J Fowler and M Chevannes, 'Evaluating the Efficacy of Reflective Practice Within the Context of Clinical Supervision' (1998) 27(2) *Journal of Advanced Nursing* 379.

30   SM Kilminster and BC Jolly, cited at footnote 12, 831.

Effective supervision can also reveal the range of uncertainties that legal professionals must address in their work. This includes uncertainty as to what has taken place and why, whether a client's account is likely to be accepted by relevant third parties, which legal doctrines are relevant to the issues facing the client, and how those doctrines are likely to apply. Assisting students to develop the ability to deal with unstructured situations has been identified as a key objective of live client clinical courses.[31]

The Carnegie Foundation for the Advancement of Teaching's 2007 *Educating Lawyers* Report (the Carnegie Report) observed that the mark of professional expertise is 'the ability to both act and think well in uncertain situations',[32] and recognised clinics as enabling the features of a practice environment to be revealed in simplified ways that can be understood by novice practitioners 'who can begin to develop their own perception and judgment'.[33] Milstein describes the contribution of clinics in developing the strategic planning skills of lawyers, involving 'making decisions about taking action or withholding action in order to maximise the likelihood of achieving the goals' of the client. 'The real-world setting of the clinic forces students to engage in the complexity of analysis that is inherent when the multiple actors who affect outcomes are identified.'[34] Supervisors should emphasise to students the importance of safeguarding client interests, and should talk through the processes used to provide advice that enables clients to make decisions.

The literature on clinical legal education also emphasises the suitability of practice contexts for fostering ethics-related learning:

---

31   Giddings (2013), 55–56.

32   Sullivan and others, cited at footnote 26, 9.

33   Sullivan and others, cited at footnote 26, 10; Elliot Milstein, 'Clinical Legal Education in the United States: In-House Clinics, Externships, and Simulations' (2001) 51 *Journal of Legal Education* 375, 379.

34   Elliot Milstein, cited at footnote 33. See also Deborah Maranville, Mary A Lynch, Susan L Kay, Phyllis Goldfarb and Russell Engler, 'Re-vision Quest: A Law School Guide to Designing Experiential Courses Involving Real Lawyering' (2011) 56 *New York Law School Law Review* 517, 533, who refer to '[d]eveloping problem solving abilities' as one of the potential goals for clinical experiences.

Decades of pedagogical experimentation in clinical-legal teaching, the example of other professional schools and contemporary learning theory all point toward the value of clinical education as a site for developing not only intellectual understanding and complex skills of practice but also the dispositions crucial for legal professionalism.[35]

Supervisors are central to harnessing the rich possibilities in the clinical environment, and should consider ethical issues as they arise with reference to the range of available frameworks.[36] Supervisors can also foster student critical analysis and awareness of a wide range of social justice issues.[37] While such teaching takes time, it can be immensely valuable to talk issues through with students.

Clinical supervision can highlight to students the importance of collaborative frameworks in legal practice. Students can develop their awareness of the team-based work performed by many modern lawyers and of the value of developing working relationships with mentors. For these reasons, supervisors need to demonstrate and model collaborative approaches in their work with students.

Supervision arrangements in Australian clinics

As we described in Chapter 5, a key driver in the development of the first Australian clinics was community service. As had happened elsewhere, student involvement in voluntary legal advice programs gave rise to clinical programs at Monash and La Trobe universities and at the University of New South Wales (UNSW).[38] There was a strong focus

---

35   See Sullivan and others, cited at footnote 26, 120. See also Liz Curran, Judith Dickson and Mary Anne Noone, 'Pushing the Boundaries or Preserving the Status Quo' (2005) 8 *International Journal of Clinical Legal Education* 104; Nigel Duncan and Susan Kay, 'Addressing Lawyer Competence, Ethics and Professionalism' in Frank Bloch (ed), *The Global Clinical Movement: Educating Lawyers for Social Justice* (2011) Oxford University Press, Chapter 12, esp. 185–87; Anna Cody, 'What does legal ethics teaching gain, if anything, from including a clinical component?' (2015) 22(1) *International Journal of Clinical Legal Education* 1.

36   For example, see Christine Parker and Adrian Evans, *Inside Lawyers' Ethics* (2013) Cambridge University Press, 2nd ed.

37   See Chapter 9 of this book.

38   Jeff Giddings, Roger Burridge, Shelley Gavigan and Catherine Klein, 'The First Wave of Modern Clinical Legal Education' in Frank Bloch (ed), cited at footnote 35, Chapter 1.

on community service and, quite understandably, limited attention was given to supervision and other arrangements designed to foster student learning.[39]

The fledgling Monash Law School clinical program drew on the experiences of the first Australian community legal centres that developed in the early 1970s. It developed a diffuse structure that generated supervision challenges. The substantial responsibility given to student volunteers and the involvement of a significant number of part-time supervisors resulted in tensions. In 1979 to 1980, the Monash University clinical program had involved 11 supervisors across three sites and faced challenges related to different approaches to supervision and a lack of shared understandings as to the extent of the responsibility expected of the predominantly part-time supervisors.[40] There was a move to a more coherent program in the 1980s with the appointment of staff focused on the clinic but then challenges arose in terms of retaining those people. The commitment to community service exemplified by the 'no appointment needed' structure of client sessions at Springvale Legal Service, the main Monash clinic site, fostered what Evans subsequently described as a superficial file-handling culture among students that presented major challenges for their supervisors.[41]

The clinical program established in the Legal Studies Department at La Trobe University in the late 1970s focused on client-service concerns in its initial years. Kevin Bell, the solicitor responsible for the La Trobe clinical program from 1981 to 1985, noted the complexity for a clinic in balancing 'three competing policy priorities'—casework, community action and legal education—and indicated that student needs were not prominent in casework selection decisions. Bell stated:

> The educational needs of the students did not figure highly in decisions made about whether a case was picked up or not. The focus was on the needs of the client, what we could do for them with the limited resources we had and whether or not a particular case was worthy of our follow up or personal attention because it had consequences beyond the immediate.[42]

---

39   Giddings (2013), 343–44.
40   Giddings (2013), 174–77.
41   Giddings (2013), 193.
42   Giddings (2013), 153–54.

The clinic at UNSW emphasised direct supervision of students with supervisors attending with the student to provide advice at the first interview. Founding Kingsford Legal Centre (KLC) Director, Neil Rees, had worked most recently for Aboriginal Legal Services where there was a focus on providing the best quality of service, and where there was also considerable scepticism about student involvement in casework delivery. In hindsight, he acknowledges that he contributed to KLC's strong emphasis on service delivery, which may have come at some cost to student learning.[43]

An interesting divide has developed among the Australian clinical programs in relation to the provision of advice to the client once the student and supervisor have determined what advice is to be provided to the client.[44] When a client is interviewed for the first time at either the UNSW or University of Newcastle clinic, the student takes instructions. Once the student and the supervisor have settled on the advice to be given, the solicitor gives advice to the client with the student present and recording that advice. Clinical programs outside New South Wales have tended to use the approach developed at Monash whereby the student, after taking the client's instructions and consulting with the supervisor, returns to the client and advises them, unaccompanied by their supervisor. All programs share a similar approach to preparing students for their involvement in interviewing clients: in the first weeks of their placement, students observe interviews conducted by their supervisor and/or former students and are then involved in intensive seminars using simulations to develop their interviewing and advising skills. Such a model allows very competent students to perform to their capacity as opposed to some artificially lower level of responsibility.

The focus on client service of Australia's early clinical programs is now shared by more recently established programs. Well-established programs have had more opportunity to develop ways in which they can use supervision and clinic design to effectively integrate service and learning

---

43   Giddings (2013), 217.
44   For international examinations of similar issues, see Carolyn Grose, 'Flies on the Wall or in the Ointment? Some Thoughts on the Role of Clinic Supervisors at Initial Client Interviews' (2007) 14 *Clinical Law Review* 415; and Hugh Brayne, 'Law students as practitioners: developing an undergraduate clinical programme at Northumbria University' in J Webb and C Maughan (eds), *Teaching Lawyers' Skills* (1996) Cambridge University Press, 167.

agendas. Newer programs will need to work through those issues and develop suitable supervision arrangements that foster reflective practices and harness the learning potential of clinical legal education.

Key issues in clinical supervision

In this section, we address what we have identified as key issues in the supervision of students involved in a range of clinic placements. Particular challenges arise when arrangements result in supervision resources being spread too thinly or in not maintaining sufficient focus on student learning.

Supervision ratios

The intense nature of clinic-based learning requires a limit on the number of students with whom each supervisor works. Staff–student ratios that enable the provision of close feedback on student performance appear to be an important indicator of the durability of a clinical program. Such ratios need to be set at realistic levels and then not increased significantly over time. Chavkin refers to students' needing the opportunity to 'regularly interact with their supervisors in a setting in which faculty members have sufficient time and energy to discuss case-related and personal issues with their students in a non-directive manner'. He argues this requires a student–supervisor ratio of no more than 8:1 where students are engaged in delivering casework services in collaboration with their supervisor and colleagues.[45]

Holland's account of the Yale clinical program refers to 'the Spring from hell' in 1989 with too many students to permit effective supervision. This led to changes and the adoption in 1992 of an in-house student-clinic supervisor ratio of between 8:1 and 10:1.[46] Wilson refers to student–supervisor ratios at the Catholic University of Chile having started in 1970 at 8:1 but, by 2000, having risen to 17:1 due to the popularity of

---

45   David Chavkin, 'Experiential Learning: A Critical Element of Legal Education in China (and Elsewhere)', cited at footnote 10, 17. See also the coverage of supervision ratios in Simon Rice and Graeme Coss, *A Guide to Implementing Clinical Teaching Method in the Law School Curriculum* (1996) Centre for Legal Education, 62.

46   Laura Holland, 'Invading the Ivory Tower: The History of Clinical Education at Yale Law School' (1999) 49(4) *Journal of Legal Education* 504, 532.

the clinic and no additional clinicians being hired.[47] In 2008, du Plessis wrote of clinicians at the University of the Witwatersrand Law Clinic in Johannesburg, South Africa, each supervising between 38 and 46 students as compared to the recommended ratio of 12:1.[48] Workloads of this kind challenge both the learning of students and the longevity of supervisors.

In the 1980s, the Warwick clinical program shifted from real client to being predominantly simulation-based, in part because of supervision concerns. 'Supervising the number of cases that became necessary to provide an adequate caseload for the increased number of students was not possible without a large increase in staff.'[49] Consistency of supervision was also an issue for the Warwick program, which had developed from a volunteer student service with supervisors taking different approaches to their work.[50]

While Australia's pioneering clinical legal educators faced some heavy supervision loads, the survey we conducted indicates that current supervision loads are more manageable. Student–supervisor ratios are generally around 6:1 or 8:1 for clinics involving engagement in client casework. In several regions, such as Queensland, Victoria and South Australia, there is a considerable consistency in supervision ratios across clinical programs. The highest ratios were recorded for clinical activities not involving direct client casework. In Victoria, the Victoria University placement program involves one academic supervisor for 30 students.[51] In Queensland, one QUT virtual clinic involves 20 students for one supervisor, while the Griffith Street Law clinic has 14 students working with the one supervisor.[52]

---

47   Richard Wilson, 'Three Law School Clinics in Chile, 1970–2000: Innovation, Resistance and Conformity in the Global South' (2002) 8 *Clinical Law Review* 515, 544.

48   See MA du Plessis, 'University Law Clinics Meeting Particular Student and Community Needs: A South African Perspective' (2008) 17(1) *Griffith Law Review* 121, 127, footnote 60.

49   Avrom Sherr, 'Clinical Legal Education at Warwick and the Skills Movement: Was Clinic a Creature of its Time?' in Geoffrey Wilson (ed), *Frontiers of Legal Scholarship* (1995) John Wiley, 108, 110.

50   Avrom Sherr, cited at footnote 49, 109.

51   *Identifying Current Practices in Clinical Legal Education: Regional Report: Victoria and Tasmania*, 6, at perma.cc/J562-X6GU.

52   *Identifying Current Practices in Clinical Legal Education: Regional Report: Queensland and Northern New South Wales*, 6, at perma.cc/257Z-6EMR.

Containing the service imperative

Clinics around the globe have faced sustained challenges in balancing the needs of students with client demands for legal services.[53] These challenges are significant in Australia too, and it is important for law schools that are developing clinical programs to understand the potential of using clinical methods and to learn from the experiences of existing clinics.

In one of the most effective accounts of this issue, Redlich wrote of his experiences in 1969–70 in running a 'relatively large service-oriented clinical program' at the University of Wisconsin, describing 'many unsatisfactory experiences' resulting from the variable nature of student supervision provided by the lawyers working in the host legal aid office.[54] Lack of experience left the staff attorneys unable to supervise, so that students were left to seek supervision elsewhere.[55] Some students did excellent work with effective supervision, but others 'came and went as they wished and abandoned files were common'.[56]

Redlich reports that while some students 'enjoyed the freedom to make decisions, give advice, and, to a high degree, practice law independently, others recognized that the clients and occasionally they, too, were being imposed upon'.[57] He suggests that many problems appeared unique to that type of placement. This experience can usefully be contrasted with the positive experience at the University of Minnesota described by George Grossman, who tells how the in-house clinic avoided the downsides associated with service-oriented clinics by careful planning and by keeping the initial educational goals relatively modest. Caseloads were limited, cases were selected to suit the clinic's purposes and close supervision was maintained. As the program became established, it gained momentum with non-clinic faculty members involving themselves in supervision in their fields of expertise.[58]

53 Giddings (2013), Chapter 3, esp. 46–50.
54 Allen Redlich, 'Perceptions of a Clinical Program' (1970–71) 44 *Southern California Law Review* 574, 575.
55 Allen Redlich, cited at footnote 54, 593.
56 Allen Redlich, cited at footnote 54, 580.
57 Allen Redlich, cited at footnote 54, 589.
58 George Grossman, 'Clinical Legal Education: History and Diagnosis' (1974) 26 *Journal of Legal Education* 162, 192.

The Monash University clinical program developed out of a telephone referral service involving students taking calls from people seeking legal assistance. Once a problem was identified, the student telephoned a member of Monash academic staff for advice and referral and these details were then conveyed to the original caller. Simon Smith was one of the participating students and subsequently became Australia's first clinical legal academic. Smith refers to the students receiving 'no formal preparation or immediate professional supervision … The academic advisers were even less regulated. The success of the telephone call for a client entirely depended on who answered the phone'.[59]

Concerns arise when those advocating the importance and value of student *pro bono* schemes demonstrate a limited understanding of the importance of effective supervision and structure in enabling students to maximise their learning from clinical experiences.[60] In writing about the emergence of Pro Bono Students Australia at the University of Western Sydney, Sappideen and Cingiloglu emphasise the contributions of students in the governance and delivery of projects. They refer to a part-time student coordinator having responsibility for activities including recruitment of volunteer students, advertising, coordination, evaluation and, perhaps most significantly, supervision.[61] This suggests a failure to fully appreciate the importance of close and supportive expert supervision in enabling students to draw useful insights from experience, and seems to underestimate the complexity of legal issues that arise in the context of *pro bono* legal work.

Reflecting on his experiences in developing extra-curricular student clinics at the Universities of Bristol and Strathclyde, Nicolson emphasises the validity of community service as a focus for clinical programs. Nicolson considers service-focused clinics to be more valuable in terms of both the services provided and avoidance of the problematic messages students absorb in education-focused clinics that prioritise student learning over community need.[62] A weakness in Nicolson's argument is his apparent

---

59   Simon Smith, 'Clinical Legal Education: The Case of Springvale Legal Service' in David Neal (ed), *On Tap, Not on Top: Legal Centres in Australia 1972–1982* (1994) Legal Service Bulletin Cooperative Ltd, 49.

60   See the coverage in Chapter 2 of this book.

61   Carolyn Sappideen and Figen Cingiloglu, 'Law Student Pro Bono: Report of the Australian Pilot' in Patrick Keyzer and others, cited at footnote 25, 21, 35–36. Endnote 139 refers to the coordinator's workload averaging out at two days per week across the semester.

62   Donald Nicolson, 'Legal Education or Community Service? The Extra-Curricular Student Law Clinic' (2006) 3 *Web Journal of Current Legal Issues* 6.

failure to recognise the importance of effective supervision in ensuring the quality of services delivered to the community and in providing students with effective frameworks for reflecting on their experiences in clinic-based work. Nicolson states that close supervision of students in education-focused clinics should reduce the risk of mistakes by students, but then refers to the lack of instances in his 12 years of involvement in voluntary student programs where mistakes had been irreparable. He has subsequently written elsewhere, referring to educational theory that indicates that 'lessons learnt from experience are likely to be far more profound and sophisticated if accompanied by reflection on the experience through dialogue with others, especially those with relevant expertise and experience, and an exploration of the relevant academic literature'.[63]

Student supervisors in Australian clinical programs have tended to come to their work with very little training, and Giddings' research has revealed that clinicians had limited understanding of the complexities of student supervision before becoming clinical supervisors.[64] Legal practitioners who become involved in supervising students as part of an externship program are also likely to have received little or no preparation for student-focused supervision. Supervisors with experience of client-focused legal practice are likely to find the transition to student-focused supervision easier to make. Clinical models involving provision of advice to clients require students to assume responsibility for their actions in a much more direct way than in other forms of legal education. In such programs, students are compelled to recognise that their actions will influence the wellbeing of others, namely their clients. 'It necessarily follows from the touchstone of "realism" that a student in role must bear responsibility for the resolution of the problem.'[65] This type of student development relies very heavily on supervision designed to support student autonomy.

---

63   Donald Nicolson, '"Education, Education, Education": Legal, Moral, Clinical' (2008) 42(2) *Law Teacher* 145, 170.
64   Giddings (2013), 69. Supervision skills workshops have been held as part of each of the last six Australian national clinical legal education conferences with a view to addressing this limited experience: 2000 (La Trobe), 2003 (Griffith), 2005 (Monash), 2007 (Griffith), 2009 (Murdoch), 2011 (UNSW) and 2013 (Griffith).
65   Andrew Boone, Michael Jeeves and Julie MacFarlane, 'Clinical Anatomy: Towards a Working Definition of Clinical Legal Education' (1987) 21 *Law Teacher* 61, 67.

Developing student autonomy

Clinical experiences direct the student into relatively uncharted waters, but do so with support structures involving preliminary preparation and close supervision. As their skills and confidence develop, the student can be provided with opportunities to take greater control over their future learning as they test for themselves the best ways to approach issues and problems. This introduces students to the norms of current legal practice but also, importantly, assists them to develop a framework for how they will approach the need for ongoing learning and development throughout their professional life.

Pioneering Australian clinicians recognised the challenges generated by student supervision. In a 1984 paper, Robyn Lansdowne and Neil Rees described their supervision of students involved in the clinical course at UNSW as involving:

> [the] difficult task of leading students to believe that they must accept responsibility for the conduct of a particular case whilst at the same time ensuring that our clients are not disadvantaged in any way by student involvement. In part, we have to create an illusion of responsibility.[66]

They had earlier referred to their approach to supervision as being 'akin to placing students on a rope. The rope is gradually let out if a student is performing well. If a student fails to perform adequately we are forced to draw in the rope and explore every minor detail of a case with the student'.[67]

In 1987 Simon Smith drew on more than a decade of experience supervising in the Monash clinical program to provide a very effective description of the clinician's supervisory role:

> Whilst on the one hand the teacher is endeavouring to develop a diagnostic/problem solving ability it has to be tempered with a benevolent power of instant veto. The supervising responsibility is a subtle animal. Exercised too harshly it can crush the student. Exercised too loosely then the client can suffer. In no other law subject is this the case. In other subjects the equation is simpler – 'the student stuffs up, the student fails'![68]

---

66 Robyn Lansdowne and Neil Rees, 'Kingsford Legal Centre: A Clinical Experience', Paper to the 1984 Conference of the Australian Law Teachers Association, 10.
67 Neil Rees and Robyn Lansdowne, 'Report to the School on Clinical Legal Education' (6 October 1983) 35.
68 Giddings (2013), 186.

Supervision issues generated disagreement in the United States in the 1990s among the advocates of different clinical models, particularly between those endorsing externships and those supportive of in-house clinics. Divergent views have been taken of the particular benefits students derive from being supervised by a practitioner-academic rather than by an external person who, while often having lengthy practice experience, must prioritise other responsibilities and may have little experience in working supportively with students. This tension is usefully highlighted in the 1991 American Association of Law Schools Committee Report that noted: 'There is a marked difference in how schools rated the level of extern supervision. Schools without in-house clinics tended to rate their level of extern supervision as high, while schools that had in-house clinics most frequently rated extern supervision as low.'[69]

Various explanations are given for these variations, the most interesting being that they 'represent self-serving statements on both sides, with schools having in-house clinics minimizing the supervision offered to externs, while schools without in-house clinics seek to defend externships as a viable alternative'.[70]

Givelber and others question the significance of academic supervision of clinic students. On the basis of their analysis of the 'co-op' externships program at Northeastern University, they argue:

> the nature and intensity of the work are at least as important as any aspect of supervision in explaining what distinguishes a good learning environment. This finding challenges one of the bedrock assumptions of clinical methodology—the centrality of an intensive, education-focused supervisory relationship.[71]

Further, they insist that there is 'absolutely no empirical support' for the notion that learning can occur only where a professional educator is present.[72] They found that 'both the characteristics of the job *and* the presence of supervision play important roles in students' evaluations of their work experiences'.[73]

---

69   American Association of Law Schools, 'Report of the Committee on the Future of the In-House Clinic' (1992) 42 *Journal of Legal Education* 508, 550.
70   American Association of Law Schools, cited at footnote 69, 550.
71   Daniel Givelber, Brook Baker, John McDevitt and Robyn Miliano, 'Learning Through Work: An Empirical Study of Legal Internships' (1995) 45(1) *Journal of Legal Education* 1, 3.
72   Daniel Givelber and others, cited at footnote 71, 47.
73   Daniel Givelber and others, cited at footnote 71, 38.

Givelber and others found that 'busy hands correlate[d] most significantly with a high rating' from students of their externship placement 'as a learning experience'.[74] Their survey notes that the statistically significant negative factors included students finding it difficult to clarify the nature of the work assigned to them, mismatches of skills and responsibilities, and the failure to honour mutual expectations.[75] They suggest that good supervision is not enough and that it is also necessary for students to receive both written and oral feedback, and to be productively engaged throughout their placement, avoiding idle time.[76] Our response is that all of these characteristics should be viewed as coming within a broad definition of supervision that is applicable to those clinical experiences, whether supervised by academics or by other practitioners.

English clinical scholar Hugh Brayne has candidly outlined how he changed his approach to sitting in on student interviews with clients.[77] For his first four years as a clinical supervisor, Brayne 'sat in on every student interview', thinking 'that I had a professional responsibility to do so'. Subsequently, following discussions with clinicians in the United States, he almost never sat in on student–client interviews. He became concerned to avoid usurping the student's relationship with the client. Brayne considered that his previous approach had come from 'a failure to separate the two goals of legal service and student learning'.[78]

Brayne's argument in favour of allowing students to conduct their interviews and provide advice without their supervisor present is persuasive. However, the best model no doubt depends on the individuals involved, that is, both the supervisor and the student. Students who demonstrate the capacity for relatively independent work will benefit from opportunities to assume greater control over the advice process. The extent of preparation of students through other developmental activities will also be significant. Students should be prepared for their work with real clients by observing and discussing interviews, advocacy activities and other client work conducted by practitioners. New clinic students can also learn from experienced students and by participating in simulated activities on which they receive feedback. It may also be useful

---

74 Daniel Givelber and others, cited at footnote 71, 32.
75 Daniel Givelber and others, cited at footnote 71, 41.
76 Daniel Givelber and others, cited at footnote 71, 38–39.
77 Hugh Brayne, cited at footnote 44, 172–73.
78 Hugh Brayne, cited at footnote 44, 173.

for students to conduct joint interviews together with another student. For such a model to work, students need to be taught how to effectively provide feedback to their peers.

Particular supervision issues generated by externships

While they have operated in Australia for a long time,[79] externship and placement programs (discussed in Chapter 3) have become more organised and much more prominent in the last decade. This has meant that students are participating in the work of a much more diverse set of law-related workplaces. Further, the external supervisors may have received little in the way of training and guidance in relation to their role and are often juggling a broader set of priorities. Academic requirements linked to external placement programs also vary considerably in terms of who organises the placement, the work students do, and the related classroom component.

The variability of externship arrangements means that the preparation of both supervisors and students is particularly important. Law schools need to provide external supervisors with advice on what constitutes effective supervision of students, together with frameworks to help them implement that supervision advice.

Those responsible for such a program need to ensure that the relationship between each student, their supervisor and the law school is based on shared understandings and realistic expectations around what each party will contribute. This tends to be more challenging for externship programs than for other clinical models where the law school retains greater control over the educational experience.

Externship students need to appreciate that their opportunities to assume responsibility for legal work on behalf of clients are likely to be limited. They also need to be realistic about the access they can expect to have to their supervisor. It is important that supervisors recognise they are engaged in an educational endeavour that needs to balance student learning with client service. Externship programs will be more sustainable if law schools also recognise the need to appropriately resource externship programs,

---

79   Giddings (2013), 89, 208–09.

especially in terms of preparing supervisors and developing an appropriate classroom program that enables students to share experiences and make sense of their placement experiences.

The greater variability of student experience that characterises externship programs presents interesting educational opportunities for students to learn as much as they can from the experiences of their colleagues as well as from their own placement work. In effect, there are two complementary learning environments—the placement site and the classroom—and supervision practices have a key role to play in revealing insights from how each student experiences their placement. Debriefing with both students and supervisors about their externship experiences will be important.

How law schools can promote effective supervision

Both the Australian and United States *Best Practices* guides (compared in Chapter 10) provide advice on the structures and processes law schools should use to foster effective supervision of clinic students. Recognising the time-consuming nature of student supervision is an important first step in building sustainable practices. The Australian *Best Practices* provides for supervision ratios of 4:1 per clinic advice session, with a limit of two sessions per supervisor in any given semester.[80]

Many of the clinicians interviewed as part of our survey identified training of supervisors as an issue needing greater attention. Training programs tailored to the structures and priorities of the program should be delivered in ways that enable those involved to develop shared understandings and practices. The Australian *Best Practices* guide specifically addresses the particular needs for effective training and support for supervisors involved in external placement programs, emphasising the need for a shared commitment to meaningful liaison between academic staff and externship agency staff.[81]

---

80 Adrian Evans, Anna Cody, Anna Copeland, Jeff Giddings, Mary Anne Noone, Simon Rice and Ebony Booth, *Best Practices: Australian Clinical Legal Education* (2013) Government of Australia, Office of Learning and Teaching, Staff, Best Practice 5, at perma.cc/2J6E-ZMQX.
81 Adrian Evans and others, cited at footnote 80, Supervision Best Practice 4.

The United States *Best Practices* guide provides useful detail in relation to supervision, focusing on how supervisors can most productively provide feedback to students and how students can be prepared for receiving feedback.[82] The framework set out in the report is particularly useful for new supervisors, and can provide a useful focus for discussion of supervision practices.

Close examination of the range of purposes of supervision will be useful in developing new ways for law students to constructively share and learn from their respective placement experiences through the classroom component of their clinical studies. As we noted above, clinicians take a purposeful approach to enabling students to learn how to learn from their experiences. Supervisors should be very clear about what the student is expected to learn from their clinical experience.[83] A purposeful approach also involves working closely with students to foster their structured reflection on what they have experienced.[84] Modelling reflective practices is an important way in which supervisors can assist students to understand how and why to use such processes. A purposeful approach further entails giving students multiple opportunities to incrementally develop the understandings and skills addressed by the clinical program.

Particular issues generated by online supervision

The use of online supervision models is likely to grow in the future. Such arrangements raise particular issues in terms of ensuring that messages are accurately conveyed and received along with needing to support effective student–supervisor relationships. Reliance on technology can generate technical issues and the absence of actual face-to-face contact alters the sense of presence between the parties. Supervisors should seek to avoid over-reliance on email and find other ways to engage with students.

If supervision occurs at a distance, then it can be helpful to use some form of video-conferencing to foster the inter-personal dimensions of the relationship. Gibson provides useful guidance on how to structure video-conferencing to make it an effective supervision tool. In essence, Gibson's

---

82   Roy Stuckey and others, cited at footnote 14, 175–77.
83   See Chapter 4 of this book.
84   See Chapter 7 of this book.

message is to concentrate on being an effective listener. She suggests using a formal structure that sees each participant speaking without interruption, then listening without interrupting, with conscious turn-taking.[85] It can also be helpful to prepare for supervision discussions by developing and sharing an agenda ahead of the meeting.

Principles to inform law school structures in support of clinical supervision

The Australian *Best Practices* includes the following principles relating to clinical supervision:[86]

> The supervision needs of students vary according to:
>
> 1.1 the objectives of the clinic and clients' needs; and
>
> 1.2 the experience and level of training the students already possess.
>
> Supervision arrangements are designed to assist students to link theory and practice and work collaboratively with supervisors on addressing clients' needs. The arrangements also enable students to encounter a range of work (both areas of law and legal tasks) during their clinic experience.
>
> Supervision is structured, with ground rules and clear learning objectives. As a system, it ensures students' right to supervision and feedback, together with support and respect for both supervisees and supervisors.
>
> Supervisors meet with each student on a regular basis as well as having the capacity to respond to unpredictable events.
>
> Development of a strong supervision relationship relies on supervisors as role models.

These student-focused principles are designed to provide a platform to assist law schools to appreciate the importance of effective supervision. They also emphasise the value of law schools engaging with both supervisors and students to make clinical experiences as constructive as possible.

---

85   Adele Gibson, 'Staying Connected: Videoconferenced Supervision for Rural Provisional Psychologists' (2007) October, *InPsych* at perma.cc/HK5Q-KED3.
86   Adrian Evans and others, cited at footnote 80, 17.

Guidance for supervisors

Supervisors face a challenging task in balancing the interests of their organisation and their duties to clients along with the interests of the students. The diversity of contexts in which student supervision takes place makes it difficult to develop universal best practices. This difficulty is reinforced by the limited time available to some supervisors to tailor their supervision to fit with program objectives and the needs of particular students.

The following guide provides a basic framework for use by supervisors, especially those who are new to working with students in a clinic context, whether in-house or as part of an external placement. It is designed both as a framework and a prompt for discussion as part of the training that should be a key part of preparing supervisors for their engagement with clinic students.

Understand the program

- Use the program objectives to frame your approach (see Chapter 4).
- Be clear about what the law school expects of you and each student (the intended learning outcomes: see Chapter 4).
- Appreciate the value of 'learning by doing and reflecting' (see Chapter 7).

Communicate clearly

- Listen carefully and encourage students to explain their views.
- Specific feedback is a key to supervision.
- Be candid and constructive.
- Be sure that students understand each task they are to complete.

Be sensitive

- Be sensitive to both clients and students. Most of us are more sensitive than we let on.
- Model an inclusive approach.

Be collaborative

- Be collaborative with students.
- Be collaborative with your clients.
- Be collaborative with your fellow workers.

Plan for student development

- Take an incremental approach to build student confidence and self-reliance.
- Often, 'less is more'. Rather than providing the answer, support students to understand the issues and identify the answer for themselves.
- Foster systematic student reflection.

Be accountable

- Elaborate on your views on the standard of student work.
- Corroborate your views with your colleagues.
- Keep a record of your key observations.
- Encourage students to be accountable.

Whenever possible, enjoy your involvement with students.

Preparing students to make the most of supervision

An aspect of supervision practice that warrants closer examination is how to best prepare students for their work with their clinic supervisor as constructively as possible. Law schools can assist their students to prepare for the learning and service opportunities they will encounter in the clinic.

Supervision issues that can usefully be addressed in preparing students for their relationship with their clinic supervisor include the following:

Prepare in a professional manner. Students should expect to receive clear instructions on the task at hand rather than have their supervisor provide them with answers to research issues. Students should check their work before consulting their supervisor and anticipate and address issues the supervisor may raise. This can be usefully summarised as 'make it easy for your supervisor to guide and support you'.

Consider the relationship from the supervisor's perspective. Mutual respect is a key to any relationship. It is also helpful for students to appreciate that good supervision is time-consuming.

Receive feedback in a constructive manner. The United States *Best Practices* guide calls on students to 'listen to the critique with care and an open mind'.

Be proactive. Taking a problem-solving approach is as important in the student–supervisor relationship as it is in the student–client relationship.

Take a reflective approach. Students should appraise their own performance and be honest about whether they have performed well.

Always remember the client. Students need to appreciate the central significance of their client in whatever work they do. Working with and on behalf of the client is central to professional work.

Ryan Cole and Wortham provide constructive advice to law students about how they can most productively approach the supervision process.[87] They emphasise the value of students being prepared, setting goals and clarifying each assignment. Clinical students should also make the most of the opportunity to learn from the experiences of their fellow students. Seminars, workshops and 'case rounds'[88] all provide valuable opportunities for students to learn from their peers as well as from their supervisors. This is particularly effective for external placement programs where the opportunities to learn from peers are reinforced by the diversity of the legal work done in a wide range of placement sites.

It is also important for students and academics to make the most of the learning opportunities provided by group discussions as part of the classroom component of placement programs. This is particularly valuable for externship programs. The diversity of legal workplaces generates significant scope for reciprocal learning with students sharing insights and learning from each other's experiences. The academic can usefully take

---

87   Liz Ryan Cole and Leah Wortham, cited at footnote 18, Chapter 3.
88   Susan Bryant and Elliot Milstein, cited at footnote 28.

a facilitative role to support the students to share their stories and then draw on the differences and commonalities of those stories to make sense of their respective placements.

Effective law student supervision project

A comprehensive set of resources to support the effective planning and conduct of law student supervision is available at the website for the Effective Law Student Supervision Project developed by Professor Jeff Giddings at Griffith Law School.[89] The website contains materials for students, supervisors and those responsible for managing programs that involve students learning through supervision.

Conclusion

Effective supervision is fundamental across all models of clinical legal education. It safeguards the interests of clients and provides the structure that supports and constructively challenges students. Supervisors have always played a central role in helping students to make sense of the complex environment they encounter. As a clinical legal education community, we need to further develop our collective understanding of what makes for effective supervision. This is especially so in relation to externship arrangements, where supervisors face competing priorities and often receive limited law school support and have had little training for their role.

Improving the preparation and practices of supervisors requires careful planning by those responsible for clinical programs. Law schools will benefit from engaging with the legal profession to promote involvement in student placement programs. As more law schools and other legal education institutions seek out placement opportunities for their students, challenges are bound to arise in terms of promoting effective practices. Clinics need to plan for the prospect that they will face expectations to further contribute to preparing students for professional relationships beyond law school.

---

89   See www.griffith.edu.au/criminology-law/effective-law-student-supervision-project.

7

Reflective practice: The essence of clinical legal education

Introduction

It is a longstanding assertion of clinical legal educators the world over that one of the most important elements of a good clinical program is reflection. Roy Stuckey, in his highly regarded and often-referred-to book, *Best Practices for Legal Education*,[1] articulates it as 'helping students learn how to learn from experience', while Milstein puts it more formally with his suggestion that the ultimate aim of clinical teaching is to develop reflective practitioners and lifelong learners.[2]

Our recent research on clinical legal education in Australia has confirmed the importance of reflection. Australian clinical legal educators from a broad range of programs consistently identified reflection as central to the clinical legal education process, many calling it a 'minimum standard' for clinical legal education programs.[3] This observation should hardly be a surprise, as clinical legal education is experiential learning and, as Stuckey has argued, optimal experiential learning involves a circular

---

1   Roy Stuckey and others, *Best Practices for Legal Education: A Vision and A Road Map* (2007) Clinical Legal Education Association.
2   Elliot Milstein, 'Clinical Legal Education in the United States: In-House Clinics, Externships, and Simulations' (2001) 51 *Journal of Legal Education* 375.
3   See *Identifying Current Practices in Clinical Legal Education,* Regional Reports, cited in Chapter 1 at footnote 6, particularly the 'Key Elements of a Good Clinical Program' section and the report responses attached as annexures.

sequence of experience, reflection, theory and practice.[4] This universal recognition within Australian clinics of the role of reflection led us to consider in more depth exactly what is meant by reflection and why it is so important to clinics.

Our research shows that reflection and reflective practice are often used to assess students in clinical programs; this is evident from the repeated reference to reflection by those we surveyed when asked about how they assess students. Our research shows that reflective workshops, debriefs, blogs and journals are all used to assess such diverse aspects of the clinical process as client sensitivity and empathy, sociolegal awareness, and even intellectual grasp of substantive law.[5] While the scope of our research was not designed to tease out the distinction between assessing reflective thought and using reflection to assess more substantive legal skills, this crossover raised some very interesting questions for us, such as what exactly is reflection within a clinical legal context? Should it be assessed and, if so, how? And finally, if reflection is relied on to measure the success of our students against a range of other criteria, is enough emphasis being placed on the process of reflection itself?

These questions could not be answered without a clear understanding of what reflective practice is and why it is considered so crucial to clinical legal education. Once we delved into these questions it became clear that while almost all clinicians see reflection as vital, there are very different views on what it is, and many clinicians were in the dark as to how to most effectively foster reflective practice in our students.

In this chapter, we will explore reflection in the clinical legal setting, drawing on the literature on reflection and our own research. We will 'think through' what reflective practice actually means and why it should be part of clinical legal programs. We then turn our attention to how it might be taught and assessed. There has been much discussion, both within clinical legal programs and beyond, as to how we assess reflection (or even if we should) and we will explore this discussion in the Australian context.

---

4   Rachel Spencer, 'Holding up the Mirror: A theoretical and practical analysis of the role of reflection in Clinical Legal Education' (2012) 17–18 *International Journal of Clinical Legal Education* 181, 186, citing R Stuckey, 'Teaching with a purpose; defining and achieving desired outcomes in clinical law courses' (2007–08) 13 *Clinical Law Review* 807, 813.

5   This is evident from a close reading of the Regional Reports, cited in Chapter 1 at footnote 6.

What our research discovered about reflection

Before we begin, a few words should be said about our research and what its findings suggest about reflection in clinical legal teaching. As canvassed in Chapter 1, the first stage of our research surveyed all the clinical legal education programs offered across the country. We did not ask direct questions about reflection and, in fact, reflection was not mentioned in our survey document. This was an unfortunate oversight, although it is of interest that reflection appeared repeatedly in the responses to our questions. For example, the first part of the survey asked for details of the program being surveyed, while the second part asked about what might make a 'good' clinical program. In that second section, our open-ended question about whether there are any minimum standards that should be achieved in clinical programs elicited responses that almost always mentioned reflection.[6]

The next section of the survey was aimed at supervision and supervision standards, and again reflection and reflective practice featured large. For example, when asked about the appropriate length of a clinical program, a typical response was that it needed to be long enough to allow reflection and the development of reflective skills.[7] However, the section in which the most references to reflection appeared dealt with questions about assessment. It is clear that almost all clinics use reflection, whether through discussions, presentations, journals or blogs, to help them assess their students.

The section of the survey headed 'Clinical Supervision Standards' again showed us how important reflection is. Respondents were asked to comment on if and how they assess a variety of capacities, understandings and skills. These ranged from client sensitivity and ethical and sociolegal awareness to intellectual grasp of substantive law, drafting, negotiating and advocacy skills, self-organisation, and comprehension of the law reform process. Reflection and reflective practices, including reflective discussions, workshops, blogs or journals, were repeatedly cited as ways in which students were assessed against all these varied competencies.

6   See Regional Reports, particularly the 'Key Elements of a Good Clinical Program' section, question 1, cited in Chapter 1 at footnote 6.
7   Again, see Regional Reports, cited in Chapter 1 at footnote 6, e.g. *Identifying Current Practices in Clinical Legal Education, Regional Report: Queensland and Northern New South Wales*, 14, at perma. cc/257Z-6EMR.

There is perhaps a lack of clarity in the way that clinicians communicate to their students the aim or role of the reflective exercises they ask of them. Because reflective exercises are often used to assess more than simply the students' ability to reflect, we may be diluting the message that reflection in itself is important. It is possible that the readiness to use reflection as a form of assessment means that we are giving our students some mixed messages about what it means to reflect, and weakening understanding of the inherent value of reflection itself. Mary Ryan has commented:

> Despite the common (and often undefined) use of the terms reflection or reflective in assessment tasks ... learners are not often taught how to reflect, which different types of reflection are possible, or how best to communicate their disciplinary knowledge through reflection.[8]

It is clear across the responses to our survey that reflection is core to clinical legal education. But is this because clinicians rely on reflection to assess other capacities, or is it because reflection is valued as a fundamental skill and an inherent part of a good clinical legal program? There is no doubt that reflective exercises, whether oral or written, are a rare opportunity to understand better the thought processes, assumptions, values and beliefs held by our students. It can also be hard to resist opportunities to test how well we have taught other aspects of our courses. However, is this really the role of reflection? To answer this question we need to be clear on what reflection is.

What is reflection?

'[Reflection] is the magic ingredient which converts legal experience into education.'[9]

There has been a great deal of writing on reflection and the role it should play in the education or development of professionals. Teaching reflective practice has long been the norm in education, nursing and social work as well as in many other disciplines, and the literature from this wealth of experience has a lot to offer the discipline of law. Law, on the other hand,

---

8 Mary Ryan, 'The pedagogical balancing act: teaching reflection in higher education' (2013) 18(2) *Teaching in Higher Education* 144.
9 Georgina Ledvinka, 'Reflection and assessment in clinical legal education: Do you see what I see?' (2006) 9 *International Journal of Clinical Legal Education* 29, 29–30.

has barely begun to explore reflection and the idea of teaching reflective practice. So what does reflection mean and what does it look like in the context of legal education?

Discussion of reflection, what it is and why it might be important to professional practice goes back many decades. In the early 1900s, Dewey looked closely at how we think and, in a book of that name, he analysed the different ways in which we think about a given issue or situation.[10] He identified several different ways of thinking, including stream of consciousness, belief, imagination or invention and, of course, reflection.

Although Dewey did not necessarily articulate it in this way, clinical students often find it helpful to think about these different ways of thinking in a progressive way. That is, when faced with an issue or, for example, a client's problem, the most immediate response of the student/practitioner[11] is a continuous stream of consciousness in their mind. This is a natural, common and, it could be argued, unavoidable response to a new experience. Dewey describes it as everything that 'goes through our minds'.[12] This stream of consciousness perhaps tries to capture as much of the information the student/practitioner is presented with as possible—but it is not yet ordered or structured.

From this stream of consciousness, the student/practitioner often then moves into another of Dewey's types of thinking: belief. Almost immediately, a student/practitioner will start to rely on belief—they may not even be able to articulate how, but the information from their stream of consciousness is triggering in them 'understandings' or beliefs they already hold. So, for example, the student/practitioner may assume that a client who presents with a legal issue about divorce is in conflict with the other party, even if that has not been said. Belief is not based on evidence, it is not proven and it is not necessarily true (although it may be), yet it is held by the student/practitioner to be true.

Almost simultaneously, the student/practitioner will also start to engage in invention or imagination. This form of thinking involves starting to extrapolate solutions or possible options out of the information they

---

10   John Dewey, *How We Think* (1910) DC Heath.
11   We use this term in this chapter to highlight that it is the student acting as practitioner whom we are describing: not yet practitioner and still subject to supervision, but trying to put themselves in the position of practitioner.
12   John Dewey, cited at footnote 10, 2.

already have. In our example, the student/practitioner may start to think 'perhaps if this client tells their spouse that they don't want child support, then they will be able to negotiate arrangements for the children'.

Reflection draws on all of these types of thinking but goes further: 'it is the … active, persistent, and careful consideration of any belief or supposed form of knowledge in the light of the grounds that support it and the further conclusion to which it leads'.[13]

Reflection is grounded in experience, as it is experience that allows the testing of the other types of knowledge. In our example, the student/ practitioner can reflect and draw together the other ways of thinking, but can also test them. They might hypothesise that the client may have some residue ill feeling towards their spouse, and then they might inquire further about the client's feelings and how they influence what the client wants. For Dewey, reflection was not possible without experience, but experience was meaningless without reflection.

Similarly, Schön, writing in the 1980s, accentuated experience or action as a fundamental prerequisite to reflection, particularly in the education of professionals. Schön explained:

> in the midst of their education for practice there was a profound sense of mystery. This feeling resulted from the fact that the students literally did not know what they were doing, and their teachers could not tell them – because what the teachers knew how to say the students could not at that point in their experience understand.

> The students had to have the experience of trying to do the thing before they would be ready to understand the kind of explanations that the teachers could give them about what they were doing.[14]

Kolb, writing at much the same time, focused very specifically on the learning process, conceptualising a cycle that involved concrete experience, active experimentation, abstract conceptualisation and reflective observation. We return to this below, but Kolb's point was that effective learning involves all four elements of the cycle in a kind of constant rotation.[15] While the learner could enter the cycle at any point,

---

13   John Dewey, cited at footnote 10.
14   Donald A Schön, 'Educating the Reflective Legal Practitioner' (1995) 2 *Clinical Law Review* 231, 249.
15   D Kolb, *Experiential Learning* (1984) Prentice Hall.

Kolb clearly linked the cycle to concrete experience, and reflection flows from that. Gibbs, in his book *Learning by Doing*,[16] also conceptualised the process in a circular way through his reflective cycle. The reflective cycle includes description, feelings, evaluation, analysis, conclusion and action plan. Description requires a simple retelling of what happened, and the reflective thinker then expresses the feelings these events produced in them. They then move to assessing the good and the bad in the situation before engaging in a deeper analysis in order to find meaning. From there they consider what they could have done differently in order to get a different (improved) outcome; and finally they consider an action plan of what they would do if the situation arose again.

More recently, Bain and others suggest a 'five Rs' framework of reporting, responding, relating, reasoning and reconstructing,[17] which Ryan[18] reduces to four through the merging of reporting and responding. This framework also begins with a concrete experience, which then becomes the subject of each action described in the four Rs. Bain's framework is very helpful in the context of clinical legal education, and is discussed in more detail in a report commissioned by the then Australian Learning and Teaching Council.[19]

For Schön, true reflective practice comes not only from action or experience but more specifically from the uncertainty, uniqueness and conflict of that experience. Schön believed that this uncertainty goes to the heart of professional work in that professionals do something more than simply apply the technical rationality of their discipline; they use judgment, experience, intuition and reflection-in-action to solve problems. It is this idea—that reflection generates uncertainty and conflict— that is most interesting for clinicians' purposes. It describes the ability of reflection to question assumptions, and acknowledges that this can be a very unsettling experience. In some cases the assumptions may even be unconscious, but they nevertheless form and influence our perspective.

---

16 G Gibbs, *Learning by Doing: A guide to teaching and learning methods* (1988) Oxford Polytechnic Further Education Unit.

17 JD Bain, R Ballantyne, C Mills and NC Lester, *Reflecting on practice: Student teachers' perspectives* (2002) Post Pressed.

18 Mary Ryan, cited at footnote 8, 144–55.

19 Mary Ryan and Michael Ryan, *Developing a systematic, cross-faculty approach to teaching and assessing reflection in higher education* (2012) ALTC.

The process of reflection, therefore, not only suggests a questioning of these assumptions, but leads to inquiry and discovery and, commonly, culminates in perspective transformation.

Why do we want to teach reflective practice?

Now that we know a little more about what reflective practice looks like, and perhaps what it aims to achieve, why do we want to teach it as part of clinical legal education? Expressed slightly differently, the question might actually be: why is clinical legal education so well placed to teach reflection? Stuckey asserts that helping students learn how to learn from experience 'may be the most important goal of legal education'.[20]

Four main reasons to teach reflection emerged from our research:

- Clinical legal education has a unique ability to provide rich and unpredictable experience that so lends itself to deep reflection.
- Reflection can offer a perspective on (and perhaps respite from) the dominance of positivist black letter law within legal education.
- Teaching reflection can develop our students' resilience in a profession that has some of the highest incidences of mental stress.
- Reflection assists students to understand and critique the law in context, which is particularly important because of the unique position that lawyers hold within the community.

We deal with each of these in turn.

Reflection aids the educative process, while experience aids reflection

Clinical legal education has a unique ability to expose students to new, strange and previously unimaginable experiences. This is particularly because it involves working with live clients; that is, when students are asked to participate in a real legal practice with clients and their actual legal cases. Unlike a case study, or even a simulation, which is selected or written by the educator, a real client enters the students' experience as a bundle of unpredictable, often contradictory, facts, feeling and impulses.

---

20   Roy Stuckey and others, cited at footnote 1.

Students must respond to all of these. Of course they need to develop the skills that will enable them to identify the relevant legal facts, just as they would in a class exercise, but they cannot do it in the kind of isolation that non-clinical methods allow.

Almost any client seeking legal advice will have a problem that encompasses different areas of law, and the facts are never presented neatly. This means that students dealing with such situations cannot simply fall back on conventional classroom teaching. They need to develop new strategies and approaches to problem-solving, through the process of reflection.[21]

If new strategies are required, then the best way for the student to learn the reflective lesson is to be exposed to these experiences over and over. We should successively ask them to respond, to think about their response, and then to alter their response the next time as a result of their thinking. The multiple layers of the clinical method allow and then stimulate a deep, rich reflection in this way.

Students often feel the weight of responsibility of working with real clients. That sense of responsibility can inspire them to put aside their focus on their own performance for assessment purposes and immerse themselves in their client's case. They become part of the experience because they are in the role of the practitioner, with a responsibility to do the best for their client; not simply a spectator with an opinion on how to proceed. Teaching students to reflect in this context has two interrelated benefits. First, it gives them a framework as they grapple with how they process this new and daunting experience and how they make sense of it. Secondly, it improves their ability to actually use the knowledge they have; to see their client's issues in the broader context and then use this knowledge to build a solution.

Reflection can be applied to a range of areas of clinical legal education. In the area of skills acquisition, reflection may be used to develop a student's client skills, such as accurate fact-gathering. Take, for example, the student who assumes a client who cannot recall detail must be lying; if the student has the opportunity to consider the experience of their client, including the client's personal history and circumstances, then the student may start to question this assumption. The student may discover

---

21 Georgina Ledvinka, cited at footnote 9, 34.

that their client is receiving counselling for post-traumatic stress, or that the client suffered a brain injury that interferes with memory or, simply, that the client fears losing their children into state care due to the circumstances they are being asked to describe. The student might acquire these extra facts as part of the process of taking instructions, but if the student can go beyond simply noting them and think about how these facts might influence or affect their client, then they have begun to reflect.

Without reflection, clinical legal education becomes simply skills acquisition or, at best, work-integrated learning (WIL).[22] WIL is undoubtedly an important part of education, and the exposure to workplace experience is an important step for students to begin to apply the knowledge they have obtained in the classroom. WIL placements may well encourage reflection; however, it is the intense and deliberate nature of the supervised clinical experience, the close relationship between the supervisor and their student and the recognition of immediate responsibility within the practice environment that particularly stimulate deeper learning through reflection.

Reflection as an antidote to the technical/positivist nature of legal education

One of Schön's major criticisms of the professions, including law, is their overemphasis on technical rationality. Technical rationality is Schön's term for the substantive knowledge of a profession. In the case of the legal profession, technical rationality refers to the legislation, secondary rules and case law. Schön argues that the legal academy has privileged the knowledge of these sources over the application of that knowledge, and therefore requires a distinction between thinking and doing.[23] In this model, professional educators first teach their students the basic relevant science, then teach them the applied relevant science and then give them a practicum in which to work on applying that science to the everyday problem of practice.[24]

This process does not sound foreign to anyone engaged in the teaching of law in the last few decades. However, the ongoing difficulty in the eyes of Schön is that it privileges basic knowledge over practice and

---

22   See Chapter 2 of this book; see also *Work Integrated Learning 2012 – Toolkit for Employers and Industry* at perma.cc/ZV4C-FKR4.

23   Donald A Schön, cited at footnote 14.

24   Donald A Schön, cited at footnote 14, 235.

narrowly defines what practice is. In this process, the basic knowledge is pre-eminent and alone gives legitimacy to the applied knowledge, which in turn legitimises the practice. But, in Schön's view, the practice is far broader than anything the basic knowledge can clearly support. He points to the reality faced by those who practise and try to teach practice: that the knowledge that seems relevant to the problems they address is often not the knowledge that is taught in the classroom.[25] It is the assumption that professional practice is merely the application of a body of knowledge to a practical situation, which is so unhelpful and inadequate yet dominant within legal education.

One possible side effect of this privileging of source knowledge over practice is the tendency of the legal academy to hold on to positivist approaches to the law. Positivists argue that the value and therefore validity of a law comes from its source—not its merit.[26] It is not difficult to see how such a doctrine could develop within an academy that is divorced from practice and therefore divorced from the people affected by the operation of the law. For Schön, this privileging of the knowledge over its application in practice was an inversion of the natural order of things because the delivery of high-quality work for the client is the reason why we have professions in the first place.[27] A shift to focus on the problem-solving that takes place in practice would allow a reconsideration of the needs of the very people that the law is supposed to serve.

A review of Australian law schools undertaken by the Pearce Committee in 1987 led to recommendations that teaching be integrated with intellectual skills,[28] while the Carnegie Report in the United States called for an 'integration of realistic and real-life lawyering experiences throughout the curriculum, and challenges [to] American law schools to produce lawyers who are not only smart problem-solvers but also responsible professionals committed to service of both clients and the larger society'.[29]

25 Donald A Schön, cited at footnote 14, 235.
26 For further discussion, see e.g. John Gardner, 'Legal Positivism: 5½ Myths' (2001) 46 *American Journal of Jurisprudence* 199.
27 Richard K Neumann Jr, 'Donald Schön, The Reflective Practitioner, and the Comparative Failures of Legal Education' (1999) 6 *Clinical Law Review* 401–26.
28 DE Pearce, E Campbell, and D Harding, *Australian Law Schools: A Discipline Assessment for the Commonwealth Tertiary Education Commission: A Summary and Volumes I–IV* (1987) AGPS.
29 William M Sullivan, Anne Colby, Judith Welch Wegner, Lloyd Bond and Lee S Shulman, *Educating Lawyers: Preparation for the Profession of Law* (2007) John Wiley and Sons.

In response to the Carnegie Report, one Australian professor observed: 'If students receive the message that intellectual capacities are prized beyond all else, then they will rely upon that in their future behaviour as legal practitioners. They will tend to be unconcerned with the impact their behaviour has on others.'[30]

The other major consequence of this approach is that it can set students up for failure. In fact, nothing they have been taught in law school, no matter how hard they have studied, can fully prepare them for practice. This is because legal practice is not just about substantive legal knowledge, it is also about processes: the process of building rapport with a client so that they can get the full picture; the process of applying the different silos of legal knowledge taught in law school to think about a holistic solution to the client's issue; the process of applying legal knowledge and thinking through the effect on the client and their situation while discussing this with the client to ensure they are acting on instructions. These are but a few of the complex processes that are part of practice, and they all rely on reflection. It is the practitioner's ability to reflect, and then to alter their part in the process to produce a better outcome, which develops them as a practitioner.

This practice-based approach to legal education sees students as active participants in their own learning. It has many benefits that respond to deficiencies in the way in which law is traditionally taught. Law is usually taught as if there is one right (correct and ethically compliant) answer to every legal problem and as if the practice of law does not need to engage in any way the practitioner's own judgment, values or ethics. This leads students to see ethical practice as something that is solely a matter of source knowledge, such as ethical rules, rather than the result of well-developed professional judgment. By ignoring the personal aspect of ethical practice, that part that relies on the practitioner's own skills and judgment, legal education leaves students ill prepared for ethical, sustainable legal practice.

---

30   Gary Davis, International Conference on the Future of Legal Education (20–23 February 2008) Georgia State University College of Law, USA; Report to Council of Australian Law Deans (April 2008).

Reflection to educate for lifelong learners and resilient practitioners

Reflection can serve as a useful link between study and practice. Students who are taught how to reflect, and who are exposed to the benefits arising from reflection, are unlikely to stop reflecting once they have handed in their last journal entry for their clinical course or graduated from law school. Properly developed, genuine reflective skills become a practice, a habit that leads the practitioner to greater understanding of themselves and their practice:

> What [an individual] has learned in the way of knowledge and skill in one situation becomes an instrument of understanding and dealing effectively with the situations which follow. The process goes on as long as life and learning continue.[31]

It is this incremental type of reflection that develops and supports lifelong learners, as it allows an understanding of how thinking and doing interact. Understanding this link then allows development that draws on both. Theorists have articulated the link between experience, reflection and learning,[32] one describing reflection as 'the bridge of meaning that connects one experience to the next that gives direction and impetus to growth'.[33]

Some studies have pointed to the fact that students feel a sense of loss because their commitment to social justice principles and public interest practice diminishes over the course of their studies.[34] The reflective dimension of clinical legal education can address this problem by inculcating a sense of belonging through involvement, engagement and connectedness with their degree, educators and fellow students.[35] During our research, we heard many anecdotal accounts of students' gratitude for feeling connected with fellow students in clinical legal settings, something many of them had not experienced in the broader law school environment.

---

31   John Dewey, *Experience and Education* (1938) Collier Books, Macmillan.
32   See e.g. D Boud, R Keogh and D Walker (eds), *Reflection: Turning Experience into Learning* (1985) Kogan Page.
33   C Rodgers, 'Defining Reflection: Another look at John Dewey and reflective thinking' (2002) 104(4) *Teachers College Record* 850.
34   T Walsh, 'Putting justice back into legal education' (2007) *Legal Education Review* 119, 120.
35   M Kenny, 'Roundtable Trends in Legal Education for Practice' (2012) Australian Academy of Law Australasian Law Teachers Association, Perth, 19 September 2012.

In addition to fostering growth, reflection can also promote resilience, which has become more important in light of recent research pointing to the particular difficulties the legal profession has with mental stress and depression. As we discussed more fully in Chapter 2, law students are susceptible to mental stress and face real challenges to their wellbeing.[36] Reflection gives students a structure and a process that can be applied not only to their legal practice but also to themselves and their experiences. For example, reflection allows a practitioner to explore their views on the legal system, or on the hierarchal structure of the firm or organisation in which they are working. They are able to step back and critique the structures in which they find themselves operating, rather than feel powerless and be swept along by them. As Kegan explains, being able to reflect 'is an active demonstration of a mind that can stand enough apart from its own opinions, values, rules, and definitions to avoid being completely identified with them. It is able to keep from feeling that the whole self has been violated when its opinions, values, rules, or definitions are challenged'.[37]

In this way, the ability to reflect and to develop from that reflection offers a lifeline for practitioners, and fosters resilience in the face of a stressful profession.

Reflection to expose students to law in context

Reflection can be a mechanism that raises the student's awareness of law in context. The phrase 'law in context' sums up the desirability of teaching law students to think critically about the law, rules and practices from a range of perspectives.[38] Teaching students this kind of critical reflection was consistently recognised throughout our research as an important role of clinical legal education. This was reflected not only in the initial process,

---

36   See, for further discussion, N Kelk, G Luscombe, S Medlow and I Hickie, *Courting the blues: Attitudes towards depression in Australian law students and lawyers* (2009) Brain and Mind Research Institute Monograph, 1; and Massimiliano Tani and Prue Vines, 'Law Students' Attitudes to Education: Pointers to Depression in the Legal Academy and the Profession?' (2009) 19(1/2) *Legal Education Review* 3–39.

37   R Kegan, *In over our heads: The mental demands of modern life* (1994) Harvard University Press, 231.

38   This phrase and more on this topic can be found in Adrian Evans, Anna Cody, Anna Copeland, Jeff Giddings, Mary Anne Noone, Simon Rice and Ebony Booth, *Best Practices: Australian Clinical Legal Education* (2013) Government of Australia, Office of Learning and Teaching, 53, at perma. cc/2J6E-ZMQX.

which recorded the views of those actively engaged in delivering clinical legal programs, but also in the focus groups and our further development of *Best Practices*.

Reflection is an important part of this kind of learning; when students are provided with opportunities to examine and reflect on their beliefs, philosophies and practices, they are more likely to see themselves as active change agents and lifelong learners within their professions.[39] This is a powerful educative tool, particularly in light of Dewey's assertion that it is the aim of progressive education 'to take part in correcting unfair privilege and unfair deprivation, not to perpetuate them'.[40]

Many students make far-reaching assumptions about the ways the law operates. For example, a student may start with a fundamental belief that the operation of the law is fair and equitable. If they accept that sometimes the outcome of legal proceedings might not be just, then they may attribute it to the poor performance of one of the lawyers, or to the absence of crucial information before the decision-maker, or to some procedural mishap that was not the intention of the law. However, reflecting on the actual experience can show that this is not necessarily the case; legal proceedings may result in an overtly or apparently unfair result exactly because of the intended operation of the law. For example, property laws are often designed to protect the rights of owners, which can lead to tenants being evicted without consideration of their housing rights or personal circumstances.

Clinical programs can expose students to what actually happens in the practice of law when they reflect on these realities. Often it is the first time that a student can see the impact of a client's circumstances, such as a lack of financial resources, a lack of cultural and linguistic knowledge, or simply a lack of knowledge of the law and how it operates. Clinics can shift the focus from the law and the legal system, which students examine in law school, to its effect on the client. The client and their experience become the central concern and, from this new position external to the legal system, students are better able to critique the legal system. It is reflection that both enhances and supports this process. This different

---

39 Jack Mezirow, as cited in Mary Ryan and Michael Ryan, cited at footnote 19, 3.
40 John Dewey, *Democracy and Education* (1944) Collier McMillian, 119 (original work published in 1916).

understanding of law and the legal system can be uncomfortable for students, but a student who can reflect is better placed to deal with these new insights than one who is never taught the reflective method we describe below.

How should we teach reflective practice?

We now have a clearer vision of what reflective practice might look like and why we want to develop it in our students. The next issue is, how do we do so? There has been some criticism of Schön for failing to satisfactorily explain exactly how the coaching for reflective practice might be conducted.[41]

This leads to one of the very common frustrations of students who are trying to become professionals, what Schön calls the 'paradox of ... having to plunge into doing – without knowing, in essential ways, what one needs to learn', in order to learn by doing.[42] In encapsulating the essence of the clinical method, Schön is also referring to the practice of reflection—it is necessary to ask students to reflect from a very early stage in their clinical experience, and possibly even before they have a full grasp of what reflection is. This process is, of course, best supported by good supervision, which we discussed in Chapter 6.

We propose three crucial aspects to teaching reflection, summarised as: value it, explain it and support it.

Value it

Reflective thinking and practice must be valued, and be seen to be valued, by practitioners and supervisors within the clinic. For some clinical teachers, who may have come from high-turnover, high-pressure practices such as legal aid or community law, reflection can be seen as a more academic pursuit and not central to the legal work. If this message is given to students, then they are more likely to consider reflection as an irritation

---

41 See comments of M Eraut, *Developing Professional Knowledge and Competence* (1994) Routledge, as referenced in Helen Bulpitt and Peter J Martin, 'Learning about reflection from the student' (2005) 6 *Active Learning in Higher Education* 207.

42 Richard K Neumann Jr, cited at footnote 27, 408.

that takes their time and attention away from the 'real' legal work, and are more likely to turn in reflective pieces that attempt to 'give the marker what they want', rather than engage in real reflection.

One crucial way that clinicians can demonstrate the importance of reflection to their students is to model it in their own practice. Clinical supervisors who are unwilling to reflect on their practice by, for example, admitting difficulties or mistakes and verbalising how it could have been done better are ill placed to extol the virtues of reflection. Reflection has to be integrated into the clinical course; it should be the work of all supervisors, and not just fall to those most interested in that 'touchy feely' stuff. It may be that for students to value reflection it must also be assessed in some way, an issue we explore below.

Reflective discussion can be a useful tool to stimulate and deepen reflection, but clinicians need to ensure that they move away from placing the teacher in the only 'power' role at the front of the class.[43] Clinicians should resist the practice of commenting authoritatively on all contributions by students and, rather, try to facilitate discussion within the group. This approach can be difficult within the traditional pedagogy of a law school. Even clinicians find it hard to break the habit of allowing their students to look to the teacher and the teacher alone for validation of students' contributions.

Explain it

To foster reflection, both supervisors and students must understand what it is, in both a theoretical and practical sense. This starts with an appreciation of the role of the clinical supervisor as facilitator.

The role adopted by the clinical teacher should be that of facilitator, rather than that of the master who can give the answers on every issue—'indeed to be an effective facilitator the teacher should resist the temptation to give answers, and try to guide the student towards finding them for themselves'.[44]

---

43 Rachel Spencer, cited at footnote 4, 196.
44 Georgina Ledvinka, cited at footnote 9, 36 and note 32.

The foundation for understanding this facilitative role is transparent discussion underpinned by a theoretical framework—both the supervisors and the students need a theoretical grounding and a commitment to open and transparent exchange. Many writers have pointed out the benefits of teaching theory in an integrated way,[45] arguing that a theoretical background enables students to better understand reflection and why it is part of their course. The Kolb cycle of learning is commonly used to illustrate the differences between concrete experience (doing), reflective observation (thinking), abstract conceptualisation (extrapolating) and active experimentation (testing).

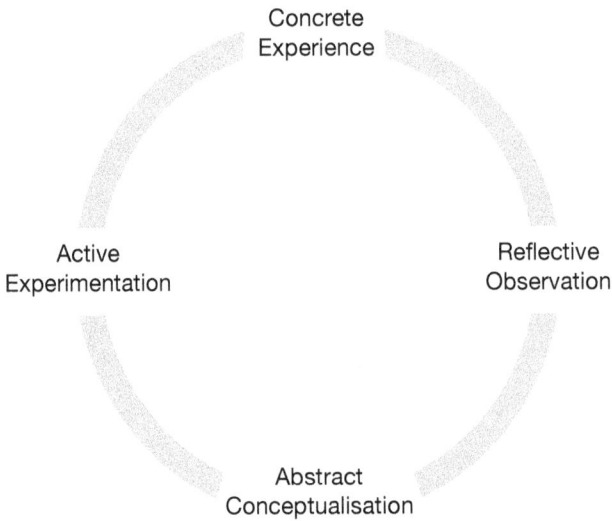

Concrete
Experience

Active
Experimentation

Reflective
Observation

Abstract
Conceptualisation

Figure 1: Kolb cycle of learning[46]

This visual representation of a cycle, through which students might pass numerous times within one interaction, can be very helpful to them while grappling with the theory of reflection. Answering criticism that this cycle oversimplified learning by reducing it to a mechanical step-by-step process, Kolb has further identified '[t]he two dialectically related

---

45 See e.g. C Maughan and J Webb, 'Taking Reflection Seriously: How was it for us?' in J Webb and C Maughan (eds), *Teaching Lawyers' Skills* (1996) Butterworths. See also the comments of Georgina Ledvinka, cited at footnote 9, 29–56.

46 DA Kolb and R Fry, 'Toward an applied theory of experiential learning' in C Cooper (ed), *Theories of Group Process* (1975) John Wiley.

dimensions of grasping experience via concrete experience and abstract conceptualisation and transforming experience via active experimentation and reflective observation'.[47]

Other students may prefer Gibbs' approach, which, with its grounding in common language and experience, is perhaps of more use to students trying to relate the concept of reflection to their own developing practice as lawyers. Gibbs also describes reflection through a cycle, but includes description, feelings, evaluation, analysis, alternative approaches and action plan.

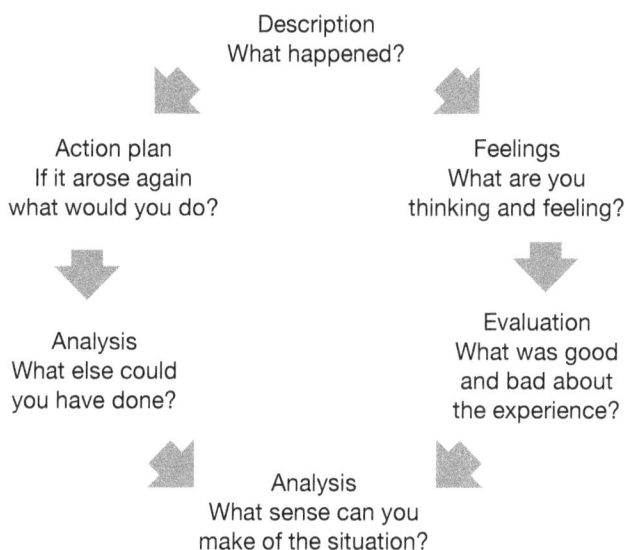

Description
What happened?

Action plan
If it arose again
what would you do?

Feelings
What are you
thinking and feeling?

Analysis
What else could
you have done?

Evaluation
What was good
and bad about
the experience?

Analysis
What sense can you
make of the situation?

Figure 2: Gibbs' learning cycle[48]

Whichever framework is chosen, there is great value in exposing students to the academic work that has been done on reflection. The exploration of the theoretical basis of reflection might serve as a starting point. However, the practical manifestations of reflection beyond the theory must also be explained to answer this ever-present question for a clinical teacher: what, exactly, are we looking for as evidence of students' reflection? Are personal ruminations enough, or are there specific criteria that can guide assessment? To answer these questions, clinicians need to clearly

---

47 DA Kolb, *Experiential Learning: Experience as the Source of Learning and Development* (2015) Pearson Education Inc, 2nd ed, 56.
48 G Gibbs, cited at footnote 16.

explain to their students why they want them to reflect, what they mean by reflection and, finally, how their reflection is being assessed (if indeed it is being assessed).

Actual demonstrations to students of reflective practice are vital. This demonstration starts with supervisors modelling good reflection in their discussion of their own practice. It should also involve tangible examples: if students are being asked to keep a reflective journal then they need to see and discuss some examples of good reflective journal writing. Such examples might come from past students, with due recognition of privacy issues, or may draw on material that, while not written for that purpose, may nevertheless provide an opportunity for analysis and critique. Looking at a literary work unrelated to law but familiar to the students, with the question 'is this piece reflective?', can also be useful.

At its essence, reflection is relatively simple: 'Reflection is a basic mental process with either a purpose, an outcome, or both, applied in situations in which material is unstructured or uncertain and where there is no obvious solution.'[49]

Dewey helps us to understand *how* we think, and subsequent theorists such as Schön and Kolb suggest the *processes* by which those ways of thinking might work together to produce new insights and action. A clinical teacher must build on this to explain to their students how such processes can support and develop their professional judgment and therefore their practice. Jennifer Moon has asserted that 'there is no point in defining reflection in a manner that does not relate to the everyday use of the word'.[50] She then observes that reflection is a means of working on what we already know.

This is a very good starting point for the use of reflection within clinical teaching. What the student *knows* prior to meeting with a client might be a collection of assumptions arising from the circumstances the client is in (that is, what legal issue they may have) and the 'truths' that student might hold about those circumstances. For example, a client seeking advice about a looming eviction from public housing may trigger in the

---

49   Jennifer A Moon, *Reflection in Learning and Professional Development: Theory & Practice* (1999) Kogan Page, 10.
50   Jennifer A Moon, *Reflection in Higher Education Learning*, PDP Working Paper 4, LTSN Generic Centre, 1.

student a range of assumptions and conclusions based on their view of public housing. Depending on their own background and experience, these assumptions may be either negative or positive.

Then the student meets the client; now they have a lot of new information. What they *know* has suddenly doubled and much of the new information may challenge what they thought they knew prior to meeting the client. Reflection is the process by which the student can make sense of this—through reflection they can identify the assumptions they held prior to meeting the client, and think through how those assumptions affected their approach. This can raise new questions, which will spark another round of fact-gathering through research or further discussion with the client. This is reflective and it can assist the student to arrive at a more nuanced and detailed understanding of their client and their legal issue. But it does not end there. Reflection can also assist the student to think about their own approach. They may ask: 'Why did I have those assumptions prior to meeting the client? What were they based on and do I see it differently now?'

Support it

The way clinicians support reflection is to allow space for it within the course they teach. Clinical programs in Australia are often highly frenetic environments. There are often too many clients to see and many complex issues to deal with. In addition, there can be a tension between addressing the educational development and skills acquisition of the student while also trying to encourage engagement with the broader social issues. In the midst of all this it is easy to overlook the structural and practical requirements to support good reflective practice. The major requirement is time; that is, ensuring there is time to properly reflect on the work being done, the observations of the students, and the assumptions and challenges that come with them.

Taking enough time may mean ensuring that time is made available for group debriefing around case issues or client work, for scheduled meetings between student and supervisor in which deeper discussion of the day's practice is encouraged, or for regular meetings where reflections are shared with peers and discussion of both the work and the students' experience of the work is encouraged. It could mean allowing time at the end of the day for students to write in their journals. It might also require each student to produce a piece of reflective writing about their experiences and then share these within the class. Whatever form it takes, taking time for reflection has to be a central part of the structure of the course, and it has to be designed so that sufficient energy can be directed towards it.

Spencer explains that paramount to teaching reflection is the establishment of an appropriate environment.[51] She suggests a set of exercises that starts with private reflection, moves on to reflection in pairs on set topics, and finally moves into encouraging the students to share their reflections with the class. Stuckey advocates a similar creation of structures and protocols in order to assist students' self-learning.[52] Spencer observes that, in her experience, '[s]tudents are prepared to take that risk if they feel supported and know that the risk will produce a positive result in the form of a validation of their feelings and encouragement for the future'.[53]

Should we assess reflective practice?

Some argue that an important way to value reflection is to ensure that it is assessed.

Regrettably, for many students learning is driven largely by assessment. If reflection is not to be assessed then there must be a risk that some students will view it as less important than assessable work, and therefore potentially expendable.[54]

While this may be true, there are two major concerns that arise from the assumption that reflection should always be assessed. The first is that any assessment risks driving students to simply express what they think those assessing them want to hear. The second is that assessing reflection becomes a kind of Trojan horse designed to 'get into our students' heads' so we can determine whether they have achieved other learning outcomes.

The first concern was well expressed by Boud in a seminar given at Sheffield University in 2001 and cited by Ledvinka in 2006: 'assessment is inappropriate because it will stultify or even destroy "raw reflection",

---

51   Rachel Spencer, cited at footnote 4, 196.
52   Stuckey's approach is set out in Rachel Spencer, cited at footnote 4, 196; see also R Stuckey, also cited at footnote 4, 813.
53   Rachel Spencer, cited at footnote 4, 196.
54   Georgina Ledvinka, cited at footnote 9, 40.

including students' confidence in expressing themselves freely and exploratively, and that it may lead to unethical levels of disclosure and confession'.[55]

In addition to this anxiety there is some concern that, if assessed, students will be searching for the 'right' thing to say or write, rather than really engaging in reflection of their experiences, thought and actions. This reservation of course leads to another question: is it appropriate to assess the content of the reflection, or simply the process of reflection? If the process is done well, then the resulting content may well reveal the core values or beliefs of a student. But is it ever appropriate for clinicians to 'assess' such material?

This dilemma leads us back to the issue raised at the beginning of this chapter: that our research revealed that reflection and reflective writings such as journal entries and blogs are often used to assess other aspects of what clinicians are trying to teach students. This purpose is inappropriate. As we repeat in Chapter 8, assessment of reflection is legitimate only to gauge whether a student understands the purpose of reflection in their learning. In other words, it is the *process* of reflection—as an aide to their learning—that we need students to comprehend and which it is legitimate to assess. If clinicians are going to use reflection to assess course content, then they are looking for the 'right answer' rather than whether the student can engage in the process. Some might argue that if the student doesn't know their supervisor is using the reflective piece in this way then they will not necessarily try to provide the 'right answer' or the content that is being sought. However, the fact that this is perhaps 'kept' from the student does not improve the situation, because it is a fundamentally dishonest use of the reflective process. Accordingly, if clinicians are seeking to identify whether students understand the content of the course or the law involved, then they need to be clear about the assessment criteria of the task and at that point it is no longer purely an exercise in reflective practice.

Our research led us to suggest some best practices: for example, that reflective practice must be informed by relevant literature and incorporated into every clinical course in a structured, planned and thoughtful way.[56] This, we suggest, includes providing students with a theoretical

---

55 Georgina Ledvinka, cited at footnote 9, 40 and note 47.
56 See Adrian Evans and others, cited at footnote 38 ('Reflective Student Learning').

underpinning and a set of relevant resources/readings. We also suggest that prompt feedback be given on the reflective practice. Included in the best practices is a suggestion that any reflective practice builds on reflection in which students have already been engaged. However, this goal is aspirational as almost no clinical programs surveyed in our research clearly articulated this practice. Finally, we also suggest that reflective practice should be assessed and that assessment be criteria-based, with criteria that focus on the process rather than the content and that are always clearly linked to the learning outcomes of the particular course or unit.[57]

How do we assess reflective practice?

There are many different ways in which reflective practice is assessed. In our research, clinicians described journals and blogs, class discussions and supervisor/student meetings among other methods. There is undoubtedly a correlation between the use of reflective practice to assess other aspects of clinical teaching and the more formal methods of reflection. For example, reflective journals were often cited as tools of assessment for a wide range of other skills and knowledge. At the same time, supervisor/student discussions were hardly ever cited as assessment tools. Although it can be argued that the role of such discussion in a supervisor's assessment of student performance is implicit, there is no doubt such discussion is a less formal and more flexible opportunity for exchange. We suggest that for this reason there may be value in keeping some space for reflection that is as informal as possible, perhaps in the form of impromptu discussions or debriefing sessions. It may further suggest the need for particular attention to be paid to the use of journals and blogs to ensure they remain truly reflective practice exercises and not just alternative forms of assessment.

Schön was very clear that eliciting and developing good reflective practice is a coaching, not a teaching, role. This idea was also articulated by Mezirow, who said that the ideal learning conditions for reflection are facilitative, with value conflict being handled effectively and underpinned

---

57   Adrian Evans and others, cited at footnote 38, 20 and 21.

by the principles of andragogy.[58] Dewey saw community as important to reflection, a point picked up on by Rodgers[59] when she identifies the following factors that highlight the benefits of collaborative reflection:

1. affirmation of the value of one's experience: in isolation what matters can be too easily dismissed as unimportant;
2. seeing things 'newly': others offer alternative meanings, broadening the field of understanding;
3. support to engage in the process of inquiry.

In relation to this last point, Rodgers observes that 'when one is accountable to a group, one feels a responsibility toward others that is more compelling than the responsibility we feel to only ourselves'.[60] We suggest, in addition, that this collaborative aspect may also play a role in deconstructing the highly competitive individualisation of legal education and this may, in turn, have a positive effect on the mental health of our graduates.

Conclusion

In this chapter, we have examined the role of reflection within clinical legal education, a role that goes beyond a simple endorsement of the importance of teaching reflective practice. Most clinicians agree that reflection should be a fundamental part of legal education, and that the clinical method offers unparalleled opportunities to develop reflective practice in our law students. Reflection is more than asking students to write down their thoughts as a way of making what they have actually learnt more visible. More importantly, it is a way in which clinicians can develop resilience in students by offering a powerful framework and process by which they can examine themselves, their role, and the system in which they are being asked to operate. In doing so, clinical legal education can produce practitioners with good ethical judgment, clear understanding of the law and a commitment to how it can benefit the broader community.

---

58   J Mezirow and Associates, *Fostering Critical Reflection in Adulthood* (1990) Jossey-Bass, as cited in Helen Bulpitt and Peter J Martin, cited at footnote 41.
59   C Rodgers, cited at footnote 33.
60   C Rodgers, cited at footnote 33.

8

Clinical assessment of students' work

Introduction

Australian clinics only occasionally spend time discussing the issue of student assessment. Clinical program leaders appear too often to face other more pressing challenges: finding suitable clinicians, dealing with academic colleagues' misgivings about the cost of clinics or their pedagogical legitimacy and, especially, just finding the time to look outside their own law school and reflect on 'what could be', as opposed to 'what is'. But when student assessment comes up in conversation or at conferences, the issues are seen to be significant and always in need of further thought.

Clinical assessment takes place against the background of general student assessment of law courses and, in this larger agenda, there is an unfortunate focus on competition as opposed to collaboration. That focus drives other debates, such as whether to grade students' performance in some law schools, episodic law school pressure to apply moderating algorithms to clinical results, and the quest for ever more precise descriptors of varying clinical performance levels. Although not all law schools are determined to apply a 'grading curve'—which operates to smooth out students' results to fit a predetermined expectation of high, medium and poor academic performance—clinicians are predictably resistant to that concept when it rears its head. On the other hand, pressure for better grade definition and better methods of self-assessment of performance is not contentious at all among law schools with grading regimes and, for those clinics where grading is in place, there is every reason to continually refine and improve them.[1] Until recently, Australian law schools have had no national set of agreed learning outcomes with which to measure their students' performance in any area of values, legal knowledge or skills, let alone those that are more specific to clinical legal education. The 2010 arrival of the Threshold Learning Outcomes (TLOs) for Law[2] rectified this omission. It is now feasible and cost-effective for clinicians to confidently assert learning outcomes for their programs that are consistent with the TLOs, and to design assessment indicators that relate closely to those outcomes. What is particularly interesting is the active-voice language used by the TLOs: they ask legal educators to define learning outcomes in terms such as 'demonstrate' and 'be able to', phrases that are well suited to the day-to-day scrutiny that supervisors bring to students' activities inside clinics. This qualitative language also sensibly allows for the possibility of grading while avoiding any insistence on metric measurement of 'demonstration' or 'ability'.

The architecture set by the Australian Qualifications Framework (AQF),[3] which requires of LLB graduates a Level 7 achievement of 'broad and coherent knowledge and skills for professional work',[4] is also essentially consistent with many current assessment practices in Australian clinics, as we discuss later in this chapter.

This chapter begins with a short discussion of the results of the regional reporting process in the *Best Practices* project described in Chapter 1. Our research shows that while assessment practices are quite diverse around Australia, with some being very sophisticated, much clinical assessment tends to the basic, intuitive and generalised rather than being developed systematically from the learning objectives of the particular course. There is little explicit pedagogy in assessment, and too few law schools have internally coherent assessment routines for their clinical

---

1   Victoria Murray and Tamsin Nelson, 'Assessment – Are Grade Descriptors The Way Forward?' (2009) 14 *International Journal of Clinical Legal Education* 59. See also Ann Marie Cavazos, 'The Journey Toward Excellence in Clinical Legal Education: Developing, Utilizing and Evaluating Methodologies for Determining and Assessing the Effectiveness of Student Learning Outcomes' (2010–11) 40 *Southwestern Law Review* 1.

2   See Council of Australian Law Deans, *Learning and Teaching Academic Standards Statement, December 2010, Threshold Learning Outcomes for the LLB degree*, at perma.cc/BY6N-6SRF.

3   The Australian Qualification Framework (AQF) is a broad, all-sector set of standards that all education and training providers are required to meet. See www.aqf.edu.au/.

4   See AQF qualification levels at perma.cc/8CWE-RF4Z.

courses. The strongest divergence of opinion occurred in relation to whether to grade students' performance beyond pass/fail, and we discuss the arguments for and against both approaches. Our research led to a series of recommended best practices for clinical assessment. We discuss the main themes of these best practices below. They lead into a wider discussion of the international and Australian literature about assessment practices for different types of clinics. The chapter concludes with a discussion of several underlying and important themes that emerge from our consideration of this important aspect of clinical method.

Australian clinicians' views on assessment: The contributions of our survey to best practices

In considering the debates about clinical assessment and their proper place in developing the best practices, it was important to survey what happens in Australian clinical programs and what Australian clinicians think about assessment issues. As the following section makes clear, there is little consistency or reflection on assessment pedagogy, and even less awareness of that gap.

All of the outcomes contained in the TLOs[5] are well suited to various types of clinical experience and live client clinics can achieve all of them, a reality that only a few highly innovative law schools have fully exploited.[6] However, survey respondents did not explicitly refer to these high-level outcomes, even though many were likely to be achieving some or all of them in practice.

Respondents were asked for their opinions about seven discrete areas involving assessment of students: levels of sensitivity to clients and communication; ethics and ethics awareness; intellectual grasp of substantive law/practical implementation; drafting, negotiation and advocacy skills; self-organisational ability; sociolegal awareness; and, finally, their comprehension of law reform processes.

---

5   See footnote 2.
6   For example, Newcastle University and the University of New South Wales (UNSW) in Australia, and Northumbria University at Newcastle-Upon-Tyne in the United Kingdom.

The edited responses[7] are instructive chiefly because they show respondents' fairly limited ability to articulate learning outcomes, as opposed to describing techniques and approaches to the mechanics of assessment. In quite a number of areas, respondent clinicians across the country said they did not attempt assessment in the designated area of enquiry. Clinical components of doctrinal courses are not listed in the table; they were identified for assessment purposes only in relation to sensitivity to client communication and ethics awareness, and for both criteria assessment occurred only through student reflection, for example, in a reflective journal.

Some minor differences were observable between regions. However, very often, clinicians appear to rely on their intuition in deciding if a student is achieving in a particular area and do not think it necessary to articulate the basis on which they exercised that intuition. These clinicians may, of course, have had explicit internal criteria for measuring different areas of achievement, but they did not see the need to be too precise in their responses. Only in a few cases were possible assessment standards articulated in a way that showed an awareness of the need to measure something according to expressed criteria, even though the survey questions asked for details of both techniques used and opinions as to appropriate assessment standards.

Approaches to assessment criteria in different types of clinical experience

Edited responses from all regions

Clinical programs in all regions of Australia are likely, in varying degrees, to be addressing quite appropriate learning outcomes and attempting to conscientiously assess their achievement or otherwise. However, most clinician respondents did not say that they recognised the critical need to directly connect their own assessment regime to those learning outcomes. On the contrary, respondents identified a range of disparate practices that they thought were relevant to measuring different learning outcomes.

---

7   Full responses are available at www.monash.edu/law/about-us/legal/olt-project.

For example, in relation to assessing students' perceived levels of sensitivity to clients and the effectiveness of their client communication within in-house clinics, respondents referred to a diverse group of techniques and concepts:

> establish relationship with students and through this assess against standards of the supervisor
>
> [observe] the way students talk to clients
>
> [use] reflective journaling
>
> [note their] instinctive reaction
>
> [note] the way the student communicates with supervisor – rely on the supervisor to pick up on that
>
> if you cannot see the student in with the client you rely on how they are talking about them
>
> we assess their reflection [on the clinical process only – see Chapter 7 of this book] and what they learn from it themselves, which is probably more valuable
>
> [a] teacher can have a view about how to deal with clients but students' views could be equally valid
>
> [conduct] grid and case conferences.[8]

In an externship context, respondents had a very different and perhaps less sophisticated set of approaches to the same assessment need, as reflected in these comments:

> [consider] feedback from solicitors
>
> sometimes informed by client feedback
>
> [the] supervisor rates the students' communication skills
>
> [the] academic supervisor does not assess these qualities. A way to do so would be to measure whether a student listens to the client, [noting] whether they responded to the client's questions, [and] whether they showed empathy.[9]

---

8   These techniques and concepts are edited and paraphrased from recorded responses to the regional surveys. See footnote 7.
9   See footnote 7.

The general state of awareness of the need for explicit assessment criteria for each identified learning outcome appears highly variable, ranging from the sophisticated, in highly organised clinics, to minimalist or non-existent in those with less history, less funding and fewer connections to the law school. The following main themes of *Best Practices* relating to clinical assessment are a part of the remedy for those deficiencies.

Preliminary statement

Clinical legal education courses offered by law schools can and should be assessed. This can be done in many ways including, where appropriate, overall clinic performance and performance of specific tasks within particular clients' cases, essays on points of law arising in clinic cases, reflective journals, the quality of court advocacy on behalf of clients, observation of students' performance in common simulated scenarios based on prior cases, the quality of law reform submissions and *vivas* based on the content of much of this previously submitted work.[10] Clinics can support students to achieve deep and active learning through the timely provision of feedback to them. Clinical assessment is most helpful when provided in a constructive manner, in close proximity to the actions of the students.

After considering the results of our survey, we determined that best practice requires the alignment of assessment tasks with identified learning outcomes, and the use of both formative (developmental) and summative (concluding) assessment. Considering the strength of views on the issue, we also concluded that assessment could be conducted on either a graded or pass/fail basis, providing that both approaches offer detailed summative and written feedback. We also thought it important to avoid standardising algorithms and to ensure that final mark moderation occurs through peer supervisor discussion.

---

10   See, generally, R Grimes and J Gibbons, 'Assessing experiential learning – us, them and the others' (2016) 23(1) *International Journal of Clinical Legal Education* 107–36.

Literature on assessment purposes and techniques

Our consideration of the link between best practice and what actually happens in clinics has also been influenced by the writing of many scholars in Australia and overseas. Their views, summarised in the following section, have allowed us to be confident that recommended best practices for assessment are internally consistent, pedagogically sound, and reasonably achievable.

In this section, we discuss scholarship dealing with several important issues in clinical assessment. Scholars' general concerns around assessment issues are numerous and varied. The best place to begin, as we discussed in Chapter 4, is with the impact of Stuckey's proper insistence on aligning assessment with learning outcomes. This is followed by the debate about grading versus pass/fail, then by discussion of the pressure to standardise clinical assessment, formative and summative assessment in clinics, and how and what to assess in clinical performance.

Each of these issues has implications for best practice, although not all are on law schools' 'must discuss' list.

A well-established United States clinician, Anthony Amsterdam, sums up the distinction between 'conventional' or academic teaching and clinical teaching in this way: 'The academic teacher seeks to enrich understanding of the general by deriving abstract principles from the particular; the clinician seeks to enrich understanding of the general by refining a capacity to discern the full context of the particular.'[11]

This distinction is commendable, although today many academic teachers and clinicians would say they use both approaches. Clinicians often help their students to generalise from their clients' cases, just as conventional teachers increasingly look for and provide a 'real world' context in explaining particular principles. But for both conventional teachers and clinicians, refining students' capacity to discern 'the full context' is no small task, particularly when it comes to assessing the depth of their understanding of the real world. Clinical teaching may well make it easier to investigate more 'depth' in issues and cases than is possible in classrooms with case reports, but the assessment of that depth of knowledge, in all

---

11   AA Amsterdam, 'Telling Stories and Stones about Them' (1994) 1 *Clinical Law Review* 9, 39.

the colour and shade of context, is complex. Though many have reflected on assessment, our research shows that clinicians themselves are uncertain about what can be clinically assessed, how best to do it and, in particular, whether graded assessments are legitimate in a clinical setting. There are few who can cut through that haze, but one of those is Roy Stuckey.

Best practices in United States legal education: Grading beyond pass/fail

Although Stuckey has focused on the United States' approach to legal education,[12] his often critical observations are highly relevant to other systems of legal education.

Stuckey is dismissive of grading in the context of first-year United States students' law courses,[13] and is also clear about the deficiencies of much clinical grading in the United States:

> In many in-house clinics and externships, grades are based mostly on the subjective opinion of one teacher who supervises the students' work. Grades in these courses tend to reflect an appraisal of students' overall performance as lawyers, not necessarily what they learned or how their abilities developed during the course. When written criteria are given to students, they tend to be checklists that cover the entire spectrum of lawyering activities without any descriptions of different levels of proficiency.

> Virtually no experiential education courses give written tests or otherwise try to find out if students are acquiring the knowledge and understandings that the courses purport to teach. Items that could be clearly subjected to more objective testing include students' understanding of theories of practice or particular aspects of law, procedure, ethics and professionalism. A student's understanding of many aspects of law practice as well as their lifelong learning skills could also be assessed, for example, by asking them to analyze recordings or transcripts of lawyers' performances. Serious efforts to assess student learning in experiential learning courses are not being made on any large scale.[14]

---

12   Roy Stuckey and others, *Best Practices in Legal Education: A Vision and a Road Map* (2007) Clinical Legal Education Association. Stuckey was the principal author, but not the only contributor to this influential work. See also Roy Stuckey, 'Can We Assess What We Purport to Teach in Clinical Law Courses' (2006) 9 *International Journal of Clinical Legal Education* 177 (cited hereafter as Stuckey (2006)).

13   Roy Stuckey and others, cited at footnote 12, 236.

14   Roy Stuckey and others, cited at footnote 12, 238–39.

In Australian clinics, it is common for students to have several supervisors for different aspects of their clinical experience. So it is not possible to apply United States practice to Australia uncritically, but the warning about one-dimensional and limited assessment practices is still relevant. Discussion about the dimensions of assessment can become very energetic. In Australia there is little contest around whether to assess students at all (decided, it seems by default, in the affirmative), but there has been a longstanding debate (and divergent practice) about whether students' performance should be graded beyond the initial classifications of fail or pass. Simon Rice has written perhaps the most impassioned and articulate article in Australian clinical legal education, in which he has argued for pass/fail grades only,[15] and that approach continues at the clinical courses run through Kingsford Legal Centre and some of the other clinical courses in the University of New South Wales (UNSW) Faculty of Law. But, to date, only a few other law schools have followed this course of action and, with the passage of time and the demands of students for competitive advantage over their peers, it is unlikely that pass/fail assessment will gain the allegiance of a majority of law schools. Clinicians need support for their programs from their more 'conventional' teaching colleagues, and a decision to move to pass/fail assessment might risk that support.

Rice's views are, however, influential, and led us to take an open position on the merits of grading clinical performance. He regards assessment as important, but not grades:

> On recognising effort, teachers will often want to acknowledge a student's efforts, or to confirm a student's lack of effort, and would feel frustrated if not able to. This does not, of itself, lead to a subject being graded. Grading is only one, and not a necessary, means of a teacher's expressing encouragement or concern. Grading is a simple and simplistic mechanism. I suspect that it is attractive to teachers precisely because it is unspecific and impersonal.[16]

---

15 Simon Rice, 'Assessing – But Not Grading – Clinical Legal Education' (2007) Working Paper No 2007–16, Macquarie University; available at SSRN: perma.cc/QR7X-7KQL.
16 Simon Rice, cited at footnote 15.

Rice does not deny the importance that students themselves place on grading,[17] but considers that clinics offer their own attraction and students do not require grades in order to enrol in a clinic.[18] He asserts that what is needed and is sufficient in clinical assessment is a calculation as to whether student awareness has been achieved or not. If students reach adequate awareness, then they should pass:

> my learning objective of the study of justice, for which I choose clinical method … This learning objective, I concede, can be measured. In fact it might usefully be measured if the goal is a student's attainment of an awareness they did previously not have. What might be best is a before and after snapshot of understandings and awareness, to confirm the occurrence of change, and hence the achievement of the learning goal. But that is to assess, not to grade.[19]

The difficulty in this formulation is that students' awareness is of a layered, multifaceted and context-rich quality. It may be possible to say that a student has reached sufficient awareness to pass a clinical course, but that judgment does not deny or necessarily rule out lower and higher levels of awareness. There is debate in some areas of experiential legal education as to whether it is possible to go beyond pass/fail assessment. For example, in relation to the acquisition of skills, practical legal training (PLT) providers have commented that pass/fail is all that can be asserted. Their argument is that, in a PLT environment at least, 'you can't grade practical training at say 85% because the 15% is the risk zone and you can't advise clients with a specified % of risk. The advice is either competent or not – [practising lawyers] must service the client and the client's needs'.[20]

It must be emphasised, however, that sufficiency and insufficiency are also, logically understood, themselves grades. To assess anything as adequate (a pass) or inadequate (a fail) involves determining one of two grades. And if it is necessary to make that choice, then is this not grading?

---

17 Stacy Brustin and David Chavkin, 'Testing the Grades: Evaluating Grading Models in Clinical Legal Education' (1997) 3 *Clinical Law Review* 299, 316; Simon Rice, cited at footnote 15, 2: 'In 1991, in a Kingsford Legal Centre Student Survey almost 60% of graduates of the clinic preferred pass/fail to graded assessment.'

18 Simon Rice, cited at footnote 15, 2: 'The Brustin and Chavkin research, at 313, showed that "the majority of students would have registered for clinic regardless of whether performance was graded on a pass fail basis"', referring to Stacy Brustin and David Chavkin, cited at footnote 17, 312–13.

19 Simon Rice, cited at footnote 15, 9.

20 Comment made at ALTC Project Stakeholder Meeting, Melbourne, December 2011. However, PLT providers would concede that other areas of experiential legal education, e.g. reflective journalling, could be graded.

But this issue of students' awareness or confusion is Rice's derivative, not primary, point. He is very clear, echoing Stuckey and many other legal educators, that learning outcomes must be reflected in assessment—and his preferred primary clinical learning outcome is the achievement of a level of awareness of justice and injustice.[21] From that perspective, Rice is making an argument for assessment-without-grading since, if clinical legal education is concerned to focus on justice and process ('from instrumentation to empowerment'), then it must avoid a vision of law and lawyering—including competitive grades—that still dominates conventional classroom instruction.[22]

However, it is difficult to see anything offensive in recognising that awareness involves shades of grey rather than only black or white. The real world of justice and injustice is not one of black and white—grey is everywhere. For example, it is difficult to point out to a student exactly how their comprehension of the justice process is mixed or in what precise way their understanding of the effect of poverty on client recidivism is patchy, but these are common situations where students' awareness may be adequate but not superior. Setting out where improvements are desirable is a formative responsibility of clinical supervision and it is perhaps a bit churlish not to recognise, at the end of the semester, students' differing progress towards higher states of awareness.

Rice also makes another important point: it should be enough for adequate clinical achievement that a student is in effect 'on the move', since when can anyone of us be said to have sufficiently 'arrived'?

> The language of the learning goal is of process, not result, of moving, not of having arrived. The goal is not the attainment of a measurable degree of knowledge of theories of justice, it is the students' [degree of] internalising of the fact of power, their sense that they are becoming a part of a system whose currency is power, their awareness of their place in law, and their potential as lawyers.[23]

In this quotation the parenthesised 'degree of' is added to beg the quantum question. Rice is content to say that such 'internalising' is a binary state. In practice, it is doubtful whether students can identify such a neat state,

---

21   As required in Threshold Learning Outcomes 1(c) and 2(c). See Council of Australian Law Deans, *Learning and Teaching Academic Standards Statement, December 2010, Threshold Learning Outcomes for the LLB degree*, at perma.cc/BY6N-6SRF. .
22   Simon Rice, cited at footnote 15, 7–8.
23   Simon Rice, cited at footnote 15, 10.

though all experienced clinicians are required to decide if they think that sufficient student internalising has occurred. The point is that, if capable of deciding whether an initial 'pass grade' of internalising has been achieved, clinicians can go on to decide if deeper internalising has also occurred, and award higher grades. Put this way, goals can address both process and results. And if that is possible, and appropriate propositional criteria are developed that reflect learning outcomes accommodating deeper levels of awareness or internalising, then why should that not be fostered?

Fundamentally, Rice is not convinced that clinicians should grade beyond pass/fail, even if they can do so at a technical level, because the necessary level of supervisor intrusion is essentially immoral:

> Grading cannot respect the internal and personal nature of the learning we are bringing to the students. The clinical experience makes demands of their emotional intelligence and they will respond to it in different ways and to different degrees. Because there is difference does not mean the difference should be measured. It is simply difference. It is not better or worse.[24]

There may be no satisfactory answer to this charge of intrusion and, if so, group agnosticism on the merit of grading beyond pass/fail is appropriate. But clinical supervisors within the one clinic must adopt the same approach and, ideally, they will support that approach intellectually and emotionally.

International practice is also relevant. Hyams has surveyed such practices and ultimately supports grading beyond pass/fail:

> It has also been argued that clinics are intended to be safe environments for students to experiment, satisfy curiosity and explore their own values, assumptions and motivations. [citation omitted] Grading students may interfere with the non-judgmental environment, [citation omitted] inhibiting students' desire to explore and test themselves for fear of 'getting it wrong' and consequently losing marks. Further, it may be an additional source of stress and preoccupation for students in an already stressful environment. [citation omitted]

> Alternatively, grading may have the opposite effect on students – it can have a motivational effect and lead to a higher level of professionalism. Grades also provide the opportunity to acknowledge the time, effort and

---

24   Simon Rice, cited at footnote 15, 13.

labour that students contribute to their clinical work. Finally, there is always the 'external' issue of the academic credibility of the clinic. Grading makes a statement to both the students and the faculty that clinic has as much academic rigour as other 'black letter law' units and students will be subjected to the same exacting regime as their other units of study. [citation omitted]

Brustin and Chavkin's rigorous investigation led them to conclude that there are 'tangible benefits' to grade students in clinical courses which, they believed, may improve the pedagogical process and augment service delivery to clients. [citation omitted][25]

Since other academics tend to have a simplistic and sometimes sceptical (perhaps cynical) view of clinic assessment, defensible assessment has become an important symbol of clinic credibility within the wider law school. That political dimension ought not to be forgotten.

As Stuckey reminds us, however, the decision as to whether higher grades are appropriate must, in the end, come back to a clinic's agreed learning outcomes.[26] And he is notable for his insistence on defining outcomes well in advance of any student commencement in a clinic. This pre-definition task includes being very clear about the minutiae of the criteria to be used to measure adequate and higher levels of achievement, not just to limit the potential for vaguely defined grading but fundamentally to make self-learning possible and empowering:

We can improve the quality of our assessments by following the approach used in other disciplines of developing and disclosing criteria-referenced assessments. Criteria-referenced assessments rely on detailed, explicit criteria that identify the abilities students should be demonstrating (for example, applying and distinguishing cases) and the bases on which the instructor will distinguish among excellent, good, competent, or incompetent performances [citation omitted] ... The use of criteria minimizes the risk of unreliability in assigning grades.[27]

Stuckey might prefer that clinical assessment were pass/fail only, and his arguments make it clear that this is not just because the dominant objective of United States legal education is to prepare students for a career

---

25   Ross Hyams, 'Student assessment in the clinical environment – what can we learn from the US experience?' (2006) 9 *International Journal of Clinical Legal Education* 77, 88.
26   Stuckey (2006), cited at footnote 12, 13, citing Judith Wegner, 'Thinking Like a Lawyer About Law School Assessment' (Draft 2003, 55; unpublished manuscript on file with Roy Stuckey).
27   Roy Stuckey and others, cited at footnote 12, 244.

in private legal practice where formal grades of law school achievement become professionally less important than word-of-mouth reputation. But he realises that grading is what happens in law schools and proposes ways and means to improve its reliability and validity:

> The use of clear criteria helps students understand what is expected of them as well as why they receive the grades they receive. Even more importantly, it increases the reliability of the teacher's assessment by tethering the assessment to explicit criteria rather than the instructor's gestalt sense of the correct answer or performance. The criteria should be explained to students long before the students undergo an assessment. This enhances learning and encourages students to become reflective, empowered, self-regulated learners.[28]

Formative and summative assessment in clinics

Much is now made of the distinction between formative and summative assessment in all education. Legal education is no exception. But in clinical contexts the distinction may be less important to the extent that formative and summative assessment can blend into each other, except for the purpose of developing detailed criteria for assessment. A United Kingdom legal educator observes that:

> The difference between formative and summative assessment is often an area of concern for law teachers. The essence of *formative assessment* is that undertaking the assessment constitutes a learning experience in its own right. Writing an essay or undertaking a class presentation, for example, can be valuable formative activities as a means of enhancing substantive knowledge as well as for developing research, communication, intellectual and organisational skills. Formative assessment is not often included in the formal grading of work, and indeed many believe that it should not be.

---

28   Roy Stuckey and others, cited at footnote 12, 245. Stuckey refers to and approves of Sophie Sparrow, 'Describing the Ball: Improve Teaching by Using Rubrics – Explicit Grading Criteria' (2004) *Michigan State Law Review* 1, 28–29. See also, generally, Adrian Evans and Clark Cunningham, 'Speciality Certification as an Incentive for Increased Professionalism: Lessons from Other Disciplines and Countries' (2003) 54(4) *South Carolina Law Review* 987–1009.

In contrast, *summative assessment* is not traditionally regarded as having any intrinsic learning value. It is usually undertaken at the end of a period of learning in order to generate a grade that reflects the student's performance. The traditional unseen end of module examination is often presented as a typical form of summative assessment.[29]

Clinical assessment 'events' tend to be more diverse and more frequent than assessments in conventional law teaching. In live client clinics they range from the fairly mechanical examination of file maintenance standards (that is, the degree to which client instructions are comprehensibly and accurately recorded, the comprehension, legibility and detail of file notes, the evidence of relevant legal research, the grammatical quality of letters, briefs and written advocacy), to more specific measures associated with the quality of client interviewing and representation (for example, client and fellow supervisor feedback, observation of test interviews, observations of interpersonal skills, portfolios of written case reports and the outcomes of hearings) and, finally (as we discussed in more detail in Chapter 7), to supervisors' overall judgments about the quality of the *process* of students' self-reflection in their learning journals. As we strongly emphasised in Chapter 7, assessment of reflection for this limited purpose is justified. Less tangible qualities, such as clinic attendance, participation, improvement and effort, are also important in these final judgments. Each of these categories of assessment should be considered for both formative and summative purposes.[30]

In externships, some or all of these criteria are also available and, in simulated clinical experiences, it is also possible to standardise formative assessments with strictly comparable case scenarios and narrowly defined instructions to students as to expected performances.

In most cases, clinicians wish to assess both students' developmental learning process and the work they actually create, but it is important for all the above reasons to be clear about the distinction. Different measures can be better for different objectives: journals are popular for assessing

---

29   Rob East, cited without further information in JP Ogilvy with Karen Czapanskiy, *Clinical Legal Education: An Annotated Bibliography* (2001), at digitalcommons.law.umaryland.edu/fac_pubs/268.
30   Useful discussions of assessment issues appear in, e.g. Hugh Brayne, Nigel Duncan and Richard Grimes, *Clinical Legal Education: Active Learning in Your Law School* (1998) Blackstone Press; Jerry R Foxhoven, 'Beyond Grading: Assessing Student Readiness to Practice Law' (2009) 16 *Clinical Law Review* 335; Karen Barton, Clark D Cunningham, Gregory Todd Jones and Paul Maharg, 'Valueing What Clients Think: Standardised Clients and the Assessment of Communicative Competence' (2006–07) 13 *Clinical Law Review* 1.

learning development, and case outcomes obviously allow some judgments about overall performance, but the interaction between these methods is also instructive and can allow assessment of the capacity to reflect. For example, a student who obtains a reduced penalty in a lower court criminal case by declining to remind a magistrate of a known prior conviction might well claim a 'successful' outcome, but if their journal entry on the same case contains no awareness that they have been reflecting on any implicit deception of the court process—that is, they do not appear to reflect on whether it is appropriate or justified to rely on the silence of the prosecution in such cases—then it might be considered that their understanding of the reflection process is itself underdeveloped. Comparing the apparent insights of different assessment approaches improves the definition and precision of each individual measure.

Assessing student formation can be addressed through some forms of feedback, providing clinicians are clear with students in advance as to what learning outcomes are at stake and how they will be assessed.[31] Feedback is discussed carefully in Chapter 6 in relation to supervision, but it is important to recognise that it cannot be realistically offered or accepted for assessment purposes unless these outcomes are clear to everyone at the start of a clinical experience.

Similarly, feedback works best as an assessment tool when accompanied and supported by students undertaking a variety of self-assessment exercises,[32] because self-assessment often allows both supervisor and student to quickly get to the heart of persistent gaps between desired outcomes and actual achievements. These exercises are most useful when they contain detailed opportunities not only to discuss a particular case file outcome, but also to talk about how the result was achieved (for example, the process used to research the law in relation to that case, as well as the case result).[33]

---

31 David J Nicol and Debra Macfarlane-Dick, 'Formative Assessment and Self-Regulated Learning: A Model and Seven Principles of Good Feedback Practice' (2006) 31 *Studies in Higher Education* 199, 200.

32 Anthony Niedwiecki, 'Teaching for Lifelong Learning: Improving the Metacognitive Skills of Law Students through More Effective Formative Assessment Techniques' (2012) 40 *Capital University Law Review* 149, 187–90.

33 Anthony Niedwiecki, cited at footnote 32, 181.

After grading

Pressure to standardise clinical assessment

It is now common practice in university assessment regimes to standardise results so that the relative performance of a particular cohort of students can be measured in a steadily ascending and descending two-dimensional gradient (or 'bell curve' or grading bands), with relatively few 'fails', a considerable number of modest 'passes' and 'credits' (the top of the bell or in the highest band) and relatively few very high grades. The standardising process is intended to smooth out anomalous high and low results that can be attributed to assessment error.

Standardising is achieved by applying an algorithm (an equation) to a set of results and modifying each result to a greater or lesser extent to fit the institutional expectation as to how many students in an average cohort should fail, pass, pass very well and achieve distinction.

The exact dimensions of each bell curve are very much the result of a policy decision by the law school and to that extent are artificial. However, they still represent well-intentioned attempts to limit inherent inaccuracies in conventional assessment of particular courses, particularly when that assessment is restricted to relatively few and crude measures of performance where teachers and students have comparatively little personal interaction.

On occasion, law schools can decide on a one-size-fits-all approach and, where the assessment regime is greater than pass/fail, apply general course algorithms to clinical courses. This is not a good idea, for several reasons. First, the algorithms applied to standardise assessment are commonly based on a mathematical premise that there will be a minimum number of students in each cohort, usually at least 50 and preferably many more. This is an application of the general statistical truth that the bigger the sample, the more reliable the analysis. If the cohort is too small, then the mathematics of the algorithm will demand too big an alteration in the marks of both very poorly performing and very strongly performing students. In other words, the ends of the bell curve will be distorted so that, instead of a bell shape, the gradient can tend to look much more like a rectangle, with the possibility of fewer fails and fewer high marks. Since most clinical courses tend to have many fewer than 50 students in any one cohort, an algorithm can result in unfair final assessment.

Secondly, clinical method is a premier method of learning and teaching. It is intensive, with frequent one-on-one teacher/student interaction. Much clinical work by nature engages students' hearts and minds in the problems of their clients, triggering a personal desire to perform. Typically, this personal element translates into significantly higher performance and the wider community notices them and their law school. Law schools increasingly see good clinics as important for their overall reputation and expect their students will achieve a great deal in a relatively short period of time. They invest in that expectation by providing a high staff–student ratio, and they expect their clinical students to work in and excel in highly collaborative professional environments. In that preparation-for-work team culture, another essential bell curve premise—that of highly individualised performance—is misplaced. A clinical bell curve embodies a contradiction, for this reason.

Thirdly—and whether or not the particular algorithm in a clinical course is unfair or misconceived—clinical students' complaints about the substantial differences between their 'raw' mark and their lower standardised mark—which can amount to 10 to 12 marks—can quickly snowball into systemic criticisms of the course. Since clinical courses often contain highly motivated, self-selecting students who receive much personal and highly targeted formative assessment through close supervision, the opportunities for student improvement and performance success are substantial. In a real sense, clinics with close supervision and mentoring arrangements could be said to be engaged in continuing assessment. High raw marks are common, and no law school can easily justify a substantial reduction in marks and be perceived by students to be competent and caring of students' experiences.

Fourthly, clinical courses—as is the case with many electives—are courses where students do better because they are choosing what to study. A bell curve does not recognise this.

Fifthly, and more fundamentally, clinical assessment is perhaps the most thorough and personal process that a law student will ever encounter. It is profoundly formative, personal and individual and contains no conceptual assessment gap requiring the generalised 'rescue remedy' of an algorithm. Clinical assessment tends to be accurate because, on average, each student is well known to their teachers.

Strengthening formation—recognising metacognition

While student reflection contributes to the wider concept of formation, the assessment of that formation requires some specific discussion, particularly if clinicians are to help students shift their focus during a clinical semester from producing a specific activity (for example, a brief to counsel, advocacy letter or written negotiation strategy) towards the process of their own current and future learning.

The objective here is to assess the degree or otherwise of students' growing understanding of their most effective learning process—that is, their 'metacognition' of how they learn best now and how they will learn best once in paid employment. Essentially, this is a reflective activity (see Chapter 7). The understanding and embedding of metacognitive awareness is emphasised by both Stuckey's *Best Practices*[34] and the Carnegie Report[35] as critically important to revitalising legal education in general. It is highly significant for legal education as a whole that clinical methods are tailor-made to achieve the best in students' metacognition.[36] Hyams observes that:

> Self-reflection is a large part of the focus of clinical pedagogy in the US and is a key aspect of the teaching in various US clinics ... The skill of self-reflection is often implicit in clinic work and is used by clinicians to assist students with their metacognitive abilities. By asking a student: 'How would you go about finding the resolution to this dispute? What might be the appropriate approach?' and 'How would you do this differently next time?', we are achieving a dual purpose: 1. modelling a lawyering practice which is careful and reflective, and 2. providing tools for improving metacognition (that is, problem solving) skills.[37]

Formative assessment is the best way, and possibly the only cost-effective way, to tackle that objective within clinics. Niedwiecki states it simply: 'Essentially, the goal of formative assessment should be to move legal education away from a focus on *an end product*—a memorandum, motion, negotiation, oral argument, etc.—to the underlying *process* of developing these products.'[38]

---

34   Roy Stuckey and others, cited at footnote 12, 192.
35   William Sullivan, Anne Colby, Judith Welch Wegner, Lloyd Bond and Lee S Shulman, *Educating Lawyers: Preparation for the Profession of Law* (2007) Jossey Bass (the Carnegie Report), 107.
36   Ross Hyams, cited at footnote 25, 83.
37   Ross Hyams, cited at footnote 25, 83.
38   Anthony Niedwiecki, cited at footnote 32, 152 (emphasis in original).

Metacognition is not difficult to grasp. Many students instinctively understand what is meant by it once they have examples in front of them. It includes basic areas of self-knowledge, for example, knowing what sort of physical environment (quiet/noisy, light/dark, close to others/separate from others) is best for an individual lawyer when trying to comprehend new written material. It also covers more cerebral issues such as visual *versus* text-based learning preferences and knowing when to revise and how to self-test one's own comprehension. Niedwiecki provides this description:

> Essentially, metacognition is the ability to regulate and control one's learning. There are many definitions of metacognition, but … put simply, it is the process of 'thinking about thinking' and the ability to self-regulate one's learning with the goal of transferring learned skills to new situations. There are many metacognitive skills that everyone employs in the learning process: monitoring one's reading comprehension, evaluating one's process of learning, understanding the influence of outside stimuli on one's learning, and knowing when one lacks motivation, just to name a few.

> … Metacognition also can be described as the internal voice people hear when they are engaged in the learning process – the voice that will tell them what they have to do to accomplish a task, what they already know, what they do not know, how to match their previous learning to the new situation, when they do not understand what they are reading or learning, and how to evaluate their learning. It is this internal reflection and conscious control of the learning process that goes to the heart of metacognition.[39]

Conclusion

In the current stringent financial climate, conscious decisions to link clinical assessment regimes to the learning outcomes of each clinic can only strengthen their graduates' experience and hence the reputation of each clinic. In most law schools it should not be difficult to strengthen and realign any clinical assessment regimes that do not approach best practice. But assessment of students' performance and development is not the only dimension to clinical assessment.

---

39   Anthony Niedwiecki, cited at footnote 32, 155–57.

It will also be necessary in time to assess clinical programs as a whole. Evans and Hyams have already jumped the boundary fence to some degree and made a case for periodic review and assessment of each clinic.[40] The potential positive flow-on effect to the particular law school is already well established. Law schools' investment in coming to grips with assessment pedagogy and then applying it consistently, not just to students' efforts but to their entire programs, is therefore an investment in the reputation and viability of the law school itself.

---

40   See Adrian Evans and Ross Hyams, 'Independent Evaluations of Clinical Legal Education Programs: Appropriate Objectives and Processes in an Australian Setting' (2008) 17 *Griffith Law Review* 52. See also Adrian Evans, 'Normative Attractions to Law and their Recipe for Accountability and Self-Assessment of Justice Education' in Frank Bloch (ed), *The Global Clinical Movement: Educating Lawyers for Social Justice* (2011) Oxford University Press, Chapter 24, which provides a possible metric for a law school to self-assess its effectiveness in delivering justice (including clinical legal) education.

9

Resourcing live client clinics

Introduction

In this chapter, we rely on the insights of respondents to the *Best Practices* survey to inform the discussion of various dimensions of clinical program resourcing. All are related to the distinctive politics of Australian law school funding. Best practices in clinical legal education programs are the main focus of this book, and we deal with the full range of clinical models. In Chapter 3 we discussed all the models but, unless otherwise made plain, 'clinic' in this chapter refers only to the live client learning setting, whether in-house or in an externship.

After discussing the directions identified by the survey and stakeholder input, we address the important role of strategic direction, on which the overall impact of a clinical program often depends. In a live client clinic of any sort, whether in-house or external, there is a profound need for clinic administrators with both strong interpersonal skills and a detailed capacity to manage money. But the core resources of an effective clinic are the clinical supervisors—the individual lawyers or cross-disciplinary supervisors who personally direct, guide and nurture law students through the maze of their own 'growth' and its interaction with the learning objectives.

Only when these central role descriptions are on track will the clinical program have any chance of making a profound difference to learning and, where it is provided, to service delivery. But infrastructure issues remain important. Adequate funding for clinical programs is a recurring headache for law school deans because of the demands of competing interest groups within law schools. Indeed, some law schools are still to be persuaded that superior legal education involves clinical integration in one way or another. There is also an obvious need to ensure that the clinical legal practice can operate to deliver both immediate and longer-term legal needs in the same way that any legal practice does—and this means all the compliance-related infrastructure of ethical systems, insurance, information technology (IT) resourcing and the like.

In respect of infrastructure (in effect, the funding of the clinic), *Best Practices* gives attention to insurance, training, IT/library access, administrative and locum support and the need to formalise the relationships between any external agency and the law school in relation to the full range of issues arising from clinical service delivery.

Apart from Giddings' recent major work on clinical sustainability,[1] there is very little other Australian scholarship on clinical quality and accountability.[2] Clinical funding remains tenuous. While almost all universities think they need a law school regardless of its cost, not all law schools see their clinical programs as indispensable. In this climate, the critical need for clinical leadership can never be underestimated, especially leadership that is emotionally and tactically sensitive to the political struggles inside law schools.

In the survey responses, infrastructure concerns almost always concentrated on the cost of running a program, and the slightly anxious desire to see that adequate professional indemnity and other insurances were fully provided by each law school. The Regional Reports make it clear that clinical programs consider their funding to be less than ideal in one way or another. These include the differences in salaries for different types of supervisors, inadequate funds for IT equipment and cramped physical conditions, even among those apparently successful clinical sites. Few respondents engaged in detailed reflection on sustainability concerns,

---

1   Jeff Giddings, *Promoting Justice Through Clinical Legal Education* (2013) Justice Press, Chapter 5.
2   However, see Hugh Brayne and Adrian Evans, 'Quality-Lite for Clinics: Appropriate Accountability Within "Live-Client" Clinical Legal Education' (2004) 6(1) *International Journal of Clinical Legal Education* 149; Adrian Evans and Ross Hyams, 'Independent Evaluations of Clinical Legal Education Programs: Appropriate Objectives and Processes in an Australian Setting' (2008) 17(1) *Griffith Law Review* 52.

but the impacts of periodic changes in law school leadership, external agency needs, required service delivery reviews and the uncertainties of government legal aid funding were a common underlying reality.

Clinic supervisors

Resourcing clinical legal education appropriately is not just a matter of money. It is also a question of recruiting and retaining staff with appropriate values, attitudes, skills and energy. To go even further, real success in resourcing consists in recruiting 'good' leaders, clinic administrators and supervisors. The statement in *Best Practices* on resourcing is divided into two categories, 'Staff' and 'Infrastructure', in order to emphasise that staffing and individuals' supervision qualities are not just a subsection of infrastructure needs. As we say there: 'The effectiveness of a clinic will depend on the strength and sensitivity of the supervision provided. Clinical supervisors require a combination of legal practice backgrounds, a concern for improving access to justice and a deep interest in student learning.'[3]

Supervisors are the main resource of a good clinical program and the main challenge. Resourcing these clinics properly requires longevity in program leadership, as well as leaders' personal acceptance of the need for succession planning. These are not contradictory qualities: the best clinics are those that have people in leadership who have the personal judgment and maturity to comprehend their interrelated nature. Often the sustainable, large and well-regarded clinical program is identified not just in its outputs—that is, in its teaching reputation, law reform impacts, delivery of services and attraction of funding—but in the broader personal qualities of its key staff. Among clinical supervisors who hold conventional academic positions, a key indicator of strength and productivity can also be the impact of their writing. *Best Practices*, as it relates to clinical supervisors, therefore responds not only to the depth and complexity of their required personal attributes, but also to their teaching status as supervisors (see Chapter 6 on supervision), equating them as far as possible to law school peers in their pay and conditions, their access to training and their relative autonomy. It is particularly important to

---

3   Adrian Evans, Anna Cody, Anna Copeland, Jeff Giddings, Mary Anne Noone, Simon Rice and Ebony Booth, *Best Practices: Australian Clinical Legal Education* (2013) Government of Australia, Office of Learning and Teaching, 63, at perma.cc/2J6E-ZMQX.

recognise the long hours and intensive nature of supervision—having regard to any research and publication expectations—by controlling the number of students for which each supervisor is responsible.

A well-established clinic, particularly one in an external agency such as a community legal centre, may have an overall director and a site director, as well as an administrator and clinical supervisors. But it is probably more common, especially in an externship program, to find one or two lawyers with mixed responsibilities—partly for their own caseload and partly for the supervision of students. Smaller programs may get by with just one lawyer/supervisor and a part-time administrator at a single site. In our regional surveys, many views were expressed by respondents about the range of qualities needed by clinical supervisors.[4] Most comments were consistent in their listing of a demanding range of personal and professional skills and attributes. However, there were some inconsistencies.

A number of respondents thought 'credentials' are necessary, so that supervisors should have postgraduate qualifications in teaching.[5] A few respondents were wary of scaring off potential supervisors, whom they see as hard to attract into the field, and these respondents thought that supervisors do not have to be 'teachers', as long as they are good mentors.[6] The difference may be minor, but the general emphasis in United States clinics on proficient supervisors as educators and not just as practitioners—together with Australian national efforts to improve the quality of all teaching at all levels—may mean that postgraduate teaching qualifications will become a precondition to identifying good clinicians as time goes by.

Perhaps unconsciously reflecting this awareness, many respondents held the view that clinical supervisors are serious educators and need to be paid at the same level as 'conventional' teaching colleagues, with the same opportunities for career advancement. It is, however, unlikely that equal status will occur without comparable ongoing education requirements. Only a few respondents seem to be aware that the extensive wish list for

---

4   Adrian Evans and others, cited at footnote 3; and refer to *Identifying Current Practices in Clinical Legal Education*, Regional Reports, cited in Chapter 1 at footnote 6. Section E of each Regional Report deals with clinical staffing issues.

5   Adrian Evans and others, cited at footnote 3; *Identifying Current Practices in Clinical Legal Education, Regional Report: Victoria and Tasmania*, Section E, at perma.cc/J562-X6GU.

6   Adrian Evans and others, cited at footnote 3; *Identifying Current Practices in Clinical Legal Education, Regional Report: Victoria and Tasmania*, Section E, at perma.cc/J562-X6GU.

good supervision is related to cost and funding, and that it could affect financial sustainability to compare salaries paid to supervisors with those paid to the comparatively few supervisors who also hold formal academic appointments in the relevant law schools.

In the survey responses the attributes of clinic leaders or directors were not generally commented on, but one respondent considered people in these roles need at least five years post-admission experience, with management experience and the capacity to run a legal practice. The following list of desirable qualities for supervisors (regardless of the type of clinic) is a synthesis of respondents' views across all the regions surveyed:

- Have a practising certificate, current practical experience and a good working knowledge of the law.
- Have excellent lawyering skills ('good natural communication and supervision skills and experience').
- Have creativity, empathy and preference for use of plain, clear language.
- Have patience, enthusiasm, compassion, respect for difference and diversity and the maturity to be able to critique work without humiliating students.
- Have the ability to balance stakeholders' expectations, so that those who are unrealistic are restrained appropriately.
- Have good client communication skills (emotional intelligence) and the ability to discuss what they are doing and why with both clients as individuals and students as individuals.
- Like people and be interested in people's problems; must like students and young people and have a sense of humour.
- Know how to teach—have an understanding of reflective practice in teaching and learning, measured by achievement of recognised training in postgraduate teaching (for example, a formal teaching qualification such as a Graduate Certificate of Higher Education), or be trained in professional supervision and/or adult education for new staff.
- Be aware of the tensions between getting to know students and having to assess them and between being organised and being able to prioritise supervision within other responsibilities.
- Have a social justice focus and perspective—be able to expose students to the idea of making the law more just and fair; to influence their practice of law in the future.
- Have ethical awareness.

- Have sufficient administrative skills (to operate in a quality accountable learning/service delivery site).
- Have an awareness of the clinical and related literature, covering overall clinical objectives, teaching technique, policy debates, law reform and critical evaluation.

Clinic program directors

Sometimes, law school leaders ask if clinical program directors[7]—those who oversee a whole program rather than just a single clinic—are actually needed. The question is often perceived by clinically aware academic staff as unfortunate, but it is understandable because of a perception inside law schools that teaching clinic is like any other teaching allocation and entails no additional roles or responsibilities. Perhaps, if clinical and conventional teaching methods were so well integrated that law academics could not distinguish them, it would be appropriate to ask if clinical direction is needed. In that world all substantive legal concepts would be finding expression in law schools helping to resolve the current problems of people, corporations and non-government organisations. But that is not the case and, as we discussed in Chapter 2, is unlikely while Australian law schools are funded at the lowest Commonwealth band for their LLB courses.[8] In the meantime, there is a struggle going on for better teaching integration of this nature, for external government and philanthropic funding of clinic to supplement law school sources, and for the law-in-context impacts that distinguish good clinical method.

Of course, there are program directors who lead single clinics and those who oversee multiple clinics, depending on the history and circumstances of the law school. But the key issue remains one of clinical leadership, which is something more than management or administration.

---

7   The term 'program director' is generic. There is a considerable variation. For example, at Monash University, the term is 'Director of Legal Practice Programs', while at Griffith University, there is a 'Director of Professionalism'.

8   JD degrees are another matter of course, since they are funded by students and often make money for law schools, in the sense that they effectively subsidise the teaching of LLB students.

What is involved in clinical leadership?

A broad educational and professional perspective is needed for the best in clinical leadership. A clinical director must have a real interest in constant liaison with law school senior leadership, seeking opportunities to achieve advances for the program as a whole. This connectivity is helped if their office is located close to those leaders so that they are 'in the loop': Kingsford Legal Centre, for example, is on the ground floor of the University of New South Wales (UNSW) law building. Correspondingly, clinic directors who may be located away from the main law school building or are obliged to report to CEOs of external agencies in which their clinics are located have a more difficult job in staying up to date with law school developments.

The capacity to lead is often witnessed in an ability to create and implement new clinics. But clinical leaders will often display many other attributes. While clinical supervisors without leadership responsibilities may not require an extensive range of skills beyond supervisory competence, that is not the case with clinical leadership.

With so much dependent on effective clinical direction, a prudent law school dean might consider using a search consultant to help recruit a new program director, and to utilise modern 360-degree analyses of potential appointees, in order to maximise the chances of a successful appointment.

Externship programs are by definition located inside agencies with their own governance arrangements and they may not engage in active casework where clients' money is transacted. But if the clinical program director is also the solicitor formally in charge of a clinic that does handle clients' money, then they will be required to hold a current, full practising certificate regardless of the Australian jurisdiction.[9] However, if the roles of program director and clinic director are separated (which is often the case in larger law schools), then it is only the clinic director—'on the ground' as it were and directly responsible for such clients' files—who needs to have the full certificate. For this reason, it cannot be essential for a clinical program director to have a background as a practising lawyer, though most applicants for such positions will have this experience.

---

9   A full practising certificate is usually described as one entitling the holder to operate a client trust account. See, generally, e.g. *Legal Profession Uniform Law Application Act 2014* (Vic), Schedule 1, Part 4.2.

Clinical supervisors ('clinicians')

As we emphasised in the introduction to this chapter, the core resource of any clinic is its staff and, among those staff, clinical supervisors perform the core function—supervision. It is essentially up to these lawyers to effectively communicate the complexities of supervision (see Chapter 6) to law students and to oversee their baptism into legal practice. Clinical supervisors have a critical role as student mentors and role models; and these attributes frame their quality as teachers, technicians and ethical, street-aware lawyers. There are few things as important to resourcing clinical legal education as the recruitment, selection and retention of appropriate clinical supervisors.

Of course, supervisors need to be eligible for current practising certificates, but there is a more fundamental list of criteria for those who will be able not just to practise law, but to teach that practice, to watch over those learning to do the same and to impart the socially conscious values that are integral to clinical methods.

Accordingly, good applicants for supervisory roles will be able to meet the following selection criteria:[10]

- Appropriate experience of legal practice.
- An understanding of the responsibilities of ethical legal practice, including an awareness of the pedagogical debates concerning competing legal ethical perspectives.
- The capacity to teach by example and encouragement, showing emotional intelligence.
- The willingness to trust students and to set reasonable boundaries around that trust so that they feel able to exercise appropriate client-related initiatives.
- An understanding of the distinction between normative and positivist theories of law (normative theory being that law must be understood in the context of its effects on justice; positivist theory being that the law simply 'is' and need not be further justified or examined, except for its likely capacity to provide loopholes for clients).

---

10   This list is based on a similar list in Adrian Evans, 'Normative Attractions to Law and their Recipe for Accountability and Self-Assessment in Justice Education' in Frank Bloch (ed), *The Global Clinical Movement: Educating Lawyers for Social Justice* (2011) Oxford University Press, Chapter 24.

- An understanding and acceptance that clinical method extends beyond skills development to promoting a normative and critical orientation in law students.

- A shared understanding with the clinic as to the base or bases in curriculum theory of the clinical program and, in particular, as to whether the clinical program is law student–education centred, client-service centred or whether it seeks to foster a conscious balance of the two.

Training, diversifying, strengthening and retaining good clinical supervisors

The strengthening of university expectations of teaching staff is such that consideration should be given to appointing clinical supervisors on probation for whatever period is common in the law school. During that period it is desirable, though not yet required by all law schools, that they undertake appropriate assessable teaching education. Typically, this will be a relatively short postgraduate teaching diploma of one or two years offered by the wider university of which the law school forms a part. New supervisors who come from legal practice environments may consider this to be prescriptive, but it is not unreasonable to require new teachers who are being employed as teachers but have no background in this craft to be so educated, particularly if they wish to attract similar employment conditions to conventional law teachers. It is also commonplace for external supervisors to be appointed, not by a law school but by the agency that manages them on a day-to-day basis. Law schools may have representatives on selection committees, but their influence will vary. In the agency environment, there will often be little encouragement of or requirement for training and teaching development among clinicians.

Sometimes there will be resistance to the concept of training at any level beyond the compulsory, but minimal, levels of continuing professional development, particularly if the agency will not or cannot support the cost of teacher development. When that resistance is encountered and the agency is indifferent or hampered by its own funding, clinic directors can lead by example, encourage and try to persuade their colleagues at a personal level of the longer-term advantages of participation in teaching training. These are slow processes and will not solve an agency's up-skilling issue overnight. However, such processes are consistent with a best practice approach that prioritises professional development not just in substantive law, but also in the discipline of teaching.

Probation periods for new staff are universal in law schools and agencies and the probation mechanism provides an opportunity to both foster the connections of a new clinical supervisor to wider legal education and normative lawyering and ensure they are handling the transition as well as possible. During probation it is desirable that a new clinic supervisor be not merely supervised by the clinic director in an operational manner, but also be encouraged to explore their potential for writing and reflecting on their clinical supervision.

However, encouragement of clinical supervisors to write about their experiences, whether they are in-house or in externships, has not been well managed by many Australian clinical programs for two reasons. First, clinics themselves are still often directed by lawyers who do not have backgrounds in writing and are unconvinced that scholarly connections are needed or are even desirable. And law schools for their part have not all been committed to ensuring that all those teaching their students are productive as lawyers as well as productive in terms of research and writing. They are still a long way from the integration ideal we spoke about in the introduction to this chapter. Indeed, as law schools offer more specialised electives in their degree programs and try to save on staff cost by employing practising lawyers as sessional and casual teachers, the *status quo* will continue, with sessional teachers and clinical supervisors in the same boat.

It is nevertheless becoming a norm for law school academics to achieve and maintain some sort of 'research active' status. Different law schools have different ways of measuring such activity, but minimum annual research outputs are not uncommon. Clinical supervisors who seek to be a part of the wider law school environment will at some point face these research output expectations. In our regional surveys, there were diverse opinions among clinical supervisors as to what could reasonably be expected of them in terms of research and writing. Most wanted the same employment conditions, including research or sabbatical leave—and the same levels of perceived respect—as conventional university teachers. However, they felt there was too little understanding by their law schools of the complexity of work associated with clinical case management. They do not always see themselves as law teachers at all, and some identify more closely as lawyers who are far busier than (conventional) law teachers because of the ever-present reality of client and case deadlines and the need to ensure that the responsible students, who have their own challenges, are on top of these events on a 24/7 basis.[11] On the other hand, the bureaucracies of modern law schools and the wider university are effective in exhausting, dispiriting and removing 'conventional' law teachers on a regular basis as well. Any precision or consensus about who is busier or has more time is unlikely because the clinical and substantive law teaching environments remain quite different.

Clinical programs will also be more successful in retaining good supervisors, rather than see them move to other occupations or legal workplaces, if they are able to offer them a career track. So, just as the provision of good supervision to law students is perhaps the critical ingredient in their learning (see Chapter 5), the encouragement of clinicians' thinking and writing demonstrates to them that they have a future in this discipline. Contrary to much present practice, new clinical supervisors in externship settings will be strengthened by deliberate linkages to the wider law school, such that they expect of themselves over time that they will research and write and will actually have fulfilling academic, as well as legal, careers. In this way, they will have a means to both combat the physical and emotional isolation from which clinical supervisors can suffer and bridge the gaps between clinical supervision and conventional law teaching.

In lobbying within law schools and clinics for greater recognition of clinical supervisors, it is worth putting several propositions that will be hard to rationally resist:

- That integrated clinical programs[12] offer best practice legal education and that global competition among legal education providers will eventually make clinics a point of differentiation among law schools (just as is beginning to happen in regional Australian settings).
- That career tracks among clinical supervisors are becoming clearer as the positive impacts of clinical methods gather more disciples.

---

11   See e.g. *Identifying Current Practices in Clinical Legal Education, Regional Report: New South Wales and Australian Capital Territory*, Section E, at perma.cc/FU7X-5TNV.

12   That is, where substantive, compulsory law subjects utilise clinical methods, including simulation and client-topic specific placements of early-year law students in clinics, as a matter of course; where these compulsory subjects are also regularly co-taught by clinical supervisors; and where all law school teachers, including clinical supervisors, are expected to develop similar capacities in theoretical and clinical teaching and in their ability to research and write.

- That new clinical supervisors need developmental support in their discipline if they are to have a career in clinical supervision and, eventually, leadership.
- That integrated clinical legal education must eventually mean that clinical supervisors themselves have an integrated approach and will publish as well as teach and practise law.

If all these things are predictable over time, then an expectation of reflection and writing by clinical supervisors is not just reasonable, it is an investment in continuing clinical integration.

Supervisors can be engaged in collaborative, team and multidisciplinary supervision of students, so that their understanding of the educational possibilities of supervision is deepened. And they will benefit by rotating in and out of clinical supervision sites and roles, alternating with otherwise conventional law school academics as supervisors, whenever the opportunity presents itself.

Rationales behind clinical supervisor–student ratios

A key factor in retaining any employee in any job is the workability of the role. For clinical supervisors, workability means being responsible for the correct or appropriate number of students, but no more. Today, clinical supervisors need to '[develop] in students a breadth of personal, interpersonal and management skills'[13] that cross over into almost every aspect of their human development. Further, the analysis of law in context within a specific legal case is more intense than in a traditional doctrinal lecture. A relatively high clinical supervisor–student ratio, ideally at no more than 1:8 for a full-time clinical supervisor in an Australian setting, is required not just to cope with students' caseloads, but also for the necessary discussion and reflection process. Significantly lower ratios undermine the depth of supervision or lead to burn out among supervisors. To take just one example, the supervisor needs to ensure that their students are making systemic connections between the drug-using client in their office and public policy related to substance addiction as a crime rather than

---

13   Jeff Giddings, 'Contemplating the Future of Clinical Legal Education' (2008) 17 *Griffith Law Review* 1, 16.

a sociomedical problem. It takes time and much concentration to manage students' critical transfer of clinical insight to effective sociolegal policy recommendations and law reform.[14]

Each of these activities demands major emotional and energy commitments from clinical supervisors year after year. If the supervision ratio required by the law school involves too many students, then the attractiveness of the role reduces and supervisors depart or, just as unfortunate, conventional law teachers have bad experiences and decline to be involved in anything but instruction in doctrinal law.

Funding

Clinical programs containing a clinic (as distinct from those confined to simulations or externships that are not engaged in client service) need to recognise a legal obligation to adequately resource the legal practice that operates in the clinic. For present purposes, the clinic includes the legal practice, but the 'legal practice' is in some ways distinct from the clinic in the sense that the former consists of the mix of regulatory and ethical protocols that a lawyer must provide and operate within. The clinic is more than that: it includes the physical facilities that are needed to accommodate students, in addition to the lawyers and support staff. This obligation may be difficult for the wider law school or university to recognise or accept, but it is set out in various pieces of legislation, in particular, the legal profession frameworks governing lawyers in all jurisdictions.[15] These frameworks are developing very slowly into a code, most notably in the beginning of a national legislative regime,[16] that covers a host of issues relevant to the funding of clinics, such as:

- The provision of a client trust account, requiring a part-time bookkeeper or accountancy-trained administrator and approximately $3,000 per year in audit fees; internal safe-keeping facilities (a safe or other secure cabinet) for cash, registers of securities and transit

---

14   Liz Curran, 'Innovation in an Australian Clinical Legal Education Program: Students Making a Difference in Generating Positive Change' (2004) 4 *International Journal of Clinical Legal Education* 162.

15   For example, see the *Legal Profession Uniform Law Application Act 2014* (Vic) (the *Uniform Law*), which has provided a uniform legal regulatory framework that took effect in Victoria and New South Wales from 1 July 2015.

16   The *Uniform Law*, cited at footnote 15.

payments, cheque books and related banking records; and risk-management staff training to prevent fraud and reduce inadvertent mistakes in trust accounting.

- Professional indemnity insurance to offset the risk of lawyer or student mistakes in their legal work. For clinics that are a part of the community legal service network, such insurance is available through the National Association of Community Legal Centres (NACLC) at a significant discount.[17]

- Continuing professional development (CPD), which typically requires each lawyer to undertake 10 hours of education annually in current legal issues. At least some of this education will be available only at a cost of several hundred dollars per hour per lawyer, but clinics commonly organise their own CPD to achieve more targeted delivery at a lower cost by drawing on internal and law school academics as presenters.

- Annual practising certificate fees (typically $300–400 per lawyer per year) and contributions to local fidelity funds, which compensate clients when their lawyers steal from them (typically $100–300 per lawyer per year for those who work in clinics). Optional law society membership can add another $300–500 per lawyer per year.

- Office procedural manuals specific to each clinic, which in turn dictate office standards for other documentation covering file maintenance (maintaining adequate details and records of each client's matter); conflicts registers; complaint handling, secure and fire-safe file storage (for a minimum of seven years),[18] practising certificate and CPD records.

- Access to an adequate law library (usually through their law school) that includes low- or no-cost access to digital 'how-to-do-it' manuals that instruct law students in the detail of model case procedures in common areas, for example, how to conduct a Magistrates' Court/ Local Court case, or how to defend a consumer debtor.[19]

---

17 There are additional costs associated with general compliance: e.g. Directors and Officers Liability Insurance for governing board members, recurring occupational health and safety training, regular fire drills, maintenance of first aid facilities and public liability insurance.

18 Cloud storage of client information is problematic for lawyers for security reasons. See Christine Parker and Adrian Evans, *Inside Lawyers' Ethics*, (2014) Cambridge University Press, 2nd ed, Chapter 4, 104–06.

19 The interstate network of *Lawyers Practice Manuals*, which have their origins in the early connections between community legal centres and clinics, is one such resource. See e.g. perma.cc/ KC5F-B65H.

Major funding needs

This table lists minimum and desirable funding levels, expressed in qualitative terms, for the major expenditure categories of a typical clinic:[20]

Category of expenditure	Minimum funding level	Desirable funding level
Clinic director (principal solicitor with full practising certificate, entitled to hold trust funds)[a]	Average for fifth-year admitted lawyer	Minimum for eighth-year admitted lawyer
Clinical supervisor	Average for second-year admitted lawyer	Average for fourth-year admitted lawyer
Clinic administrator (F/T)	Equivalent to administrative staff classification applicable to mid-level law school manager	Equivalent to administrative staff classification applicable to second-tier law school manager
Support staff (depending on the number of law students)	Equivalent to administrative staff classification applicable to first- to second-year law staff	Equivalent to administrative staff classification applicable to second- to third-year law staff
Locums for above staff categories[b]	Equivalent to four weeks per year for annual leave plus any agreed study leave	Equivalent to four weeks per year for annual leave plus any agreed study leave
Ancillary staff costs	Allowances for periodic increments and long service leave from the start of employment	Three weeks conference leave and the cost of attendance. Allowances for periodic increments and long service leave from the start of employment

---

20 The authors are grateful to Gai Walker, Managing Director, SCALES Community Legal Centre, Western Australia, for her helpful comments on the items included in this table.

Category of expenditure	Minimum funding level	Desirable funding level
Office and associated accommodation space[c]— equivalent rental cost per m²	One interview room per four students; one terminal or desk space per two students in shared workroom Separate offices for clinical director and clinic administrator; shared offices for clinical supervisors Shared offices for support staff Staff toilet facilities Joint meeting and staff room Quiet or reflection space for staff and students Client waiting room and separate toilet facilities Client file storage (enough for at least seven years) Parking facilities at local municipal standard ratio	One interview room per four students; one terminal or desk space per student in shared workroom Separate offices for clinical director, clinic administrator and clinical supervisors Shared offices for support staff Staff toilet facilities Meeting room, staff room and shared purpose teaching and function room Quiet or reflection space for staff. Two hot-seat terminals away from clinic workroom for visitors, volunteers and graduate placements Client waiting room with internet, children's playroom and separate toilet facilities Client file storage (enough for at least seven years) Parking facilities at local municipal standard ratio
Information Technology[d]	Multi-port Asynchronous Digital Subscriber Line2 + access for all fixed terminals (or NBN fibre link if available) Unlimited access to main law school library and law intranet (including full access to all law school online subscriptions, for example, the local *Lawyers Practice Manual*)	As for minimum funding level In addition, multi-node security-enabled wi-fi access throughout the clinic, including client waiting room

[a] Clinic directors who are not law school academic staff members may nevertheless seek access to study leave from time to time. Typically, such leave can cost the clinic up to six months' annual salary.

[b] Locum expenditures are often overlooked in clinic budgetary discussions, but they are essential for sustainable clinic operations. A supervisor who routinely returns to work after annual leave to find that their students were effectively unsupervised or poorly supervised in their absence will become dissatisfied and start to look for other employment. Since good supervisors are difficult to find in the first place, their loss for this sort of reason has many implications for clinic reputation and clients' outcomes.

[c] Gai Walker (see footnote 20) has contributed several specific suggestions to the detail of office accommodation. For example, the university or other funders will have a square-metre-staff-required-space formula that may be applicable. Walker states that the Western

Australian Government requires 13m² for each person employed. Further, since the law school will expect and even require a closely related clinic to apply for external funds, it ought to seek additional space above and beyond the recommended m² allowance, to cope with the extra accommodation required if external fundraising is successful. Note that it is not realistic to cost externship accommodation using this measure because the organisations in which externships are located will share their own facilities with students, other organisations and any external (law school) supervisors.

ᵈ Gai Walker (see footnote 20) suggests also that 'workstations need to be set up appropriately' for occupational health purposes, ideally through the university; that 'IT support from the University is invaluable' and is far less expensive than through private providers. She adds 'replacement provisions for equipment within the university programs is important. Interview rooms should be cabled so that a laptop can be taken into the room to help with internet access forms ... [and] phone equipment should ALWAYS include headsets for EACH phone ... with voicemail on staff phones'.

Conclusion

'Clinic' is perceived to be expensive,[21] but that perception is a clichéd consequence of unfair comparisons. The per-student direct cost of a large conventional lecture taught by one person to 300 students (or to thousands of students, via the massive online open course or MOOC) is lower than that of a legal clinic, but both of these delivery methods measure direct costs only and presume satisfactory learning outcomes. Learning outcomes from conventional lectures may also be focused on intellectual understanding. They are as unsuitable to the development of lawyers' professional expertise as they would be to developing similar capacities in hospital residents facing their first nervous exposure to an emergency room. Properly resourced clinical programs are perhaps the most reliable, holistic and sustainable contributors to future lawyers' professional competence, versatility and integrity.

---

21 The federal Attorney-General, who is responsible for the Commonwealth's national contributions to the states' legal aid funding, wrote to CALD in late 2008 encouraging all law schools to provide both clinical education and *pro bono* opportunities for law students and advising of his intention to involve the federal Minister of Education in that effort, in an attempt to broaden the bureaucratic and Cabinet support base for law school clinical programs: Letter from the Federal Attorney-General Mr McClelland to Prof William Ford, Chair of the Council of Australian Law Deans, 10 September 2008.

10

Australian best practices—a comparison with the United Kingdom and the United States

Introduction

Efforts to develop clinical legal education in Australia, the United Kingdom (UK) and the United States of America (US) have gradually evidenced a common goal: to develop consciously the best practices of clinical legal education in each country. In doing so, there is an effort to provide clinicians with guidance to improve law student education in the essential lawyering skills and in their ability to analyse and critique the law and legal system. We use the term 'best practices' throughout this book to describe what experience and, to varying degrees depending on the country, research have shown to be the most effective practices, or approaches, to clinical legal education in the countries compared in this chapter. As noted in our Australian *Best Practices*, 'there will always be debate about what is "best"'.[1] In the UK, for example, clinical legal education practices are described as 'standards', though they do not serve a regulatory function. For comparison's sake, this chapter will refer to the UK 'standards' as 'best practices' or 'best practices standards'.

---

1   Adrian Evans, Anna Cody, Anna Copeland, Jeff Giddings, Mary Anne Noone, Simon Rice and Ebony Booth, *Best Practices: Australian Clinical Legal Education* (2013) Government of Australia, Office of Learning and Teaching, 7, accessible at perma.cc/2J6E-ZMQX. Accessed 19 August 2016.

While each country has a different system of legal education, and a different process for determining how a person qualifies for admission to practise law, the core pedagogy of clinical legal education in each country emphasises involving students in the work that lawyers perform in service to clients with legal problems. In a clinical course, 'clinic students confront the same types of issues they will confront after becoming full-fledged lawyers, [and] they do so under the supervision of faculty who engage the students in the process of critique, self-critique, and self-reflection'.[2] This pedagogy focuses on assisting students not just to learn how to learn from their experiences, but also to appreciate how that knowledge will assist them in their development as effective, ethical lawyers or other professionals, as well as to reflect on the role of law and the legal system in achieving justice.

In Australia, the UK and the US, clinical legal education principally developed as an emerging pedagogy in the 1960s and 1970s,[3] though, especially in the US, the origins of clinical legal education are much earlier.[4] In some jurisdictions, the focus of clinical legal education has been on client service and, in others, on legal education. However, both objectives are commonly recognised as important in all three countries. Other notable differences in clinical legal education among countries have included law reform *versus* client service in program goals, systemic advocacy *versus* individual advocacy in legal service delivery and, increasingly, the academic status of clinicians both within their individual law schools and the legal academies in their countries.

In this chapter, we compare the efforts in each country to establish best practices in clinical legal education, and the resulting best practices that were developed. We hope that the material in this chapter may aid clinicians in other countries as they consider whether to develop their own best practices in light of their cultures, legal institutions, and systems of legal education.

---

2   Peter A Joy, 'The Law School Clinic as a Model Ethical Law Office' (2003) 30 *William Mitchell Law Review* 35, 43.
3   See e.g. Jeff Giddings, *Promoting Justice Through Clinical Legal Education* (2013) Justice Press, 5–11 (cited hereafter as Giddings (2013)); William M Rees, 'Clinical Legal Education: An Analysis of the University of Kent Model' (1975) 9 *Law Teacher* 125, 125–26.
4   Giddings (2013), 5–8; and Chapter 2 of this book.

Why best practices?

The development of best practices reflects a level of maturity in clinical legal education, and represents an effort to move from the implicit and often anecdotal understanding concerning teaching and organising clinical legal education to a more systematic and explicit articulation of its effective qualities. By identifying and explicitly communicating educational practices and organisation of clinical legal education, best practices identify achievable goals and practices for individual clinicians, their clinical programs, and clinical legal education within each country. The articulation of best practices also supports the development of clinical legal education more broadly and documents existing good practices.

Best practices provide clinicians, law school deans, and other academic staff with criteria or guidelines for strengthening their clinical programs. Not only do best practices serve to enhance existing clinical programs, but they are also an important resource for law schools initiating such programs. In addition, for countries that have law school accreditation standards, such as the US,[5] best practices for clinical legal education can be influential. For example, efforts to identify best practices for clinical education in the US, especially in the areas of externships and status of clinical faculty, have had a beneficial effect on accreditation standards.[6]

Before best practices for clinical legal education can be developed in any country, there first needs to be a perceived need or benefit. In the US, where legal educators developed the first set of best practices (called 'guidelines for clinical legal education') in the late 1970s and early 1980s, the need was originally motivated by the growing importance of clinical legal education in legal education.[7] By the early 1990s, clinical faculty compiled data on reported practices of in-house clinics in areas such as student–faculty ratios, hiring criteria for clinicians, and structures for in-house clinics.[8] The more recent version of best practices for clinical legal

---

5   American Bar Association Section of Legal Education and Admissions to the Bar, *ABA 2016-2017 Standards and Rules of Procedure for Approval of Law Schools* (2016), at www.americanbar.org/groups/legal_education/resources/standards.html. Accessed 19 August 2016.

6   See e.g. Peter A Joy, 'Evolution of ABA Standards Relating to Externships: Steps in the Right Direction?' (2004) 10 *Clinical Law Review* 681, 696–704; Peter A Joy and Robert R Kuehn, 'The Evolution of ABA Standards for Clinical Faculty' (2008) 75 *Tennessee Law Review* 183, 191–213.

7   Report of the Association of American Law Schools and American Bar Association Committee on Guidelines for Clinical Legal Education, *Guidelines for Clinical Legal Education* (1980), iii.

8   'Report of the Committee on the Future of the In-House Clinic' (1992) 42 *Journal of Legal Education* 508.

education in the US is the result of an effort that addresses best practices for all of legal education, and was motivated by the principle that US law schools could and should better prepare students for the practice of law. In the UK, which developed best practices first in 1995 and then revised them in 2007, the need was to provide guidance to those active in clinical legal education as well as to those setting up new clinical programs.[9] In Australia, the development of best practices responded to the need to integrate clinical legal education better into the academic focus of law schools, as well as to promote better unity between the academic and clinical dimensions of legal education.[10]

Comparing the scope of clinical best practices in Australia, the United Kingdom and the United States

The scope of best practices, and the nomenclature, differs in each country, in part due to the underlying need or motivation for identifying best practices. Our 2013 *Best Practices: Australian Clinical Legal Education* addresses clinical legal education through in-house live client clinics, external live client clinics ('agency clinics'), externships and clinical components of doctrinal law courses.[11] The 2007 UK *Model Standards for Live-Client Clinics* addresses live client clinical legal education that occurs in-house or through an external agency.[12] The 2007 version partially relied upon work published in 2004 by Richard Grimes and Hugh Brayne identifying and mapping best practices in clinical legal education through a project funded by the UK Centre for Legal Education.[13] The 2007 US *Best Practices for Legal Education* addresses all of legal education,[14]

---

9   Clinical Legal Education Organisation, *Model Standards for Live-Client Clinics* (2007), 3, at perma.cc/HR7Y-HSY5. Accessed 19 August 2016.
10   Adrian Evans and others, cited at footnote 1, 7.
11   Adrian Evans and others, cited at footnote 1, 7.
12   Clinical Legal Education Organisation, cited at footnote 9. For comparison's sake, our chapter uses the 2007 version of the CLEO *Model Standards for Live-Client Clinics* (updated from the 1995 version) because it represents the most current understanding of best practices for clinical legal education in the UK.
13   Richard Grimes and Hugh Brayne, *Mapping Best Practice in Clinical Legal Education* (2004), at perma.cc/ZM2T-NU6S. Accessed 31 January 2017.
14   Roy Stuckey and others, *Best Practices for Legal Education: A Vision and a Road Map* (2007) Clinical Legal Education Association.

devoting a chapter to 'Best Practices for Experiential Courses',[15] which include simulation courses, in-house live client clinics and externships, and another separate chapter to 'Best Practices for Assessing Student Learning'.[16] In our chapter, the comparisons of standards or best practices in each country will focus primarily on live client clinical legal education, in both in-house and external clinics or externships, because the live client element is the common denominator in those three models of clinical legal education.

An additional consideration for comparison's sake is the fact that in the US there are formal accreditation standards for law schools promulgated by the American Bar Association (ABA).[17] One standard and its interpretations address requirements for externships,[18] another standard defines a 'law clinic',[19] and another standard and its interpretations require that the terms and conditions of employment for full-time clinical faculty members be reasonably similar to those for other full-time academic faculty.[20] Because the ABA standards address conditions of employment for clinical faculty, the best practices in the US do not. The best practices in the US also do not include all of the requirements for externships found in the ABA standards, though they do cover many, and include some best practices for externships not in the ABA Standards.

---

15   Roy Stuckey and others, cited at footnote 14, Chapter Five: 'Best Practices for Experiential Courses', at 165–205. For comparison's sake, our chapter uses the experiential learning chapter from *Best Practices for Legal Education* because that chapter represents the most current understanding in the US concerning best practices for clinical legal education.

16   Roy Stuckey and others, cited at footnote 14, Chapter Seven: 'Best Practices for Assessing Student Learning', at 235–63.

17   American Bar Association Section of Legal Education and Admissions to the Bar, cited at footnote 5.

18   American Bar Association Section of Legal Education and Admissions to the Bar, cited at footnote 5, Standard 305 and Interpretations 305-1, 305-2, 305-3.

19   American Bar Association Section of Legal Education and Admissions to the Bar, cited at footnote 5, Standard 304.

20   American Bar Association Section of Legal Education and Admissions to the Bar, cited at footnote 5, Standard 405(c).

In Australia, the Council of Australian Law Deans (CALD) has adopted voluntary standards addressing matters related to the operation of law schools and law courses.[21] In Chapter 2, we provided an explanation of the regulation of law schools and the roles played by CALD and governmental regulatory bodies in Australia.

In contrast to the US, there is no overarching regulatory body for law schools in the UK, nor is there voluntary regulation similar to the CALD standards in Australia. As a result, one of the authors of the 2007 UK *Model Standards for Live-Client Clinics* refers to the document as largely consensual and 'a description of a range of good practices rather than necessarily best practices'.[22]

Process

Clinical researchers in each country employed different processes to study and obtain input to the development of best practices. While the processes differed, in each country the processes included efforts to solicit contributions from as many clinicians as possible so that the resulting best practices would serve the function of addressing important aspects of clinical legal education, utilising the lessons learned from clinicians with broad-ranging experiences. In each country, broad input was key to developing best practices that would reflect areas of consensus, as well as identify guidelines and practices for important issues facing clinicians where consensus had not yet formed. In Australia and the US, other legal educators not teaching clinical legal education provided additional input and perspectives.

The process of developing best practices in each country also involved research into the theoretical and practical dimensions of clinical legal education. The research component was very important in order for best practices to reflect something more than existing practices, especially where existing practices varied among clinicians and law schools. As a

---

21   Council of Australian Law Deans, *The CALD Standards for Australian Law Schools*, as adopted 17 November 2009 and amended to March 2013, available at perma.cc/FTX6-HGML. Accessed 19 August 2016. An introduction explaining the context for the CALD standards is available at perma.cc/C4ML-R2WS. Accessed 19 August 2016.

22   Email from Philip Plowden, Pro Vice-Chancellor, University of Derby, to Peter A Joy, Henry Hitchcock Professor of Law, Washington University School of Law (24 December 2013, 10:01:21 CST).

result, the best practices in each country also represent aspirational goals for clinicians, their law schools, and for clinical legal education in their countries. The balance of this section outlines the processes.

Australia

The development of best practices for clinical legal education in Australia has been distinct from the development of best practices in the UK and the US. The Office for Learning and Teaching (previously known as the Australian Learning and Teaching Council) funded this effort after a competitive grant process that required the project team to identify the project's rationale, methodology, and outcomes.[23] The grant process therefore required the project team to approach the development of best practices in a well-thought-out and systematic way. The grant also required periodic reports and a timetable for achieving various aspects of the project that served to keep the project focused and adhering to a schedule. The grant support provided funds for staff support and expenses related to the project.

The project team consisted of representatives from six law schools closely associated with experiential learning in law.[24] In addition to the project team there was both a national reference group and an international reference group that provided input throughout all phases of the project.[25] The project team investigated current practices in clinical programs throughout all of Australia and held workshops across Australia in order

---

23   After the grant award, the Australian Learning and Teaching Council was renamed the Office for Learning and Teaching, and information about the Office for Learning and Teaching is available on its website www.olt.gov.au/. Accessed 23 September 2014.

24   Members of the project team were Professor Adrian Evans, Monash University; Associate Professor Anna Cody, Director of Kingsford Legal Centre, University of New South Wales; Anna Copeland, Director of Clinical Legal Education Programs, Murdoch University; Professor Jeff Giddings, Director of Professionalism, Griffith University; Professor Mary Anne Noone, Coordinator, Clinical Legal Education and Public Interest Law Postgraduate Programs, La Trobe University; and Professor Simon Rice, ANU College of Law, The Australian National University.

25   Members of the national reference group were Professor Stephen Billet, Griffith University; Judith Dickson, Director, Practical Training, Leo Cussen Centre for Law; Professor David Dixon, Dean of Law, University of New South Wales; and Professor Sally Kift, Deputy Vice-Chancellor, James Cook University. Members of the international reference group were Professor Peter Joy, Washington University School of Law, US; Kevin Kerrigan, Executive Dean of the Faculty of Business and Law, University of Northumbria, UK; Professor Philip Plowden, Pro Vice-Chancellor, University of Derby, UK; and Professor Emeritus Roy Stuckey, University of South Carolina, US.

to understand the different approaches to clinical legal education and to identify effective practices. The project was a broad-based team effort that lasted 27 months.

The project team's methodology began with developing a single research instrument to survey Australian clinicians. Project team members interviewed clinicians and interested legal academics concerning the survey instrument, and utilised their input to refine the survey instrument. The project team next created a database of clinicians in Australia. Preliminary colloquia were held in some of the regions to introduce the survey instrument.

Once the survey instrument was finalised, the project team conducted interviews with clinicians and local stakeholders, principally in person but occasionally via telephone and webcam. Altogether, the project team interviewed representatives of 26 law schools over a 12-month period. The survey sought information on 'what are existing practices' and 'what should be best practices' for clinical legal education in Australia.

Using the responses from these surveys, as well as drafts of regional reports from participants at colloquia throughout Australia, the project team produced five Regional Reports identifying current practices in clinical legal education in 2011: one each for New South Wales and the Australian Capital Territory; Queensland and Northern New South Wales; South Australia; Western Australia and the Northern Territory; and Victoria and Tasmania.[26] Regional colloquia introduced key contributors to the initial findings of the Regional Reports. Before finalising the reports, the project team received feedback and evaluation from both the national and international reference groups.

Initially, the project envisioned the development of 'standards' for clinical legal education. The project team members utilised the information they gathered through the survey interviews and colloquia to develop an initial set of standards. These standards were circulated to an international audience at a joint conference of the Global Alliance for Justice Education (GAJE) and the *International Journal of Clinical Legal Education* in Valencia, Spain, in July 2011, and to a domestic audience at the Australian Clinical and Experiential Education Conference in September 2011. The conference workshops generated helpful feedback. After the

---

26   The Regional Reports are cited in Chapter 1 at footnote 6.

conference in Australia, the project team decided that characterising their recommendations as 'best practices' (rather than 'standards') was likely to be more productive and would better serve their acceptance by clinicians, law faculty, law deans, and others. Some thought 'standards' suggested a prescriptive approach.

The project team used material from the international and domestic conferences, as well as the reference groups, to develop best practices around the following seven themes: course design; law in context in a clinical setting; supervision; reflective student learning; assessment; staff; and infrastructure. Additional drafts of the best practices organised around these seven themes were presented to a stakeholder project workshop in December 2011, to CALD in July 2012, and to the Australasian Law Teachers Association (ALTA) Conference in July 2012.

The project team finalised the best practices in a document entitled *Best Practices: Australian Clinical Legal Education,* in September 2012, and presented the final version to CALD. CALD resolved unanimously to endorse the final version of the clinical best practices in November 2012.

United Kingdom

In the UK, the Clinical Legal Education Organisation (CLEO) developed an initial set of standards for live client clinics in 1995 at a time when some law schools were considering implementing clinical courses. Although CLEO refers to 'standards' rather than best practices, as noted at the start of this chapter, we will use the term 'best practices' or 'best practices standards' because they function as such.

CLEO's best practices standards resulted from the work of experienced clinicians who had identified good practices in developing clinical legal education in the UK. CLEO then adopted the best practices standards at its 1995 Plymouth Conference in the UK.[27]

Although active in the 1990s, CLEO then became dormant for a period of time.[28] However, it was revitalised and in 2006 it undertook to review and update its best practices to reflect developments due to the expansion

---

27 Richard Grimes and Hugh Brayne, cited at footnote 13, 78, Appendix 1.
28 Richard Grimes and Hugh Brayne, cited at footnote 13, 78.

of clinical legal education in the UK. The process involved discussion of revisions at CLEO meetings and the circulation of multiple drafts to CLEO members and others interested in clinical legal education.

Eventually, a general consensus was reached and CLEO adopted the *Model Standards for Live-Client Clinics* in 2007. These revised best practices standards state that they 'are intended to provide a benchmark for those active in or setting up clinics, and reflect the wide experience of those already running clinics both in the UK and abroad'.[29]

United States

In August 2001, the US Clinical Legal Education Association (CLEA) Board of Directors initiated the Best Practices Project. This followed a much earlier effort of a committee of the Association of American Law Schools (AALS) and the ABA that developed guidelines for clinical legal education published in 1980,[30] as well as another effort of an ABA taskforce that resulted in a report commonly known as the MacCrate Report,[31] which emphasised the important contribution of clinical legal education in teaching lawyering skills and professional values in law schools.

The CLEA Board appointed Professor Roy Stuckey to chair the project and created a steering committee consisting of 14 members representing a cross-section of clinical teachers and some interested non-clinical faculty. The steering committee determined the scope of their work.[32] Early in the project, the steering committee decided that the overall aim should be to focus on how law schools could and should better prepare students for the practice of law.

Better preparing students for the practice of law is extremely important in the US, because US law schools are professional schools, and graduation from an ABA-accredited law school enables graduates to sit for the bar in every US jurisdiction. As a result, almost all law school graduates take the bar examination and seek to be admitted to the practice of law.

---

29   Clinical Legal Education Organisation, cited at footnote 9, 3.

30   Report of the Association of American Law Schools and American Bar Association Committee on Guidelines for Clinical Legal Education, cited at footnote 7.

31   Task Force on Law Schools and the Profession: Narrowing the Gap, American Bar Association Section of Legal Education and Admissions to the Bar, *Legal Education and Professional Development – An Educational Continuum* (1992).

32   Roy Stuckey and others, cited at footnote 14, ix–x.

Because the primary mission of every US law school is to prepare students for the practice of law and entrance into the legal profession, Professor Stuckey and the steering committee determined that focusing solely on best practices for clinical legal education would be insufficient to fulfil the overall project aim.

Professor Stuckey was the principal author, and much of the best practices for clinical legal education reflect his research into best practices for all aspects of legal education. The process of formulating the best practices involved several meetings of the steering committee and other faculty interested in the project throughout the different parts of the US in which drafts of the best practices were presented. Each new draft of the best practices was posted on a website, usually three times a year, and notices of the new drafts were distributed through various clinical and other law faculty listserves. This process spanned nearly six years. Literally hundreds of clinicians, legal educators and others provided suggestions and assisted with drafting what was eventually published as *Best Practices for Legal Education: A Vision and a Road Map*.[33] As the book containing the best practices was being finalised in 2007, CLEA appointed a Best Practices Implementation Committee to publicise the best practices and to encourage law schools to adopt them.

The chapter devoted to best practices for experiential courses relied on scholarship and teaching materials from more than 40 clinicians, as well as on the work of educational theorists and the results of surveys and clinical committee reports.[34] The chapter also drew on the work of a joint committee of the AALS and the ABA that published *Guidelines for Clinical Legal Education* in 1980.[35]

Reinforcing the work on best practices in the US was the publication in 2007 of a study by the Carnegie Foundation for the Advancement of Teaching that called for the 'integration of student learning of theoretical and practical legal knowledge and professional identity'.[36] The Carnegie Report observed: 'Clinics can be a key setting for integrating all the

---

33 Roy Stuckey and others, cited at footnote 14, ix–x.
34 Roy Stuckey and others, cited at footnote14, 165–205.
35 Report of the Association of American Law Schools and American Bar Association Committee on Guidelines for Clinical Legal Education, cited at footnote 7.
36 William M Sullivan, Anne Colby, Judith Welch Wegner, Lloyd Bond and Lee S Shulman, *Educating Lawyers: Preparation for the Profession of Law* (2007) Carnegie Foundation for the Advancement of Teaching, 3 (the Carnegie Report).

elements of legal education, as students draw on and develop their doctrinal reasoning, lawyering skills, and ethical engagement, extending to contextual issues such as the policy environment.'[37] The Carnegie Report's ultimate conclusion was that clinical legal education can and should play a key role in preparing students for the practice of law.[38]

Best Practices for Legal Education and the Carnegie Report have helped to shape thinking in the US about the development of legal education and the importance of clinical legal education. Since their publication, there has been an increased emphasis on clinical legal education at many law schools.[39]

Conclusion

Each country employed a different process for identifying best practices, although the goals in each country were largely the same—to identify existing practices that are generally accepted as preferable ways of organising and delivering clinical legal education. In Australia, the process was very structured and systematic, soliciting input not just from clinicians in Australia but from other legal educators in Australia and in other countries. The process for identifying best practices in the US was not as systematic as that in Australia, but was structured to provide an opportunity for as much input as possible from clinicians and other interested educators. It was also very research-based, drawing on scholarship and research into teaching and learning, empirical studies about negative effects of current legal educational practices on the emotional wellbeing of students, and was informed by the work of the Law Society of England and Wales in developing a new training framework for solicitors.[40] In contrast to both the processes in Australia and the US, the best practices standards developed in the UK were less informed by research into teaching and learning but, rather, reflected a consensus among UK clinicians concerning the best approaches for developing clinical legal education.

---

37 William M Sullivan and others, cited at footnote 36, 121.
38 William M Sullivan and others, cited at footnote 36, 197–98.
39   Mark Yates, 'The Carnegie Effect: Elevating Practical Training Over Liberal Education in Curricular Reform' (2011) 17 *Journal of the Writing Institute* 233, 233–34.
40   Roy Stuckey and others, cited at footnote 14, 1.

General scope of best practices: Live client clinics

The best practices developed in all three countries share a focus on best practices for live client clinics—that is, clinics in which students represent, or assist in the representation of, real clients with legal problems. The reason for this shared focus is not explained, though it may be because those involved in developing the best practices in each country had experience primarily in this form of clinical legal education. While the best practices share a particular focus on live client clinics, the general scope of each set of best practices varies from all of legal education in the US, to all of clinical legal education in Australia, to focusing solely on live client clinics in the UK.

The organisation of the best practices also differs. Australian best practices are organised around seven themes, with a short discussion of each theme followed by underlying principles and then best practices with illustrations. There is also a bibliography of books and articles for each theme. The UK best practices are organised around 24 standards with subsections, without a bibliography or references. The UK best practices standards do not prescribe learning outcomes or take a position on student assessment, but do provide appendices with an example of learning outcomes and the 'pros and cons' of assessing student performance. The US best practices identify a set of 10 best practices for all experiential courses (simulations, externships, and live client), eight best practices specific to in-house clinical courses, and 11 best practices for externships, as well as the underlying principles for the best practices.

The following table provides an overview of the general focus of each set of best practices relating primarily to live client clinics, whether in-house, external or externships. Where distinctions between best practices for in-house clinics and external clinics or externships are important, those distinctions are noted. The main themes are identified using the best practices headings in each country, though some paraphrasing is used when necessary.

To assist interpretation, the table uses the assigned numbering systems used in Australia and the UK, and lists the most equivalent US best practices, which rely on letters and numbers. In the US, those best practices for all experiential courses are labelled A.2.a–j; best practices for in-house live client clinics are labelled C.2.a–h; and best practices for externships are labelled D.2.a–k.

Comparison of general themes of best practices for live client clinics

Australia	United Kingdom	United States
Course Design		
1. Specify learning objectives 2. Design curriculum to achieve learning outcomes 3. Live client experience follows observation and simulation 4. Students develop reflective practice 5. Classroom component 6. Clinical component reflects course objectives 7. The nature of work to be conducted by an agency clinic and externships is to be negotiated to address priorities of both the agency and the law school and to support the course objectives 8. Simulations are used to prepare students for clinical experience 9. Students read relevant academic and practice materials 10. Student selection is consistent with university policy 11. Supervisor has discretion in casework selection consistent with learning outcomes (in agency clinic course to agency's right to choose cases and projects, preference should be given to matters addressing learning objectives) 12. Clinical course requires student engagement over sustained period of time 13. Clinical courses run over a semester to give students necessary time to reflect on their experience 14. Clinical course design has regard to best practices in regard to Law in Context, Supervision, Reflective Learning, Assessment, Staff, and Infrastructure 15. Periodic review of law school curriculum should include a review of all clinical courses	1. Educational Objectives 1.1 The substantive law and legal process 1.2 Professional responsibility and ethics 1.3 Legal and transferrable skills 1.4 The role of law and justice in society 21. Training 21.1 Minimum – build to live client clinic through training 21.1.1 That supports the general educational aims of the program and is appropriate to the stage of development 21.2 Recommended – structure training to be case focused and use clinical manuals 21.2.1 Appendix A – Learning Outcomes (examples)	A. Experiential Courses Generally 2. Best Practices for Experiential Courses, Generally a. Provide students with clear and explicit statements about learning objectives and assessment criteria b. Focus on educational objectives that can be achieved most effectively and efficiently through experiential education – includes helping students appreciate their ethical obligations – includes helping students how to learn from experience c. Meet the needs and interests of students d. Grant appropriate credit e. Record student performances i. Give students repeated opportunities to perform tasks if achieving proficiency is an objective C. In-House Clinical Courses 2. Best Practices for In-House Clinical Courses a. Use in-house clinical courses to achieve clearly articulated educational goals more suited to those goals than other methods of instruction – this includes emphasis on the importance of seeking justice and providing access to justice, fostering respect for the rule of law, the essentiality of integrity and truthfulness, the need to deal sensitively and effectively with diverse clients and colleagues b. Be a model of law office management d. Approve student work in advance and observe or record student performances f. Have a classroom component D. Externships

Australia	United Kingdom	United States
		2. Best Practices for Externship Courses
		a. Use externship courses to achieve clearly articulated educational goals more effectively and efficiently than other methods of instruction could
		b. Involve faculty enough to ensure achievement of educational objectives
		d. Establish standards to assure that work assigned to students will help achieve educational objectives
		f. Consider students' needs and preferences when placing students
		h. Approve student work in advance and observe or record student performances
		i. Ensure that students are prepared to meet obligations
		j. Give students opportunities to interact with externship faculty and other students
Law in Context in a Clinical Setting		
1. Case work selection preference to students analysing context of law's operation (in agency clinic subject to agency's right to choose cases and projects preference is given to matters that best enable students to critically analyse the context of law's operation) 2. Client-focused approach to skills training includes cultural awareness 3. Students responsible for work with clients 4. Instructors engage students in structured analysis of their experiences 5. Supervision draws out law-in-context dimensions of client interactions 6. Classes include examination of broader context of law and the legal system 7. Readings encourage broad, critical analysis of law in context 8. Assessment includes assessing students' ability to reflect on how law operates from a range of perspectives and their own role in the legal system	12. Integration – Structure clinical program so that it enables students to better understand concepts and principles of law in the context in which they operate – Clinics should be integrated with the rest of the curriculum – The role of law and justice in society should be a course objective	C. In-House Clinical Courses 2. Best Practices for In-House Clinical Courses c. Provide malpractice insurance e. Balance student autonomy with client protection h. Respond to the legal needs of the community

Australia	United Kingdom	United States
Supervision		
1. Supervisors are able teachers and practitioners 2. Clinic designed to advance clients' interests while supporting students' education 3. Students are prepared and trained for work 4. All supervisors are trained (in agency clinics and externships, training is provided by the law school in conjunction with agency) 5. Law schools effectively support supervisors (in agency clinics and externships, supervisor training includes provision of feedback to students) 6. Supervisors are accessible to deal with unexpected events (externship supervision agreements include regular meetings involving clinical academic) 7. Supervisors provide constructive feedback to students in a timely manner	2. Supervision 2.1 Use competent and experienced supervisors 2.2 Adhere to special qualification and registrations necessary for practice areas 2.3 Designate one or more persons as director(s) of clinic 2.4 Solicitors should be well qualified 2.5–2.7 Supervision has to be adequate at all times, includes law office management	2. Best Practices for Experiential Courses, Generally f. Train those who give feedback to employ best practices j. Enhance effectiveness of faculty in experiential courses, includes using qualified faculty and assigning reasonable workloads D. Externships 2. Best Practices for Externship Courses c. Establish criteria for approval of sites and supervisors e. Establish standards to assure that field supervisors will help achieve educational objectives
Reflective Student Learning		
1. Course is structured to emphasise reflective learning 2. Course provides students a framework for reflecting on experience 3. Clinical legal education pedagogy involves planning, reflection (self-critique and feedback), and planning next step 4. Prompt feedback 5. Reflective learning builds on students prior learning 6. Reflection is assessed	20. Student Activity 20.1 Minimum 20.1.1 Orientation to clinic operating practices 20.1.3 Weekly meetings with supervisors 20.2 Recommended 20.2.1 Keep record of each student's expectations and performance to enhance formative feedback through feedback 20.2.3 Encourage group work 20.2.5 Structure work so students assume responsibility	2. Best Practices for Experiential Courses, Generally g. Train students to receive feedback h. Help students identify and plan how to achieve individually important learning goals

Australia	United Kingdom	United States
Assessment		
1. Assessment is aligned with learning outcomes 2. Formal assessment uses publicised criteria and combined with informal feedback 3. Summative and formative assessment are used 4. Assessment is graded or assessed on a pass/fail basis 5. In externships 'Learning Contracts' or some other mechanism are used to ensure shared understanding of learning outcomes and assessment among the agency, the students, and the law school 6. Clinical assessment practices are criteria-referenced and in accord with law school policies 7. Clinics incorporate mid-semester review 8. Clinical assessments are not subject to large class algorithms 9. Clinical supervisors consult with each other in assessing the same students	10. Learning Outcomes – Identify learning outcomes appropriate for the academic level of the student 11. Assessment – Explicitly takes no position on assessment noting that some live client clinics do not use assessment Appendix B – Assessment (pros and cons of assessing student performance)	[Chapter Seven of *Best Practices* focuses on assessing student learning] – Effective assessment exhibits qualities of validity, reliability, and fairness 1. Be clear about goals of each assessment 2. Assess whether students learn what is taught (validity) 3. Conduct criteria-referenced assessments, not norm-referenced (reliability) 4. Use assessments to inform students of their level of professional development 5. Be sure assessment is feasible 6. Use multiple methods of assessing student learning 7. Distinguish between formative and summative assessment 8. Conduct formative assessments throughout the term

Australia	United Kingdom	United States
Staff		
1. Clinical supervisors have status consistent with their positions (in agency clinics a clinical supervisor/teacher with academic status has overall responsibility for the course) 2. Clinical staff (supervisors and professional staff) are appointed with comparable terms and conditions of employment as law school peers (agency clinic supervisors receive appropriate training) 3. Workload allocation and research expectations recognise actual hours spent in clinical supervision 4. Clinical supervisors have discretion as to student loads depending on the number and complexity of files 5. Clinical supervisors with academic positions requiring research and publication should have student ratios adjusted 6. The university should support clinical academics' scholarship to the same degree as non-clinical academic staff 7. Appointment criteria for clinical supervisors includes practice experience 9. The law school should encourage suitable academic staff to rotate into clinics as clinical supervisors	15. Supervision and Staffing 15.1 Minimum 15.1.1 No more than 12 students in teams of two per supervisor 15.1.2 At least two supervisors per clinic 15.1.3 Supervisor available at all times clinic is open 15.1.4–6 Describes supervision 15.1.7–12 Describes supervisory practices and staffing 15.2 Recommended 15.2.1 Dedicated administrative/clerical staff 15.2.2 Describes client appointment process 23. Management 23.1 Minimum 23.1.1 Clinic supervisors have overall management authority 23.1.2 Supervisors report to director or person with overall responsibility 23.1.3 Management ensures students meet stated learning outcomes 23.2 Recommended 23.2.1 Use a clinic advisory committee that includes members of the bar and public	C. In-House Clinical Courses 2. Best Practices for In-House Clinical Courses g. Provide adequate facilities, equipment and staffing [The issue of status for clinical faculty is addressed by the ABA.][a]

Australia	United Kingdom	United States
Infrastructure		
1. Insurance	Infrastructure Standards	C. In-House Clinical Courses
2. Policies for ethical and fiduciary obligations to clients	3. Stationery and Publicity	2. Best Practices for In-House Clinical Courses
3. Written policies for supervision, assessment, and conflicts of interest (memorandum of understanding with agency clinics and externships)	4. Basic Client Care	b. Be a model of law office management
	5. Insurance	c. Provide malpractice insurance
	6. Confidentiality	g. Provide adequate facilities, equipment and staffing
4. Access to university library	7. Ethics	D. Externship Courses
5. Access to university IT services	8. A Professional Standard of Service	2. Best Practices for Externship Courses
6. Sufficient staffing for casework	9. Conflict of Interest	g. Provide malpractice insurance
7. Compliance with all health and safety requirements	13. General Representation	k. Ensure that adequate facilities, equipment, and staffing exist
8. University support for replacing clinicians on leave	14. Operational Practice	
	16. Maintenance of Files and Records	
	17. Premises	
	18. Equipment	
	19. Funding	
	22. Referrals to Other Agencies	
	24. Review of Clinical Procedures	

[a] ABA Standard 405 and its Interpretations define the professional environment in the law school, and Standard 405 provides: 'A law school shall afford to full-time clinical faculty members a form of security of position reasonably similar to tenure, and non-compensatory perquisites reasonably similar to those provided other full-time faculty members.' American Bar Association Section of Legal Education and Admissions to the Bar, cited at footnote 5. Information about status, staffing, student–faculty ratios, and other aspects of supervision and staffing of in-house clinics and externships in the US is collected and made available by the Center for the Study of Applied Legal Education (CSALE) through surveys and reports published every three years. The most recent data and reports are available at www.csale.org/. Accessed 19 August 2016.

Observations from comparing best practices

The comparison of best practices for clinical legal education in Australia, the UK and the US demonstrates points of unity and divergence that reflect, in part, the differing motivations to create best practices in each country. All three sets of best practices address issues of importance to designing and delivering effective clinical legal education. All three explicitly reflect a commitment to educating students to become effective, ethical practitioners. In addition, each set of best practices involves differing levels of input from clinicians not directly involved in the drafting, and therefore reflects different approaches to addressing the issues identified.

The best practices standards in the UK are explicitly characterised as setting forth 'a minimum requirement, and one that might be exceeded where resourcing and pedagogic aims permit'.[41] Given the underlying motivation to provide guidance to new clinical programs as well as to reflect extant good practices, the best practices standards take a very nuts and bolts approach to what is minimally necessary to structure live client clinical legal education, focusing solely on live client clinics.

In contrast to the UK best practices standards, the best practices in Australia are explicitly characterised as reflecting 'what should be' best practices based both on empirical research into existing practices and engagement with relevant literature.[42] While some of the best practices reflect basic requirements for clinical legal education, many of the best practices go much further and are aspirational in terms of defining the elements of effective, excellent clinical legal education. The best practices in Australia look at wholly law school–funded in-house live client clinics, in-house live client clinics with some external funding, external live client clinics ('agency clinics'), externships, and clinical components, such as simulations of legal practice activities, in other courses.

In contrast to the best practices in both Australia and the UK, the US best practices that focus on clinical legal education are part of the larger project to define best practices for legal education as a whole. Like the best practices in Australia, the US best practices address all forms of live client clinics, externships, and simulation courses or course components. In addition, the US best practices also look at all other aspects of the law school curriculum and include non-clinical legal education courses. Given the broader scope of the US project, many of the best practices for clinical legal education are not as detailed or specific as those in Australia, and they do not focus on as many aspects of clinical legal education as the best practices in either Australia or the UK. The resulting document is large and reflects 'a thoughtful and deliberate search for ways to improve legal education that are consistent with sound educational theories and

---

41   Clinical Legal Education Organisation, cited at footnote 9, 3.
42   Adrian Evans and others, cited at footnote 1, 7.

practices'.[43] The resulting set of best practices includes some 'proposals call[ing] for significant changes in the content and organization of the law school curriculum and the attitudes and practices of law teachers'.[44]

Conclusion

Each set of best practices serves as an important resource for clinicians in each of the countries where they were created. The best practices reflect a common understanding in each country about the practices that best develop and deliver effective clinical legal education. Clinicians should compare their own practices with the best practices. Then they should decide whether and how to use their country's best practices to improve their clinical course, discuss with colleagues changes to the clinical program, and discuss with members of their law school's administration changes that may require institutional support.

Despite the different aims or purposes for best practices for clinical legal education in Australia, the UK and the US, the best practices from these three countries have many points of agreement on what is important to delivering effective clinical legal education. These points of agreement represent a shared understanding of important aspects of clinical legal education that transcends the system of legal education in each country. In this regard, the best practices from these three countries may serve as useful resources for clinicians in other countries as they structure their own clinical programs. In particular, the UK best practices standards address issues important to creating new live client clinics, and the Australian best practices address in some detail course design, law in context in a clinical setting, supervision, reflective student learning, assessment, staff and infrastructure for different forms of live client clinics, externships, and clinical components in other courses. In contrast, the US best practices primarily address issues of the curriculum in general, and are important for clinicians in countries in which law schools are primarily focused on preparing students for the practice of law because nearly all law school graduates are admitted to practise law. The US best practices also serve as a useful resource for clinicians in any country interested in structuring law school curricula to prepare students better for the practice of law.

---

43   Roy Stuckey and others, cited at footnote 13, 4. At present, clinical legal education in the US is sponsoring an effort to develop a companion book to *Best Practices for Legal Education*.

44   Roy Stuckey and others, cited at footnote 13, 4.

In other chapters in this book, we have addressed in depth many of the issues identified in the best practices from these three countries, including course design, supervision, reflective practice, law in context and assessment. In additional chapters, we have examined related issues such as costs and resources, non-traditional clients, and other issues of justice in clinics. These chapters are very important to understanding both the practical and theoretical underpinnings of creating best practices for clinical legal education.

11
Conclusion

Clinical legal education in Australia is dynamic. There are frequent new developments, regular improvements, changes in partnerships and, sometimes, curtailment of programs. As we discussed in Chapter 2, Australian clinical legal education is making multiple contributions to the study of law and the education of future legal practitioners. This book provides a critical foundation for future growth. It makes the case for empowering Australian legal education with the best clinical legal education practices available to contemporary law schools. It seeks to deepen the understanding of clinical pedagogy.

In the preceding chapters, we have not only provided a comprehensive and detailed account of the critical aspects of *Best Practices: Australian Clinical Legal Education*, but we have also expanded and illuminated these aspects. Chapter 2 clearly sets out the various factors affecting legal education (and consequently clinical legal education). For those new to clinical legal education and those wishing to review their own programs, Chapters 3 to 9 highlight the central role of social justice in Australian clinics, set out the merits of various models of clinical legal education, clarify the benefits of good course design and the role of assessment, detail critical aspects of effective supervision and discuss processes to foster reflective practice, and address infrastructure requirements. Chapter 10 concludes with an international perspective on approaches to best practice in clinical legal education.

In this final chapter, we provide illustrations of the links between some recent developments in Australian clinical legal education and emerging trends in legal education, legal practice and provision of legal aid services. The surveys of Australian clinical programs conducted as part of the Australian Learning and Teaching Council Priority Project, referred to regularly throughout this book, were completed in 2010–11.[1] At the time, the number of clinical legal education subjects/programs was increasing and different formats were developing. We have referred to examples of recent developments in the preceding chapters; however, the instances discussed in this concluding chapter are highlighted as they reinforce the potential and the challenges of advancing best practice in Australian clinical legal education.

As we discussed in Chapter 1, there is growing concern in Australia (and elsewhere) about the numbers of students currently studying law.[2] This increasing number presents both an opportunity and a challenge for clinical legal education. It is reported that students graduating with some form of undergraduate or postgraduate law qualification increased from 6,149 in 2001 to 12,742 in 2012.[3] The Bachelor of Laws (LLB) or Juris Doctor (JD) are the Australian academic qualifications that enable law graduates to become lawyers. The LLB is increasingly being seen as an undergraduate generalist degree and LLB graduates are employed in a wide variety of industries and occupations, not only legal,[4] whereas the JD is a postgraduate professionally oriented qualification.

---

1   See Adrian Evans, Anna Cody, Anna Copeland, Jeff Giddings, Mary Anne Noone, Simon Rice and Ebony Booth, *Best Practices: Australian Clinical Legal Education* (2013) Government of Australia, Office of Learning and Teaching, at perma.cc/2J6E-ZMQX. This website also includes summaries of the Regional Reports. For the full Regional Reports, see *Identifying Current Practices in Clinical Legal Education*, Regional Reports, cited in Chapter 1 at footnote 6.

2   For a critical assessment of this view, see Productivity Commission, *Access to Justice Arrangements* (2014) Inquiry Report No 72, Volume 1, 244–47.

3   Edmund Tadros, 'Law degree the new arts degree, students warned' (14 February 2014) *Australian Financial Review*, at perma.cc/48YC-PN7F.

4   Edmund Tadros, cited at footnote 3; Edmund Tadros, 'Misa Han University no "trade school" for lawyers' (24 October 2014) *Australian Financial Review*, at www.afr.com/p/national/legal_affairs/university_no_trade_school_for_lawyers_kkPYJ4zuhupDTxn4tTVpCK. Accessed 24 October 2014.

Growth in Juris Doctor degrees

The growth of the JD qualification in Australia has begun to positively influence the development of clinical legal education. This postgraduate professional degree is common in the United States but only in the last decade has the JD become a feature of law school offerings in Australia.[5] In 2014, 13 (out of 36)[6] Australian law schools offered this degree.[7] Most of these law schools continue to offer an LLB, but three universities offered law studies only at the postgraduate level.[8] The number of students completing JD courses increased 330 per cent from 1,635 in 2001 to 7,036 in 2012.[9]

Relevantly for those interested in clinical legal education, according to the Australian Qualifications Framework (AQF), the JD is categorised as level 9, Masters Degree (Extended).[10] The AQF descriptor for the Masters Degree (Extended) is:

> The [qualification] is designed so that graduates will have undertaken a program of structured learning with some independent research and *a significant proportion of practice related learning*. As this qualification is designed to prepare graduates to engage in a profession the practice related learning must be developed in collaboration with a relevant professional, statutory or regulatory body [emphasis added].[11]

---

5   Donna Cooper, Sheryl Jackson, Rosalind Mason and Mary Toohey, 'The Emergence of the JD in the Australian Legal Education Marketplace and its Impact on Academic Standards' (2011) *Legal Education Review* 23.

6   The University of Sunshine Coast in South East Queensland offered a law degree for the first time in 2014. Neil Rees (formerly of UNSW and the University of Newcastle law schools) is one of the co-Deans and they have developed a first-year clinical experience with the Sunshine Coast Legal Centre. A new law school at Swinburne University in Victoria opened in 2015 with a commitment to providing 20 days external placement to each student per year.

7   The Australian National University, University of Canberra, Bond University, Macquarie University, RMIT, Monash University, University of Melbourne, University of New South Wales, University of Notre Dame Australia, RMIT University, University of Southern Queensland, University of Sydney, University of Newcastle, University of Technology, Sydney, University of Western Australia, University of Western Sydney and Murdoch University. At least two others, La Trobe University and Deakin University, are offering a JD from 2016.

8   University of Melbourne, RMIT University and University of Western Australia.

9   Edmund Tadros, cited at footnote 3.

10   Australian Qualifications Framework (January 2013), at perma.cc/A4ME-RQBM. Accessed 16 October 2014.

11   Australian Qualifications Framework (January 2013) 61, at www.aqf.edu.au.

As Cooper and others comment, 'the requirement that a JD include "a significant proportion of practice-related learning" may potentially have resource and logistical implications for law schools'.[12] Obviously, having a range of clinical legal education subjects within the JD enables a law school to fulfil this requirement of the AQF. However, Cooper and others argue that 'practice-related learning' could be interpreted to include a range of experiential type learning opportunities, for instance: 'problem-based learning, mooting and role-play activities related to legal interviewing, negotiation and mediation'.[13] Recent developments suggest law schools see the added benefit of including some clinical legal education experience within the JD. Universities with established clinical legal education programs have expanded their offerings to include specific subjects for JD students.[14]

The most explicit illustration of the impact of the AQF (and United States' influence) are developments at the University of Melbourne Law School. Despite its being one of the leading law schools in the country, there has, until recently, been no clinical legal education program at the University of Melbourne.[15] However, since 2012, the law school has launched the Public Interest Law Initiative, which enables 'students to contribute to the work of our community law partners and learn by working with real clients to solve real legal problems'.[16] Currently Melbourne Law School offers its JD students clinical experiences in its Public Interest Law Clinic, an externship program where students work at Victoria Legal Aid or a community legal centre, a Street Law subject and a Sustainability Business Clinic based at Melbourne Law School supervised by lawyers from large commercial law firms. In 2015, a new subject, the Disability Human Rights Clinic, was offered. It has a multidisciplinary focus that brings together the fields of disability studies and international human rights law.[17]

---

12   Donna Cooper and others, cited at footnote 5, 45.
13   Donna Cooper and others, cited at footnote 5, 45.
14   Monash University – Professional Practice (JD) (LAW7423), based at Monash-Oakleigh Legal Service Inc; UNSW – A comprehensive and established social justice program of internships and clinical legal practice onsite at Kingsford Legal Centre (KLC) or at a range of other local and international organisations.
15   For detail of the attempt to establish a program in 1994, see Jeff Giddings, *Promoting Justice Through Clinical Legal Education* (2013) Justice Press, 145–46 (cited hereafter as Giddings (2013)).
16   See www.law.unimelb.edu.au/students/jd/enrichment/pili. Accessed 4 February 2017.
17   See perma.cc/6U32-DVCN. Accessed 6 January 2016.

Although these subjects are electives, these developments at Melbourne University suggest that the adoption of the JD within law schools can have a positive impact on the expansion of clinical legal education. This could be the result of a range of factors, including the impact of the AQF and the professional practice focus of the degree, student demand, additional revenue generated by the high fees charged for the JD or the need to be seen to be a 'global' (United States–style) university. It is also noteworthy that this high-status law school has continued the Australian clinical legal education focus of developing programs that aim to improve access to justice and provide services to disadvantaged clients.[18]

Globalisation of legal practice and legal education

Globalisation has had, and continues to have, a significant impact on legal practice[19] and legal education.[20] Law schools are responding to the requirement to educate future lawyers to work in this globalised environment.[21] One of the reasons for the adoption of the JD is the globalisation of legal practice. In a 2012 research project, Bentley and Squelch developed a framework for internationalising the Australian law curriculum. The purpose of this framework was 'to better equip graduates to work in a global, international context and across multiple jurisdictions; and to enable graduates to contribute in an international setting to the articulation, nurturing and transmission of values'.[22] The conclusions of that project included the need for law schools wishing to internationalise their law curriculum to develop a multifaceted approach and to focus on the knowledge, skills and attributes identified as essential for a global

---

18   See our discussion of social justice in Chapter 5 of this book.
19   In 1989–90, Australia's export market for legal services was worth $67m and by 2006–07 it had increased to $675m, cited in John Corcoran, 'The State of the Profession', 36th Australian Legal Convention, Perth (2009); Steve Marks, 'Harmonization or Homogenization? The Globalization of Law and Legal Ethics – An Australian Viewpoint' (2007) 34 *Vanderbilt Journal of Transnational Law* 1173.
20   VI Lo, 'Before competition and beyond complacency – The internationalisation of legal education in Australia' (2012) 22(1) *Legal Education Review* 3–49.
21   Duncan Bentley and Joan Squelch, *Internationalising the Australian law curriculum for enhanced global legal practice* (2012) Office of Teaching and Learning.
22   Duncan Bentley and Joan Squelch, cited at footnote 21.

multijurisdictional environment.[23] It is not yet clear whether the values mentioned by Bentley and Squelch will include the historic Australian clinical focus on improving access to justice, but Australian law schools are well placed to influence this issue.

An example of how the pedagogy of clinical legal education can facilitate multiple learning outcomes, is the development of cross-jurisdictional clinics. In the International Social Justice Clinic at The Australian National University (ANU), law students engage in non-government organisational activity in developing countries. Students work in teams to carry out human rights policy research for a partner non-government organisation (NGO), under supervision by staff both at ANU and at the NGO. Students are supervised regularly by NGO staff through online communications technology.[24] Similar clinics have been run at other universities.[25]

Another aspect of the internationalisation of legal practice has been the increasingly important role played by clinical legal education in legal education worldwide. The extent of this global reach is illustrated in the many examples detailed in Bloch's *The Global Clinical Movement*.[26] Many Australian clinicians are part of a global network and are members of the Global Alliance for Justice Education (GAJE). Membership of GAJE consists of not only law teachers but also law students, judges, lawyers and others interested in advancing and promoting justice education around the world.[27] One of the consequences of GAJE membership is collaboration in the development of international clinics. For example, clinical staff at a number of Australian universities have worked with Bridges Across Borders Southeast Asia Community Legal Education Initiative (BABSEA CLE). BABSEA CLE's aim is to help establish, strengthen and support university-based and community-based clinical legal education programs and it works collaboratively with universities, law students, law faculties, lawyers, members of the legal community,

---

23   There have been a number of innovations as a consequence of the internationalisation of legal education. See Ben Saul and Irene Baghoomians, 'An experiential international law field school in the sky: Learning human rights and development in the Himalayas [online]' (2012) 22(1/2) *Legal Education Review* 273–315.

24   See perma.cc/CK29-27CV. Accessed 8 January 2016.

25   For example, the International Social Justice Clinic at University of Sunshine Coast and programs at Monash University.

26   Frank Bloch (ed), *The Global Clinical Movement: Educating Lawyers for Social Justice* (2011) Oxford University Press.

27   For further information, see perma.cc/TS7W-K55A. Accessed 22 January 2015.

and justice-related organisational partners throughout Southeast Asia.[28] Australian law schools have run 'virtual' clinics with BABSEA, hosted international law academics in Australian clinical legal education programs[29] and Australian clinical staff have participated and run courses in Thailand, Vietnam and Myanmar.[30] It is likely that, with an increasing focus on producing graduates who are global citizens, universities will encourage their law schools to pursue these types of collaborations.

Changes in legal service provision to the disadvantaged

As we have detailed in several chapters of this book, most Australian clinical legal education programs are based in, or rely on externship placements in, community legal centres or legal aid organisations. Our survey found that the current features of Australian clinical legal education are a strong focus on service to the community; of law-in-context discussions; involvement in a range of legal activities including individual case work, law reform, legal research and community legal education; location in not-for-profits, community legal centres and legal aid organisations; and growth in externships.[31]

Consequently, any changes and developments in the legal assistance sector will affect clinical programs. For instance, the federal government response to the recommendations of the 2014 report of the Productivity Commission into Access to Justice Arrangements[32] and subsequent alterations to the infrastructure of legal assistance services across Australia will have significant repercussions for current clinical legal education programs. Reduction in funding to community legal centres or legal aid commissions threatens the viability of clinical programs and may lead to pressure on some programs. The strong focus on access to justice and social

---

28   See perma.cc/94R9-YH9N. Accessed 22 January 2015.

29   Griffith University, Monash University and UNSW clinical programs have all hosted Southeast Asian clinical teachers through BABSEA initiatives.

30   For example, Helen Yandell, a Monash University adjunct, volunteered with BABSEA CLE during 2014: see perma.cc/K2PN-H8AG. Accessed 8 January 2016.

31   Adrian Evans and others, cited at footnote 1.

32   Productivity Commission, *Access to Justice Arrangements Inquiry Report* (2014), at www.pc.gov. au/inquiries/completed/access-justice/report. Accessed 26 January 2015.

justice (discussed in Chapter 5) may also be challenged by changes to the priorities for how funding is to be allocated, the limitations placed on the scope of work and prohibitions on legal policy and law reform work.[33]

Impact of funding crisis: Victoria Legal Aid example

Since 1994, La Trobe University's law school had worked in partnership with Victoria Legal Aid (VLA) in an 'external live client' clinic providing additional legal services to VLA clients. The educational focus of this clinic was legal ethics and completion of the subject satisfied the professional requirement of Ethics and Professional Responsibility.[34] In 2013, the program underwent modification as a consequence of changes at VLA.

The changes at VLA during 2013 were a response to a significant budget shortfall, caused by increased demand for legal aid services. This led to a dramatic reduction in legal aid services to the Victorian community. VLA curtailed services in a variety of ways; for example, limitations on types of legal matters and aspects of legal work eligible for assistance; and internal staff reductions.[35] The budgetary response included the closure of a metropolitan regional office (Preston).[36] The rationale given for the closure was the financial situation, changed demographics of the area (reduced need) and closure of a local court. The Preston VLA office closed on 28 June 2013.[37]

Partly as a consequence of the closure of this office, La Trobe University's unique clinical legal education program, based at this VLA regional office and focused on teaching legal ethics, ceased.[38] However, it was not only the physical closure of the office that affected the clinical program; changes

33 Community legal centres claim the current National Partnership Agreement (NPA) contains a 30 per cent funding cut in 2017. Additionally the NPA restricts legal aid organisations using Commonwealth funds for lobbying or public campaigns. This is a specific concern for community legal centres as systemic advocacy and law reform work has been an integral aspect of their work since they began. See Federation of Community Legal Centres, *The Facts about Federal Cuts – Community Law Blog* (2015), at perma.cc/AAN7-NFW2. Accessed 30 November 2016.
34 *Legal Profession Admission Rules 2008* (Vic), Schedule 2.
35 For a summary of the changes, see Mary Anne Noone, 'Legal aid crisis: Lessons from Victoria's response' (2014) 39(1) *Alternative Law Journal* 40.
36 Victoria Legal Aid, 'Preston office closure' (5 March 2013), at perma.cc/JUV7-D9SG. Accessed 27 October 2014.
37 Victoria Legal Aid, *Annual Report 2012–13*, 77.
38 Victoria Legal Aid, cited at footnote 37; Mary Anne Noone and Judith Dickson, 'Teaching towards a new professionalism: Challenging law students to become ethical lawyers' (2001) 4(2) *Legal Ethics* 127.

to the VLA guidelines, the decision that the organisation would no longer conduct 'minor work' files and the increased pressure on availability of physical office space all contributed to the cessation of the program. The combination of these issues also put paid to any relocation of this clinical program to another section of VLA.[39]

Nevertheless, the ethics-based clinical subject continues. The coherence of the course design and the adaptability and resourcefulness of the clinical staff involved meant that the program could be transposed to another location. This experience highlights the need for vigilance and awareness of features that ensure sustainability of clinical programs. Giddings provides a comprehensive account of factors impacting clinics' sustainability,[40] as summarised in Chapter 2 of this book. The development of resilience and a capacity to adapt to changing external factors is a crucial part of best practice. Clarity of the purpose and aims of a clinical program, as discussed in Chapter 4, can assist in sustainability. Importantly, the creativity, resilience and commitment of clinical staff (as discussed in Chapter 9) should never be underestimated.

New models: Multidisciplinary clinics

One area of innovation within the legal assistance sector offers exciting potential growth for clinical programs and enhancement of clinical pedagogy. Given the proven connection between clients' legal problems and health issues, there is increased activity in the delivery of integrated legal services within a health care setting.[41] Additionally, the Law and Justice Foundation (NSW) research shows that legal professionals are consulted only in relation to 16 per cent of all legal problems, whereas people often turn to their trusted health and welfare professionals for advice and assistance with issues that have legal aspects.[42]

---

39   Victoria Legal Aid continues to take a small number of La Trobe students as part of another clinical externship subject.
40   Giddings (2013).
41   Christine Coumarelos, Pascoe Pleasence and Zhigang Wei, *Law and disorders: illness/disability and the experience of everyday problems involving the law* (2013) Justice Issues Paper 17, Law and Justice Foundation of NSW.
42   Christine Coumarelos and others, *Legal Australia-Wide ('LAW') Survey: Legal need in Australia* (2012) Law and Justice Foundation of NSW.

This health care delivery model integrates legal assistance as an important element of the health care team. In the United States this approach is described as Medical Legal Partnerships and in Australia they are referred to as Advocacy-Health Alliances or Health Justice Partnerships.[43] The model is built on an understanding that the social, economic, and political contexts of an individual's circumstances impact upon their health, and that these social determinants of health often manifest in the form of legal needs or requirements. Research in the United States increasingly indicates positive benefits from an integrated service approach.[44]

There are a number of longstanding examples of the provision of legal services in a health setting in Australia.[45] Recently, there has been a resurgence of interest in this delivery model and a number of innovations based in large public hospitals and community health organisations have emerged. Funders such as the Legal Services Board Victoria are actively supporting this approach[46] and this growth of health justice partnerships presents new opportunities for clinical legal education to work with other medical, allied health and welfare disciplines in developing multidisciplinary clinics. In the United States, 46 law schools have clinics working in medical-legal partnerships.[47]

Although not an example of a Health Justice Partnership, a related recent innovation in the provision of multidisciplinary clinical legal practice in Australia is the Monash University multidisciplinary clinic. In this clinic, law, social work and finance students work together to provide services to clients. This approach also entails joint supervision from the three disciplines. The clinic provides a model of legal practice for future lawyers as well as a model for future clinical legal education innovations. The opportunity for legal clinicians to learn from working with supervisors from other disciplines enhances the quality of clinical legal education.

---

43   See National Centre for Medical Legal Partnership at perma.cc/V8JJ-5JY5. Accessed 8 January 2016. For recent Australian examples, see perma.cc/5DRE-RN4P; perma.cc/M9A4-JRQA. Accessed 8 January 2016.
44   See perma.cc/K4BV-98GP. Accessed 8 January 2016.
45   Mary Anne Noone, 'Towards an integrated service response to the link between legal and health issues' (2009) 15 *Australian Journal of Primary Health* 203; MA Noone, '"They all come in the one door". The transformative potential of an integrated service model: A study of the West Heidelberg Community Legal Service' in Pascoe Pleasence, Alexy Buck and Nigel Balmer (eds), *Transforming Lives: Law and Social Process* (2007) The Stationery Office.
46   Legal Services Board Major Grants at perma.cc/VB6F-4CCB. Accessed 25 January 2015.
47   See perma.cc/K4BV-98GP. Accessed 26 January 2015.

Additionally, the scholarship generated from this endeavour is furthering our understanding of clinical pedagogy, including those critical aspects, supervision and reflection (discussed in Chapters 6 and 7 of this book).[48]

Australian clinical legal education is an evolving and exciting field where new, evidence-based initiatives are proliferating. Australian clinical teachers and their supporters continue to be innovative, adaptable, resilient, rigorous and scholarly. As the legal landscape alters, so will legal education. Clinical legal education in Australia is a powerful exemplar of good legal education and is responding to both local and global challenges with many new ideas and approaches. Reference to the contents of this book will enhance and enable these developments to be the best possible.

---

48   RL Hyams, GA Brown, R Foster, 'The benefits of multidisciplinary learning in clinical practice for law, finance, and social work students: an Australian experience' (2013) 33(2) *Journal of Teaching in Social Work* 159; RL Hyams, 'Multidisciplinary clinical legal education: the future of the profession' (2012) 37(2) *Alternative Law Journal* 103; RL Hyams, FE Gertner, 'Multidisciplinary clinics – broadening the outlook of clinical learning' (2012) 17 *International Journal of Clinical Legal Education* 23.